BETWEEN ONE AND ONE ANOTHER

BETWEEN ONE AND
ONE ANOTHER

Michael Jackson

UNIVERSITY OF CALIFORNIA PRESS

Berkeley   Los Angeles   London

University of California Press, one of the most distinguished
university presses in the United States, enriches lives around
the world by advancing scholarship in the humanities, social
sciences, and natural sciences. Its activities are supported
by the UC Press Foundation and by philanthropic
contributions from individuals and institutions. For
more information, visit www.ucpress.edu.

University of California Press
Berkeley and Los Angeles, California

University of California Press, Ltd.
London, England

Library of Congress Cataloging-in-Publication Data

Jackson, Michael, 1940–
    Between one and one another / Michael Jackson.
       p.   cm.
    Includes bibliographical references (p.   ) and index.
    ISBN 978-0-520-27233-0 (cloth : alk. paper)
    ISBN 978-0-520-27235-4 (pbk. : alk. paper)
       1. Philosophical anthropology.   2. Ethnopsychology.
3. Intersubjectivity.   4. Self-perception.   5. Other minds
(Theory of knowledge).
    I. Title.
    BD450.J235   2012
    128—dc23
                                                    2011025178

Manufactured in the United States of America

21   20   19   18   17   16   15   14   13   12
10   9   8   7   6   5   4   3   2   1

In keeping with a commitment to support environmentally
responsible and sustainable printing practices, UC Press has
printed this book on 50-pound Enterprise, a 30% post-
consumer-waste, recycled, deinked fiber that is processed
chlorine-free. It is acid-free and meets all ANSI/NISO
(z 39.48) requirements.

Here we have the paradox, the potentially tragic paradox, that our relatedness to others is an essential aspect of our being, as is our separateness, but any particular person is not a necessary part of our being.

—R. D. Laing, *The Divided Self*

All of being is in touch with all of being, but the law of touching is separation; moreover, it is the heterogeneity of surfaces that touch each other. . . . There is no *mi-lieu* (between place). It is a matter of one or the other, one and the other, one with the other, but by no means the one in the other.

—Jean-Luc Nancy, *Being Singular Plural*

CONTENTS

1. Preamble   *1*

2. The Philosopher Who Would Not Be King   *22*

3. Hermit in the Water of Life   *33*

4. Writing Workshop   *59*

5. How Much Home Does a Person Need?   *69*

6. Clearings in the Bush   *79*

7. The Gulf of Corinth   *94*

8. It's Other People Who Are My Old Age   *110*

9. Objects in Mirror Are Closer Than They Appear   *116*

10. I Am an Other   *131*

11. Yonder   *141*

12. Reading *Siddhartha* to Freya at Forest Lake   *156*

13. On the Work and Writing of Ethnography   *167*

Acknowledgments   *189*

Notes   *191*

Index   *215*

CHAPTER I

Preamble

Lived experience is always simultaneously present to itself and absent from itself.
—Jean-Paul Sartre

In the late 1930s, Gregory Bateson and Margaret Mead did pioneering ethnographic fieldwork in a Balinese village, using still and movie cameras to capture some of the "intangible aspects" of Balinese culture and everyday life, including trance, eating, gesture, mourning, family interactions, children's play, art, and shadow-play puppets. In her introductory essay to their 1942 monograph, Mead speaks of a Balinese passion for being part of a noisy, festive crowd. Whether a marketplace, temple court, theatrical event, elaborate carving, or close-packed array of offerings on an altar, "the crowd preference is seen everywhere in Balinese life."[1] Women are said to love crowds and crowdedness even more than men, "and to be less able to stand the silence of empty fields."[2] However, every four hundred days, Bali falls silent for the new year. At this time, the roads are deserted, families withdraw to their houses, markets are closed, and no music is heard. This change from convivial boisterousness (*rame*) to silence and calm (*njepi*) echoes another change that Bateson and Mead document in compelling photographic detail—the Balinese "habit of withdrawal into vacancy—letting themselves suddenly slip into a state of mind where they are, for the moment, no longer subject to the impact of inter-personal relations."[3] One photo shows a carver who, having completed a difficult piece of work, sits staring into space, "utterly empty and spent." Other photos show children, with dreamy and absentminded expressions on their faces, sitting or standing close to a parent. Entitled *Awayness*, this page of photographs also includes a "psychopathic vagrant" sitting incommunicado in the anthropologists' compound.

When I first encountered this innovative ethnographic work in the early 1970s, I failed to see what was singularly Balinese in these images. As Herman Melville observes in *Moby Dick*, this oscillation between moments of association and dissociation is as true of whale calves as of human infants. "As human infants while suckling will calmly and fixedly gaze away from the breast, as if leading two different lives at the same time; and while yet drawing mortal nourishment, be still spiritually feasting upon some unearthly reminiscence; —even so did the young of these whales seem looking up towards us, but not at us, as if we were but a bit of Gulf-weed in their new-born sight."[4] Active one minute, an infant will grow still the next, as if taking stock of one experience before seeking another. Crying will give way to calm, and a bout of vigorous kicking, grasping, or smiling will be followed by a period of passivity, the infant seemingly absorbed by something far off or deep within. Recent research on primary intersubjectivity speaks of an infant's threshold of excitability. Beyond a certain level of arousal or stimulation, an infant will use "gaze aversion to cut out stimulation," just as it will invite interaction when bored. Thus, from two to six months, the infant is actively regulating its relationship to the world around, alternating periods of intense interaction with periods of quietness and withdrawal.[5] It may be, as Bateson and Mead suggest, that in Bali the "state of dreamy-relaxed disassociation" becomes the basis of trance and thereby is assigned a positive social value that it may not attain in the West, where children are discouraged from daydreaming and told to snap out of it—though prayer, meditation, days of rest (Sabbath/Shabbat), fasting (Lent/Ramadan), and remembrance, or moments of silence for the dead, may be compared to the Balinese silent and trance states. Unfortunately, Bateson and Mead—like many anthropologists— are so focused on what is culturally unique that they overlook what is existentially universal, in this case a capacity for "non-personal concentration" that is present in all human beings, even though it finds expression in manifold ways. Moreover, this alternation of zoning in and zoning out echoes the rhythms of work and relaxation, waking and sleeping, and focused and aimless action that characterize life in every human society and are essential to well-being.

This book explores some of the variations on this interplay between being a part of and being apart from the world. As such, it builds upon my previous existential analyses of elementary forms of intersubjectivity and of the indeterminate relationship between experience and behavior or experience and belief.[6] R. D. Laing pointed out many years ago that existential phenomenology implies that existence "may be one's own or that of another," and that, moreover, "each and every [person] is at the same time separate from [others] and related to them. Such separateness and relatedness are mutually necessary postulates."[7] But, Laing concludes, our being with another can never be completely physical, any more than our being apart from another can ever be psychologically viable. We therefore find ourselves in the "potentially tragic paradox, that our relatedness to others is an essential part of our *being*, as is our separateness, but any particular person is not a necessary part of our being."[8]

By implication, neither complete detachment nor complete engagement is a real ontological possibility, despite early anthropologists' claims that primitive people live in a state of mystical participation with significant others—a collective consciousness, a group mind—or the claims of sages for a transcendental and mystical fusion with the divine. Rather, these contrasted terms suggest that while human existence is profoundly social (*comprising relationships with others*), it always entails a sense of our own singularity and aloneness (a *relationship with oneself*).[9] My method of exploring this oscillation between sociocentric and egocentric consciousness is dialectical. This implies that the movement between being preoccupied by others and being preoccupied by oneself is experienced as an ethical problem that seldom admits of any final resolution, as in the parable of the tragedy of the commons, in which a number of herdsmen find it impossible to work out a balance between maximizing their individual profits and preserving the environment.[10] And though our awareness continually oscillates between self-interestedness and commitment to the common weal—being on stage and off stage, seeing things from without and seeing things from within, associating with others and dissociating ourselves from them—we remain, paradoxically and inescapably, *both* islands *and* parts of the main, entire of ourselves as well as involved in all mankind.[11] This does not imply that we are divided selves, or that one mode of consciousness is to be preferred over another; it simply means that consciousness is continually shifting from one register to another, and that these varying perspectives have quite different existential and epistemological entailments.[12] While psychoanalysis is often portrayed as a process of getting in touch with oneself and one's emotions, "getting into oneself" is productive only if it enables a person to escape "the solipsistic strait-jacket that is used to maintain a fixed image of who we are in our own eyes and what we are thus willing or able to perceive as 'reality.'"[13] As Henry James observed, to get out of one's self and stay out one "must have some absorbing errand."[14]

FIELDWORK AS AN ABSORBING ERRAND

It is part of the received wisdom of social anthropology that fieldwork is an initiatory rite. Unless one proves oneself in the field, one has not earned the right to call oneself an anthropologist. Little wonder, then, that novice ethnographers, about to leave the sanctuary of college life and submit themselves to the perils of fieldwork, experience considerable anxiety. Daunted by the prospect of speaking a foreign language, eating unpalatable food, living in uncomfortable quarters, and questioning strangers on potentially inappropriate matters, anthropological neophytes seek assurances that they will survive this ordeal and succeed in their goals. "What should I read on ethnographic method?" I am asked. "What did you do when you first went into the field?" "How do I know that people won't reject me?" In responding to such questions, I have recourse to humor. I recount how my academic advisor at Cambridge sent me to see Dr. Hawtrey May, a physician who had been dispensing medical advice and survival tips to expedition members, colonial administrators, and research scientists since the 1930s. "Always send your beater ahead of you in case of snakes," Hawtrey May advised. "Kaolin for dysentery. Bungs you up but stops the runs. Quinine ahead of the fever, not after, and always boil your water."

In a more serious vein, I downplay the exoticism of fieldwork. Books on method, from *Notes and Queries* to the most recent manual, give the impression that one is about to enter a laboratory rather than another lifeworld in which human beings are going about their lives, caring for their children, struggling to make ends meet, getting along with neighbors, visiting friends, meeting ritual obligations, seeking respite from the daily grind. I suggest to my nervous students that they think of fieldwork as they would any other transitional experience in life—starting school, leaving home for the first time, moving to another town, falling in and out of love. Such experiences seem insurmountable when contemplated in advance but comparatively straightforward in retrospect. The anxiety of doing fieldwork is a form of stage fright or first-night nerves. As soon as one is on stage, one's panic vanishes. Finally,

I tell my students to place their trust in the protocols of hospitality, which are basically the same throughout the world. As a guest, you are expected to be unobtrusive and respect the rules of the house; in return, your hosts are bound to take care of you. Moreover, abstract knowledge of quantitative and qualitative methodologies, of great books and foreign languages, will not help you reach an understanding of others unless you share in their lives as a fellow human being, with tact and sensitivity, care and concern.

AGAINST THE VIEW FROM AFAR

I have never believed that standing back from the world is the best way to see it for what it is, and I have always felt an affinity for thinkers who sought to understand the world through active engagement with it, even at the risk of appearing ridiculous. For Marx and Engels, the purpose of this engagement was to change the world, to save humanity from itself, and I spent several years in welfare and community development work endeavoring to do just this. But my real interest, I discovered, was in neither making the world an object of contemplation nor changing it for the better, but in making myself the subject of an experiment, allowing the world to work on me, reshaping my thinking and guiding my actions. Undoubtedly it was this impulse to test and transform myself in interactions and conversations with others that drew me to ethnography. So when I left the Congo in late 1964, disenchanted with the United Nations agenda for controlling and developing the newly independent, mineral-rich, and anarchic country that Leopold II had brutally subjugated eighty years earlier, I naively hoped that anthropology would provide me a way of returning to Africa as a learner rather than a master, an equal among equals.

At Cambridge it took me a year to decide on a field site and secure funds. During this time, I felt cut off from what I called the "real" world and impatient to reimmerse myself in it. Cambridge felt cloistered and claustrophobic, a place of ivory towers, antiquated rituals, and donnish privileges. It was not without irony, therefore, that six months into fieldwork in northern Sierra Leone, I found myself gazing nostalgically at the postcard my wife's friend Didi had sent us from Cambridge of Kings Chapel under snow. Driven by a felt need to visit every Kuranko village, observing critical events, interviewing informants, transcribing stories, covering every aspect of social life, as well as meeting the incessant demands of neighbors, I was quickly exhausted and fell prey to fantasies of Cambridge, where I might find asylum and indulge the Wordsworthian luxury of writing down experiences recollected in tranquility.

Since that first arduous year of fieldwork, I have returned to Sierra Leone many times and done stints of fieldwork in Aboriginal Australia and elsewhere. Every one of these forays has recalled the first: the sense of immense relief, such as Ishmael describes on the opening page of *Moby Dick*, when one dismounts the treadmill of a landlocked existence and can "get to sea . . . take to the ship." Yet I am always mindful of the irony that, having escaped the confines of the academy and cast myself adrift in the world, I find myself, within a few weeks or months of labor-intensive fieldwork, longing to get back to the sheltered precincts from which I so elatedly sallied forth.

John Dewey argued that this dialectical movement between home and the world is the natural rhythm of human life, for we are constantly forced to rethink our lives in the light of new experiences that unsettle what we once took for granted or regarded as tried and true. Empirical method in science is simply the systematic implementation of this familiar mode of testing what we think we know against what we don't. For Dewey, philosophy should be understood in the same way—testing a hypothesis against experience in a controlled environment in order to arrive at a provisional conclusion *that demands further testing*. It follows that the good of philosophy is a matter of its ability to do justice to life. And so Dewey asks:

> Does it end in conclusions which, when they are referred back to ordinary life-experiences and their predicaments, render them more significant, more luminous to us, and make our dealings with them more fruitful? Or does it terminate in rendering the things of ordinary experience more opaque than they were before, and in depriving them of having in "reality" even the significance they had previously seemed to have? Does it yield the enrichment and increase of power of ordinary things which the results of physical science afford when applied in every-day affairs?[15]

There are, of course, many ways in which one can absent oneself from the world, and many reasons for doing so, including disenchantment, dread, disablement, or a desire for intellectual or spiritual illumination. And there are just as many ways in which one can be actively present in the world, gregarious and engaged. But the task of balancing these modes of thinking and of being—rather than ranking them or emphasizing one at the expense of the other—is difficult. In the following pages I explore this problematic through a set of portraits of thinkers I have known, many of whom would not recognize thinking as a self-conscious, systematic activity at all. My interest is in their ways of negotiating the vexed relationship between being part of and standing apart from the world. My aim is to show the limits of what is practically possible rather than describe what is abstractly conceivable. Naturally I was drawn to these individuals because I saw something of my own struggle in theirs, particularly the struggle to integrate my thinking with my life, to make thought worldly rather than merely wordy, and to clarify the relationship between how one thinks and who one is. As an anthropologist, I have never sought the kind of knowledge of others that purports to transcend the world of their experience, reducing human lives to cultural representations, innate imperatives, social rules, traditional values, or global processes; my interest is in the knowledge that may contribute to tolerant coexistence in a world of entrenched divisions and ineradicable differences. To this end one needs an ability *both* to think for oneself *and* to be open to the thinking of others, and a capacity for both self-analysis and social critique.

PARTICIPANT OBSERVATION

The tension between philosophy conceived as a conversation with oneself or within a closed community and philosophy conceived as an open-ended conversation with the world at large reflects a tension that is natural to consciousness itself, which oscillates constantly between a sense of being apart from the world and being a part of it. On the one hand, the world constantly invades my consciousness, breaking into my thoughts, disturbing my dreams, and sometimes subverting my sense of who I am or would seem to be. On the other hand, I experience a countervailing impulse to leave the world behind, to put my dealings with it on hold, opening up a space in which the rhythms of my inner life govern the way the external world appears to my consciousness. I regard this tension between turning toward the world and turning away from it as an expression of a deeper existential dialectic between being acted upon and being an actor. For the world can be so overwhelming that one is swept away by it, with no time to think, no sense of being in control, no opportunity to be still or silent. But in stillness and silence we may become estranged from the joys and obligations of our worldly life. Hannah Arendt's distinction between the *vita contemplativa* and the *vita activa* captures this antinomy, though, like Dewey, she favored the latter over the former, prefer-ring the activist to the contemplative, the man of the world to the ascetic, even though both modes of thought and modes of being are, in practice, mu-tually entailed.

It is to the anthropologist Bronislaw Malinowski that we owe the term participant-observation.[16] Strictly speaking, Malinowski's coinage is an oxy-moron, since one cannot be *at one and the same time* actor and audience, player and spectator, deeply involved in an event and disinterestedly observing it. In reality, of course, an ethnographer plays these roles successively, not simulta-neously. At times, one sets aside one's notebook and engages socially with others, sharing a meal, assisting with farmwork, tending a sick child, or par-ticipating in a ritual event without much thought of academic gain. At other times, one is an outsider, standing back, observing an event from a discreet distance, taking notes, making a film, recording a story. Even though one's initial separateness becomes, in time, transmuted into a nominal kinship or genuine feeling for the world into which one has ventured, one never ceases to stand out in that world—by one's appearance, accent, idiosyncratic interests, and transience. What gives anthropological writing its unique character is its interleaving of these very different modes of being-with-others—relating to the other as a fellow subject (a friend) and relating to the other as an object of intellectual interest (a stranger).[17]

This oscillation between being a part of and being apart from is, as I have noted, not peculiar to ethnographic or empirical methods. It is in the nature of human consciousness itself, for our minds are continually and spontaneously moving between absorption in a task and reflection on it—between doing something without thinking and thinking about what we are doing. What is true of thinking is also true of being.[18] Although we some-times experience ourselves as singular or solitary, this experience is always predicated upon a sense of what it means to be with another. This is what Paul Ricoeur means by the phrase "oneself as another." It "suggests from the outset that the selfhood of oneself implies otherness to such an inti-mate degree that one cannot be thought of without the other."[19] We are thus analogues of one another. Anthropology is the systematic application of analogical thought to a pluralistic universe, a way of understanding the other as oneself in other circumstances.

We compare and contrast ourselves with others in the same way that we use metaphors to compare and contrast the body of the world with the human body—speaking of the brow or foot of a hill, the head of a river, the eye of a storm. Analogies provide "objective correlatives" of our subjective states, and as such they carry us beyond ourselves. By likening moods to colors (blue for depression, red for anger, green for envy), to physical conditions (up or down, light or heavy, mobile or stuck), or to the weather (calm or stormy), we can grasp experiences that might otherwise be inexpressible and connect with others who share the same repertoire of images.

There is always a risk, in making comparisons, of not finding in the other anything that bears comparison with what one can find in oneself. Confronted by what appears to be the unthinkable alterity of the other, or the uninhabitability of his or her lifeworld, one may retreat into one's own world and make it the measure of all things. This is the danger of the nonempirical philosophy against which Dewey rails. It suggests a loss of balance between the need to distance ourselves from a situation that proves too overwhelming to manage[20] and the need to engage with a situation in order to test our assumptions about it.

This tension between evasion and engagement plays out in the way we think as well as the way we live.

Just as there are many languages and dialectics in the world, so there are, within in any one social universe, numerous subsets of the lingua franca, comprising argots, jargons, idiolects, and restricted codes[21] that effectively create closed communities. Although all these languages depend on analogies and metaphors (including logico-mathematical and computer "languages"), people tend to assume that their preferred manner of speaking corresponds to a privileged field of experience that marks them out, not just as specialists but as special. Schizophrenia is an extreme example of this illusion, in which the conflation of words with things leads to the conviction that one's very life, if not the life of the world, depends on the making and maintaining of one's own "successful" arrangement of objects, images, numbers, and words.

HOW WE THINK

Our ways of representing the world to ourselves give us a consoling sense that the world is within our grasp, both cognitively and practically. But our representations tend to take on a life of their own. They are felt to possess the same concreteness as the experiences and processes to which they refer. Moreover, it is believed that some representations are better than others at capturing the exact nature of those experiences and processes. While common metaphors are often dismissed as amateurish or intellectually impoverished ways of spelling out the nature of the world about us, philosophical constructions allegedly provide superior pictures of that world, while mathematics captures its essence even more perfectly. These notions that there are superior and inferior ways of grasping the essence of reality tend to lose sight of the fact that different kinds of analogical thought serve different purposes, and that the only way we may know whether or not a particular mode of thought has value is to test it against the experience we are trying to make sense of. Thought is a tool, a technique, a distinctively human capacity for managing the vicissitudes of life. As such, it offers itself up to a speculative thinker like Newton as a way of comprehending the nature of what he will call "gravity" as much as to an Indonesian subsistence farmer working out how to make the most of a steep slope to irrigate his fields. Newton's model is not intrinsically superior to the farmer's model, since their problems are different, and the proof in either case can only be measured by the success with which the thinker, whatever mode of thought he or she deploys, solves the problem at hand. And while we tend to draw a distinction between concrete thinking, that serves "some end, good, or value beyond itself," and abstract thinking, that serves "simply as a means to more thinking," we should not rank one above the other but learn to judge when each is required.[22] This pragmatist conclusion reminds one of Lévi-Strauss's insistence that scientific thought and nonscientific thought "require the same sort of mental operations" and differ "not so much in kind as in the different types of phenomena to which they are applied."[23] At the same time, in both "science" and "magic" "the universe is an object of thought at least as much as it is a means of satisfying needs."[24] People classify and order plants, animals, objects, and persons not simply out of practical interest but because such bricological arrangements are potentially good to think with. For example, it is easier to think of the two moieties of a Western Australian Aboriginal people as *both* one *and* not one if the relationship is likened, say, to the relationship between eaglehawk and crow, since both are carnivorous birds, yet the first is predatory while the second is a scavenger.[25]

Our ability to grasp the world cognitively *supplements* our ability to grasp it practically and physically, which may explain why so many metaphors for thinking are drawn from bodily processes—grasping, understanding, seeing, comprehending, and knowing.[26] And it is typically when practical and physical modes of acting fail us that thought comes into its own. When we have difficulty understanding someone, we begin imagining what he or she might be trying to tell us. When we are physically disabled, we intensify efforts to think our way around the problem that we cannot solve by physical means alone. As Dewey notes:

> The origin of thinking is some perplexity, confusion, or doubt. Thinking is not a case of spontaneous combustion; it does not occur just on "general principles." There is something specific which occasions and evokes it. General appeals to a child (or to a grown-up) to think, irrespective of the existence in his own experience of some difficulty that troubles him and disturbs his equilibrium, are as futile as advice to lift himself by his boot-straps.[27]

A corollary of Dewey's observation is that when life follows familiar routines and certain patterns, we give little thought to what we are doing or saying. Our behavior is habitual, not intellectual. It is when a routine is interrupted, when a calamity befalls us, when our expectations are not met, when a familiar person behaves out of character, and when we are suddenly unsure of our footing that we typically turn inward, thinking of a way out of or around the difficulty that has arisen. As Ed Tronick puts it, "when an impelling certitude is violated, it comes into awareness." This is true from the first year of a child's life. Faced with a depressed, anxious, or emotionally unresponsive mother, a child's thoughts will become detached and take on a life of their own.[28] Instead of existing in relationship with the mother, the child learns to live within itself, thinking of the mother and of itself as separate, disconnected entities. In effect, the child compensates for the absence of a *dyadic* consciousness (in which mother and child collaboratively construct a coherent, mutually regulating neurological system) by developing isolated conceptions of self and others that may have pathological consequences. That is to say, when we cannot be a part of another's world, we are prone to think of ourselves as apart from it, and this may then deepen the estrangement unless we are helped back into the world from which we have withdrawn.

In November 1932 Aldous Huxley began writing *Eyeless in Gaza*, a technically ambitious novel that was also autobiographical. After two years' work, Huxley was at an impasse. Not only was he unable to resolve the issues that plagued his protagonist and alter ego Anthony Beavis; Huxley was suffering from depression and insomnia. It was as if the general sense of dissociation, intellectual detachment, physical ungainliness, nearsighted-ness, and world-weariness that had oppressed him from childhood now immobilized him completely. In the fall of 1935, on the advice of a friend, Huxley began daily consultations with the therapist F. M. Alexander. As a result, his health improved, his morale lifted, and he completed *Eyeless in Gaza*, writing into the text a doctor and self-styled "anthropologist" called James Miller whose practical philosophy transforms the life of the purblind "detached philosopher"[29] Anthony Beavis, just as Alexander "made a new and unrecognizable person"[30] of Aldous Huxley who, according to his wife, became a better man, more socially adroit and sensually engaged, and in "constructive conscious control of the self."[31] As Anthony Beavis explains this transformation, after rereading D. H. Lawrence's allegory of rebirth, *The Man Who Died*: "Thinking and the pursuit of knowledge—these were purposes for which he himself had used [his] energy. . . . Thought as an end, knowledge as an end. And now it had become suddenly manifest that they were only means—as definitely raw material as life itself."[32]

A second and not unrelated example of a thinker redressing the imbal-ance between his personal and social life is that of John Dewey. Around the period 1914–1915, Dewey found that he could not write for more than a few hours without suffering fatigue and deep depression. After consulting with F. M. Alexander, Dewey realized that while philosophy was relatively easy for him, he wrote, as he lived, without much thought. This habitual discon-nection of mind from body, or thought from activity, was the probable cause of his enervation and depression. Under Alexander's guidance, Dewey not only improved his vision, posture, breathing, and general well-being; he received immediate sensory confirmation of his relational theories of body-mind, thinking-within-activity, the organism-in-nature, ideas-in-context, and schooling-in-society. One of Dewey's most compelling ideas, confirmed by practicing the Alexander technique, was that we do not act on the basis of ideas; rather, ideas are retrospective commentaries on actions that have paid off. For example, it is impossible for a golfer to learn to keep her eye on the ball by being told to do this and becoming self-conscious of her tendency to lift her head when swinging the golf club. She must first acquire new hab-its of using her body—a series of small, mindful, controlled movements that will, as a matter of course, involve keeping the head still and the eye on the ball. Speaking of the difficulty of learning how to stand up straight, Dewey writes:

Only when a man can already perform an act of standing straight does he know what it is like to have a right posture and only then can he summon the idea required for proper execution. The act must come before the thought, and a habit before an ability to evoke the thought at will.[33]

To behave decently, lose weight, stop drinking, or sit straight we cannot simply conceive the idea and then will or wish it into being; we must first have the experience, and this demands that we stop thinking about *what* we want to achieve in order to acquire, "through a flank movement,"[34] techniques for how we may inhibit old habits and instill new ones.

Does this mean that reason is synonymous with rationalization—a way of providing ex post facto justifications to actions that were not principled, pondered, or chosen? And if thought is more often afterthought than forethought, how does it differ from storytelling, which is another way we give retrospective form to experiences that defied our understanding and lay outside our control?

Consider *Totem and Taboo*, a work that Freud regarded as one of his greatest achievements. Despite its intellectual ingenuity and scientific pretensions, this work goes well beyond the little that was known about early hominid evolution, even in 1916, and must be read as largely mythological.[35]

In the earliest state of human society, according to Freud's scenario, "a violent and jealous father . . . keeps all the females for himself and drives away his sons as they grow up." One day, the excluded sons band together, kill their father, and, since they are cannibals, devour him. In consuming the body of the father, the sons "accomplished their identification with him, and each one of them acquired a portion of his strength. The totem meal, which is perhaps mankind's earliest festival, would thus be a repetition and a commemoration of this memorable and criminal deed, which was the beginning of many things—of social organization, of moral restrictions and of religion."[36] Freud assumed that the sons felt contradictory emotions toward their father. The sexual desire and lust for power that led them to hate and then murder him was followed by a resurgence of the affection and respect they had also felt toward him. Filled with remorse, the sons attempted to revoke their deed by forbidding the killing of the totem, "the substitute for their father; and they renounced its fruits by resigning their claim to the women who had now been set free. They thus created out of their filial sense of guilt the two fundamental taboos of totemism, which for that very reason inevitably corresponded to the two repressed wishes of the Oedipus complex."[37]

It is a central tenet of psychoanalytic theory that even when our thinking appears to represent the external world as it actually is, it is freighted with subjective meanings. In effect, experience-distant language, or the invocation of history, prehistory, or societies remote from one's own, subtly disguises experience-near preoccupations that analysis may be able to disclose. What unconfided, personal issues, then, lie buried in Freud's *Totem and Taboo?*

In a remarkable essay, Derek Freeman proposes that Freud projected his own ambivalence toward his father onto the "imagined parricidal sons of the primeval Cyclopean family" in order to alleviate his own Oedipal guilt.[38] Though he had written *Totem and Taboo* in a state of "certainty and elation," Freud became depressed after completing it as though, writes Freeman, he felt guilty at having succeeded in doing something his relatively uneducated father could never have done or understood, even though he had long been driven to demonstrate to his father (who often told Sigmund that he would amount to nothing) that he was worthy of his respect. Freud's reaction, how-ever, was to doubt and demean his achievement, as though this might restore the filial piety and submissiveness appropriate in a son. Even though Freud expressed uncertainty as to whether his thesis in *Totem and Taboo* was a fantastic hypothesis or based on an actual event, he clung to the reality of the primal deed, writing in the last year of his life that, "I hold firmly to this con-struction."[39] Modern prehistory provides no evidence that Freud's descrip-tions of early hominid social life were correct. Modern genetics refutes his assumption that psychical experiences like guilt can be genetically transmit-ted from one generation to another. And Freud's conflation of contemporary "primitive peoples," children, and obsessional neurotics is absurd. Yet one has to allow that thoughts generated by a thinker's own inner conflicts can serve as ways in which the thinker works through those conflicts and as ways in which others, whose personal situations are quite different, may compre-hend and cope with their particular issues. Such is the case with Freud's model of the Oedipus complex. For though it may have had its genesis in Freud's relationship with his own father, it has served countless others since Freud's time in understanding their own vexed relationships with authority figures, as well as the poignant paradox of the human condition—that the advent of all new life heralds the inevitable passing of the life that made it possible.

Whether our thoughts are concrete or abstract, fantastic or factual, they inevitably reflect who we are and the situations in which we live. Thought is a coping strategy, a way of getting some purchase on experiences that elude our grasp, some distance from experiences that are too close to be clearly seen. But though thinking, like storytelling, begins within our hidden or intimate lives, it finds consummation in the public realm—connecting with others whose incipient thoughts and stories spring from comparable experiences. This is the only sense we can give the term objective—the sense not that our thinking or storytelling has attained a final or an eternal truth, but that it has connected with the thinking and storying of others, and thus made co-existence more possible in a plural world. "This is what I call philosophizing," writes Henry Miller in his essay on Herman Keyserling. "It is something other than making philosophy—*something plus*."[40]

I confess that it is this "plus" that has always fascinated me as much as the manifest content of any philosophical or anthropological work; the sense that it is the work of a person struggling to become what she is before she is a thinker, to make sense of her situation, to speak rather than be silent, to act rather than remain passive, and, above all, to connect with precursors and contemporaries and so create a sense of human solidarity in a world that is all too often chaotic, incomprehensible, and divided.

These considerations inform James Miller's great biography *The Passion of Michel Foucault*. Not only does the word "passion" suggest that this thinker, who had erased the subject from the anonymous field of discourse "like a face erased by sand at the edge of the sea,"[41] had, ironically, constructed himself as a subject in the course of his intellectual labor; it presages an exploration of how profoundly Foucault's philosophy (*logos*) implicated a biography (*bios*). "His oeuvre . . . seemed to incorporate both his books *and* his life," James Miller writes, "and the one could not be understood—least of all philosophically—apart from the other. Indeed, some kind of biographical approach seemed warranted by Foucault's own final thoughts on the unusual kind of 'philosophical life' he had evidently led."[42]

These thoughts were recorded in June 1984, during Foucault's dying days, by one of his closest friends, the young artist Hervé Guibert. "Evoking his childhood and its dreams, [Foucault] volunteered what he felt to be the deepest truths about himself."[43] These truths centered on three primal scenes, or "terrible dioramas." In the first, Foucault, as a small boy, is led by his father, who was a surgeon, into an operating theatre in the hospital at Poitiers to witness the amputation of a man's leg. The father's motive? To "steel the boy's virility." In the second diorama, the boy walks past a courtyard in Poitiers in which a woman has been living for decades on a straw mattress. She is locally known as "the Sequestered of Poitiers," and the boy experiences an unforgettable chill as he passes by. The final scene is set in the war years. The life of the precocious young student is suddenly interrupted by an invasion of arrogant young Parisians, "naturally smarter than anyone else." "Dethroned, the philosopher-child is seized by hate, damns the intruders, invites every curse to rain down upon them." Soon after, these Jewish children, who had found momentary refugee in Poitiers, did in fact disappear in transports to the death camps of the Third Reich.

James Miller glimpses in these anecdotes many of the themes that will preoccupy Foucault for the rest of life: wanton power (the father forcing his son to witness an amputation); erotic transgression (the woman on the mattress had been confined in a pitch-dark room by her mother and brother, given little food, mired in her own shit, plagued by lice, maggots, and rats, and driven insane, allegedly because she had given birth to an illegitimate child when she was younger); and crushing guilt (for the fascism Foucault had discovered in himself, and the fate of the powerless students he had wanted to disappear).[44] Miller's analysis is confirmed, if only obliquely, in the final interview Foucault gave before he died. In a Nietzschean vein, he confesses that all his work amounted to a kind of autobiography, and he abjures the "rhetorically evasive" form of philosophy in which he had disguised the truth about himself.

In the sketches and portraits that comprise this book, I claim no definitive understanding of the thinkers whose lives have engaged my interest. But while they are tentative and tangential, these essays touch on the question of how we might balance modes of thinking, speaking, writing, and living that have, since the Enlightenment, been seen as antithetical. When a trainee social worker or psychotherapist is told not to get too emotionally involved with his or her client, when an ethnographer is counseled not to lose sight of his or her academic objectives by going native, when an analytical philosophy has recourse to symbolic logic when working out what can be reasonably stated or defended rather than adducing examples from the world of which he or she is a part, and when a scientist speaks of subjective experience as a regrettable disturbance that must be neutralized in order for objective observations to be made, we are carrying the burden of culturally and historically determined distinctions that cannot be sustained in reality and that overlook the different contexts in which these modes of being and thinking find a useful place.

We come here to the limits of social science. To understand in depth and detail what transpires within our relations to others, we draw upon the work of social scientists, psychologists, and ethologists to be sure, but it is to the work of artists, novelists, biographers, and nonspecialists that we must also turn for techniques that help us do greatest justice to lived experience. In venturing beyond the borders of orthodox science, we may be accused of departing from empirical truth and being unprofessional, or, worse, of pure invention. But there may be a middle ground, where anecdote enriches rather than invalidates our work.

Let me elaborate by referring to a largely forgotten essay by Lionel Trilling, introducing a 1952 American edition of George Orwell's *Homage to Catalonia*. Trilling begins by observing how rare it is that a writer's personal identity is fully acknowledged or fully felt in his or her writing. Indeed, both literature and science tend, conventionally, to background or occlude the author's own biography in order to give his or her characters, concepts, and conclusions greater presence and weight. But like Mark Twain and William James, Orwell "presides" over his work, eschewing any false authority and focusing on "fronting the world with nothing more that one's simple, direct, undeceived intelligence, and respect for the powers one does not have, and the work one undertakes to do."[45] Trilling goes on to speak against an etherealizing tradition, dating from the Enlightenment, that privileges abstract, rational thought over the commonplace bodily, emotional, and mental realities of our everyday lives. There are overtones of John Dewey's empirical naturalism and Bakhtin's grotesque realism in Trilling's argument against reification.

> The prototypical act of the modern intellectual is his abstracting himself from the life of the family. We have yet to understand the thaumaturgical way in which we conceive of intellectuality. By intellectuality we are freed from the thralldom to the familiar commonplace, from the materiality and concreteness by which it exists, the hardness of the cash and the hardness of getting it, the inelegance and intractability of family things. It gives us power over intangibles, such as Beauty and Justice, and it permits us to escape the cosmic ridicule which in our youth we suppose is inevitably directed at those who take seriously the small concerns of the world, which we know to be inadequate and doomed by the very fact that it is so absurdly conditioned—by things, habits, local and temporary customs, and the foolish errors and solemn absurdities of the men of the past.[46]

Inevitably, a mode of address that remains faithful to the facts of experience—pedestrian, unsystematic, ill-focused, and inchoate though they often are—resists the intellectual's demand for analytical coherence and the conventional expectation of narrative closure. It also departs from a long-standing orientation in European philosophy that Ricoeur characterizes as "the school of suspicion." In the work of the three great "masters of suspicion"—Marx, Nietzsche, and Freud—consciousness is mostly false consciousness. By implication, the truth about our thoughts, feelings, and actions is inaccessible to the conscious mind and can only be brought to light by experts in interpretation and deciphering.[47] Although Henry Ellenberger traces this "unmasking trend" back to the seventeenth-century French moralists,[48] it finds ubiquitous expression in the suspicion that "true reality is never the most obvious, and that the nature of truth is already indicated by the care it takes to remain elusive."[49] Among the Mehinaku (Upper Xingu region, Amazonia), "all the things/beings of the world are not what they seem, in a sense they are shells." The world is a world of surfaces, "of masks ('mascaras'/shepeku), houses ('casa'/pái), skins (umay) and most importantly clothing/covering (ënai)." In the Mehinaku view, gifted individuals can change skins as ordinary people change clothes. Even more extraordinary is their view that everything in the world is an inferior copy of an archetypal form that is the "true version" of the replicas that appear before us in the everyday world.[50] In Papua New Guinea, the contrast between what is evident and what is obscure is likened to a leaf, one side of which is always turned away from the light. Among the Kuranko of Sierra Leone, the socio-spatial distinction between kenema (open to the public gaze) and duguro (ground in) or duworon (covert, hidden, underhand) echoes the Latin distinction between the res publica (whatever belongs to or concerns the people as a whole) and the res privata (the domain of the domus, or house). At the same time it evokes the European distinction between the open space of the agora (marketplace) and the space of oblique meanings and of allegory (allos, "other," + agoreuin, "speak openly, speak in the assembly or market—the agora") and thus implies a wide array of differences between activities that take place in the light of day—within the hearing and sight of others and are common knowledge—and activities that are clandestine, duplicitous, or veiled by secrecy and darkness.

These non-Western perspectives suggest we might move from our preoccupation with the unconscious as a deep recess of interior being and focus on the penumbral field of being that lies about us. Accordingly, consciousness is not so much a mask that must be stripped away to reveal true intentions, ulterior motives, or real essences: the mask mediates our *relationships* with an encompassing world of others—precursory and contemporary, familiar and foreign.[51] Foucault states this beautifully, arguing that we might think of the unconscious as an "obscure space," an "element of darkness," which lies both inside and outside thought. "The unthought (whatever name we give it) is not lodged in man like a shrivelled up nature or a stratified history; it is, in relation to man, the Other: the Other that is not only a brother but a twin, born, not of man, nor in man, but beside him and at the same time, in an identical newness, in an unavoidable duality."[52]

In Plato, light and shadow serve as metaphors for the difference between reality and mere appearance. In Plato's allegory of the cave,[53] a group of chained prisoners have, from the day they were born, known only the shadowy shapes of animals and objects thrown by firelight on the cavern walls. Unable to see the fire, or the things that cast the shadows, the prisoners assume the shadows to be real and give them names, ponder their attributes, and debate their worth. For Plato, art and poetry do not get us beyond such appearances. "A stick will look bent if you put it in the water, straight when you take it out, and deceptive differences of shading can make the same surface seem to the eye concave or convex; and our minds are clearly liable to all sorts of confusions of this kind."[54] But, says Plato, reason and calculation can save us from mistakenly supposing that such magical effects are real and enable us to render the world truly intelligible. My own phenomenology is an attempt to get beyond the play of shadows without assuming that reason is necessarily superior to art. Instead of invoking the antinomies of reality and appearance, clear reason and blind emotion, or unconscious and conscious, I follow Hannah Arendt's notion of the human condition as both plural and paradoxical. Every human being possesses a unique identity *at the same time* as he or she may be identified with various modes of collective or species being.

Inevitably, this means that we find difficulty in reconciling our first-person points of view with the views that constitute the world we share with others. As Arendt observed, though private experiences "lead an uncertain, shadowy kind of existence unless and until they are transformed, deprivatized and deindividualized, as it were, into a shape to fit them for public appearance,"[55] many private experiences, such as love, are degraded by being made public, and the public sphere may assume a minatory, blob-like,[56] totalitarian form, such as Heidegger described as *Das Man*.[57] One also thinks of Baudelaire's despair at being lost in a soulless crowd, an experience with which Walter Benjamin clearly identified ("Lost in the base world, jostled by the crowd, I am like a weary man whose eye, looking backward into the depths of the years, sees only disillusion and bitterness, and looking ahead sees only a tempest which contains nothing new, neither instruction nor pain").[58] But as Edith Piaf's compelling song, "La Foule (The Crowd), reminds us, crowds can exhilarate as well as alienate. In this song, two lovers are suddenly separated by the crowd in which they had been happily borne along, singing and dancing. One moment they and the crowd are a single body; the next the woman is swept away, sundered from the man she loves.[59] In a classical novel of the Meiji period, Natsume Soseki expresses his ambivalence toward twentieth-century civilization, identifying it with the steam train, roaring along, "packed tight with hundreds of people in the one box, merciless in its progress." Though Soseki is writing thirty-four years before the transports of the Third Reich begin delivering their human freight to the death camps of northern Europe, the Japanese writer recoils at the thought of the "hundreds crammed in there," travelling at the same speed, stopping at the same places, submitting to the same "baptismal submersion in the same swirling stream." The train signifies a loss of agency and autonomy. "Some people say that people 'ride' the train, but I would say they are thrust into it; some speak of 'going' by train, but it seems to be they are transported by it. Nothing is more disdainful of individuality."[60]

Clearly, a tension always remains between the selves we construct together and aspects of ourselves that cannot be made over to the public sphere, calling conventional wisdom into question, resisting recognized roles, refusing to fit in or swear fidelity to another sphere. Otto Rank wrote of this anxious relationship between the will to separate and the will to unite[61] and, deeply influenced by Rank's thinking, Ernest Becker summarized our human dilemma as follows:

> Man wants the impossible: He wants to lose his isolation and keep it at the same time. He can't stand the sense of separateness, and yet he can't allow the complete suffocation of his vitality. He wants to expand by merging with the powerful beyond that transcends him, yet he wants while merging with it to remain individual and aloof.[62]

It is this struggle *between* aspects of ourselves that pull away from the public realm and aspects that engage and identify with it that I am concerned with in this book. In trying to capture these shifts among personal, interpersonal, and transpersonal modes of apprehending reality, I have recourse to a style of writing that juxtaposes biographical, autobiographical, and abstract reflections, interleaving narrative and essay.

CHAPTER 2

The Philosopher Who Would Not Be King

I have spent 40 years looking for a coherent and convincing way of formulating my worries about what, if anything, philosophy is good for.

—Richard Rorty

The day was hot. Trudging up the long avenue toward the university, I kept to the shade. The figs and eucalypts reminded me of Australia, bark stripped and straggling, or littering the dry ground. The oaks, myrtles, and phoenix palms took me back to the South of France. I imagined that I could feel at home here, this commingling of antipodean, Mediterranean, and American flora, this winterless climate. But the buildings, colonnades, tiled terra-cotta roofs, and open courtyards were a less congenial mix. Inexplicably, Rodin's *Burghers of Calais* had been made strangers to one another, standing alone rather than grouped as they are in Calais and London, willing hostages prepared to give their lives to save their besieged city. At the entrance to the university there was an inscription dedicating the campus to the memory of Leland Stanford Jr., "born to mortality, passed to immortality," a mother's undying love metamorphosed into an institution of timber beam, plaster walls, reinforced concrete, and carved stone. So we convert our tragedies into objects that will withstand corrosive rain, seismic upheavals, and time. We place memorial urns in the cloisters, a chapel at the heart of it all, columns and commemorative plaques that lift our eyes from the ground. Even our intellectual labor aspires to the condition of permanence and transcendence, though our lives are transitory in comparison, our miseries commonplace, our labors unavailing. I felt a strong desire to testify to the struggle of those who lacked the means to pretend that life was otherwise. In about an hour I would present a paper about the life of a Kuranko woman for whom this place might well appear to be paradise but whose thoughts were always under duress, bound by the obligations of parenthood, the struggle to make a farm, to pay her children's school fees and provide food for her children, and to overcome the debilitating effects of an undiagnosed illness. I was also thinking that this was where Richard Rorty taught from 1997 to 2005; Palo Alto was where he died.

That any philosophy mirrors the life of the philosopher is an assertion from which many thinkers would recoil,[1] since it seems to reduce thought to the prejudices, preoccupations, and persuasions that supposedly character-ize the musings of mere mortals. If every great philosophy is, as Nietzsche avows, "an involuntary and unconscious memoir" reflecting who the philoso-pher is before he or she takes up philosophy, then thought is but an adventi-tious by-product of one's life rather than the disciplined, disinterested work of reason. I thought of Nietzsche when I first met Richard Rorty. There was something disarmingly vulnerable about him. Though renowned for his groundbreaking critique of philosophy as a quest for the foundations of true knowledge or accurate representations of the essence of the world,[2] and his MacArthur "genius award," Dick Rorty seemed socially unsure of himself and nonplussed whenever the talk turned from academic to mundane matters like Australian wines, the films of Werner Herzog, or the best Vietnamese restaurant in Canberra.

The year was 1982. The place was the Humanities Research Centre at the Australian National University. We were there on visiting fellowships—myself, Dick Rorty, Don Hirsch, Zygmund Baumann, Paul Connerton, Russell Keat, Patrick McCarthy, and others I got to know less well. I was writing essays on embodiment, profiting from long conversations with Paul, who was writing his book on bodily social memory, and Russell, who was preparing his critique of Merleau-Ponty's *Phenomenology of Perception*. It was my hatha yoga practice that had inspired my explorations of body conscious-ness; unfortunately, it had also turned me into an obnoxious fundamentalist who believed that the respiratory and psycho-physical disciplines of yoga enabled one to achieve a truer and more realistic relationship with the world, and that discursive thought was largely illusory. Rorty objected to the essen-tialist overtones of my view, arguing that efforts to ground knowledge in the body *or* the mind, in reasoned discourse *or* strong intuition, were equally misguided. And he cautioned me against explaining any human experience in terms of some prior cause or first principle. In my defense, I pointed out that a philosophical argument against foundationalism could not be transferred to the real world, since all human beings have recourse to notions of firstness, foundations and fundamentals in their everyday lives. If it is existentially the case that life is insupportable without such notions, what is the point of making philosophical arguments to the contrary? Moreover, I felt that the Deweyan argument, to which Rorty subscribed, against Platonic dualisms like body-mind, true-false, and subject-object left unconsidered the way we deploy these antinomies to capture different modes of experience. Making epistemological claims for such distinctions is absurd, but recognizing the phenomenological differences they communicated was, I thought, vital to understanding human experience.

I suppose I was ineptly asking whether philosophy has anything to say that might make a real difference to our lives, and whether its insights had value only within the academic circles where they served as currency. I quickly learned that these were also burning questions for Rorty, for beyond the philosophical issue of whether we can ever truly represent what lies outside our minds—whether human thought can mirror nature—lies the much more pragmatic issue of whether the insights of thinkers can change the world.

Though Rorty's parents broke with the Communist Party in 1933, they turned to the political philosophy of Leon Trotsky, even sheltering John Frank, one of Trotsky's secretaries, for several months following Trotsky's assassination in Mexico in 1940. "I grew up knowing that all decent people were, if not Trotskyites, at least socialists," Rorty would later write, reflecting on the influence of his parents. For even as a boy, he believed that the very "point of being human was to spend one's life fighting social injustice."[3] One wonders whether this shy, bookish, and precocious twelve-year-old appreciated the ironic contradiction between his desire to reform the world and his reclusive personality that would incline him to understand the world from afar.

In an interview that first aired on Dutch TV, Rorty is asked to describe himself as a child.

Appearing almost ingenuous, Rorty searches for the right words. "Shy, withdrawn, ingrown, " he says carefully. "Um, constantly afraid of being beaten up in the schoolyard. Hmm. Not playing much of a role in any activities. Hoping to get away from school as soon as I could."

"Why?"

"Because . . . I just felt awkward and unable to join in things."

"For what reason?"

"Because . . . dunno. It's just a fairly early memory of being asocial."

Watching this video, I am immediately struck by Rorty's matter-of-factness—his refusal to reduce his shyness to some sinister cause, to find fault with his parents and upbringing, to judge his behavior as either good or bad. But the interviewer is determined to press him, to pin him down, to fathom this solitary behavior and use it as a key to unlock the secrets of the man.

"The schoolyard, then. You're standing alone, or . . ."

"You know, actually my memories aren't very strong until about the age [of] eight or seven . . . something like that. I was always being moved from school to school. I think I went to seven or eight different primary schools. In each one I would always wonder if I was going to make any friends, and then never did."

"But do you know why? This shyness, where did it come from?"

"Dunno."

"Did it accompany you all your life, or . . . ?"

"I've never been very easy in my dealings with people. I'm a lot better than when I was a child, but still I tend to avoid parties because I can't think of any small talk to make."

"As a shy boy, escaping the schoolyard, escaping the others in the classroom, going from school to school seven or eight times, you might suppose there's somebody who reads books in the silence of his room, at home? Am I correct?"

"Yeah, yeah. According to my parents I pretty much taught myself to read when I was four or thereabouts and spent most of the rest of my life reading books."

If Rorty is bored or irritated by the interviewer's probing, he is at pains not to show it. He listens to the question and tries to answer it, even if the picture that he is allowing to emerge is of a nerd who felt indifferent to the rough-and-tumble of the world.

"The world in these books, was it perhaps more important to you than the world outside?"

"Yeah, much more. The world outside never quite lived up to the books except for a few scenes in nature, animals, birds, flowers."

Rorty is alluding to his childhood passion for collecting wild orchids, flowers that may have attracted him because they were "hard to find," "socially useless," and made him feel, at certain Wordsworthian moments, that he had been "touched by something numinous, something of ineffable importance."[4]

But the interviewer wants to know "what kind of world" this boy was "creating by reading books and combining them."

"Oh, fantasies of power . . . ah . . . of control . . . um . . . of omnipotence. The normal childhood fantasies . . . um . . . you know. Turning out to be the unacknowledged son of the king, that kind of thing."

"Power. Control. The control and power you missed in the schoolyard?"

"And I think I was basically looking for some way to get back at the schoolyard bullies by turning into some kind of intellectual and acquiring some kind of intellectual power. I wasn't clear how this was going to work."

"Did you manage to come back to them as the intellectual?"

"No, I just lost touch with them by living in a world of intellectuals."

"After primary school, did the situation remain the same, that is, you were escaping, escaping into a world of books and fantasy?"

"Well, actually, I was very lucky, because when I was fifteen I went to the university. And it was a particular program in a particular university where no one talked about anything except books, so it was, you know, ideal for me, and it was the situation in which I felt more or less at ease and in control of things."

"Was there any feeling in your childhood or early adulthood that you would become a philosopher?"

"I think philosophy was somewhat accidental. I think that I could equally well have become an intellectual historian or a literary critic, but it just happened that the course I was most intrigued by when I was sixteen was a philosophy course, and so I sort of kept taking more and more philosophy courses and signing up for more and more degrees."

"Why were you intrigued?"

"I think because of the sense of mastery and control you get out of philosophical ideas. You get the impression from reading philosophy that now you can place everything in order or in a neat arrangement or something like that, and this gratifies one's need for domination."

The interviewer, it seems, is determined to have the last line.

"Compensation for shyness?"

"Yep."

If the truth of a statement lies neither in its correspondence to a preexistent reality nor in its logical coherence but in its capacity to help a person cope with life, to carry him or her into a more fulfilling relationship with others, what kind of truth is established by this interview? Given Rorty's philosophical position, his reclusive childhood did not cause him to become a thinker, doomed to converse with himself *because* no one would talk to him. What he is telling the interviewer is that books and philosophy were not escapes from the harshness of the world but ways in which he coped with this world. "I wanted a way to be both an intellectual and spiritual snob and a friend of humanity," he writes, "a nerdy recluse and a fighter for justice."[5] In pragmatism he would find a viable compromise between the life of the mind and the life of the social activist. And by placing philosophy on a par with art and craft, storytelling, religion, bird-watching, and life skills, he could simultaneously puncture the pretensions of academics who regarded intellectual cleverness as intrinsically superior to all other forms of cleverness and affirm a solidarity with men and women whose skills were practical, social, or aesthetic.

My wife and I invited Dick and his wife Mary to our house for dinner. Since Dick and Don Hirsch were close friends, we invited the Hirsches as well. It was a convivial evening, and though I have a clear memory of cooking Indian food I cannot now recall much of our conversation. A few weeks later, Dick and Mary invited us to their house for a meal. They rented a monocrete bungalow in Deakin, and their two children, Patricia and Kevin, were preparing for bed when we arrived.

From the start of the evening, it was clear that Dick had decided to assume the role of host. Moreover, I had the distinct impression that Dick had had to persuade Mary against her better judgment that this strict division of labor was a good idea. Not only did he cook and serve the food; he ensured that our wineglasses were filled and that we were properly introduced to the other guests, who included Tamsin and Ian Donaldson. Even now, twenty-nine years after the event, I retain a poignant memory of Dick's determination to prove himself equal to the occasion. But what moved me most was his obvious struggle with tasks that most of us take for granted—cooking a simple meal, bantering about the weather, commenting on current events, discussing travel plans. That none of this came easy to him was obvious. Perhaps he had never before cooked a meal for eight guests. The food was not very good, but the determination to please was overwhelming, and we responded as parents might respond to a child bringing them breakfast in bed, the toast burned, the egg underdone, the tea cold. I don't want to sound condescending, for when I later reflected on the evening, I felt only admiration that someone should push himself so hard to perform tasks that did not come naturally to him. For it seemed to me that the labor of producing a meal was greater, for him, than the labor of writing an essay on Dewey's critique of metaphysics.

After Canberra I did not see Dick Rorty again, though we corresponded for a couple of years. He sent me an inscribed copy of *Consequences of Pragmatism*, and I reciprocated with a copy of *Allegories of the Wilderness*, which also appeared in 1982. And when my wife died in September 1983, Dick sent his condolences with a phrase that conveyed that passionate acceptance of contingency without which it is difficult to survive any loss, yet communicating that sense of hope without which it is impossible to envisage a future: "I only wish there was something useful I could do."

As it turned out, his work proved to be more useful than he, or I, could have imagined, for in the months after Pauline's death I spent several hours every day methodically reading, and taking notes on, the collected writings of William James and John Dewey. Had Richard Rorty not introduced me to these writers, I would perhaps never have realized how directly and profoundly pragmatism speaks to our struggle to recover a raison d'etre in the face of catastrophic loss. Unlike Boethius, whom I also read at this time, I found no consolation in thought as "the one true good"; rather, it was the realization of the limits of abstract thought that enabled me to yield to the natural processes of mourning, which always occur in their own good time.

One can never know for certain how one's actions or words will impact on others. But sometimes it is a person's struggle to be good, or decent, that impresses one more than his or her achievement of such virtues. In my observations of Kuranko initiation rites, I was impressed by the concerted effort of preceptors and neophytes alike to realize manhood or womanhood. So completely did social order and continuity depend on this transformation of sexually amorphous children into gendered adults (and, by implication, the strict separation of men and women in everyday life) that any failure to achieve this goal doomed a person to be a butt of jokes for the rest of his or her life. But the apotheosis was impossible. No one could fully realize the gender stereotypes and the ethical codes associated with them. Personal dispositions and the vicissitudes of life made it inevitable that men and women would sometimes fail in their duties or fall short of what was expected of them. As with gender, so with rank—one could only gesture ritualistically toward the ideal. This impossibility of ever closing the gap between collective ideals and real individuals may explain the theatrical plays on gender identity with which initiation rites are replete: men presuming to give birth to the male neophytes, nurturing them without the need of mothers; women aspiring to inculcate the stoic virtues they associate with men. In the many role reversals that occur in the course of public performances—women acting as hunters or soldiers, men obliged to perform tasks normally done by women—one sees the physical impossibility of the transformations to which initiation aspires. But the dramatic power of these performances lies in the very clumsiness and ineptitude with which the actors pretend to be someone they are not. The blurring of role distinctions ironically sharpens our sense of these distinctions, reminding us that identity is partly pure artifice. Something similar is true of philosophers who aspire to change the world. Not only are our philosophical pictures of the world artificial, as Rorty points out, but the world itself lies largely beyond our linguistic and intellectual grasp. Yet it is in those moments when thought struggles to become worldly or the world seems to conspire in our struggle to understand it that we most clearly see the impossibility of the unity of mind and matter but find in that disappointment a sense of oneness with those who have travelled the same path, engaged in the same struggle, and come to the same conclusion. Rorty once wrote that "the meaning of one human life may have little to do with the meaning of any other human life, while being none the worse for that."[6] But it is gratifying nonetheless to recognize affinities, sympathies, common ground when divergent backgrounds, affiliations, and intellectual capacities led one to expect none. In such recognitions we realize the usefulness of Rorty's observation that discovering unity beneath appearances may be less exciting than discovering that comity is compatible with radical and contradictory variousness, and that there is nothing necessarily wrong with bringing Trotsky and wild orchids together in a single story without first explaining what they have in common.

Not long before his death in June 2007, Richard Rorty wrote a piece called "The Fire of Life"[7] in which he meditates on being diagnosed with pancreatic cancer and speaks of the consolations of poetry. He concludes, "I now wish that I had spent somewhat more of my life with verse. This is not because I fear having missed out on truths that are incapable of statement in prose. There are no such truths; there is nothing about death that Swinburne and Landor knew but Epicurus and Heidegger failed to grasp. Rather, it is because I would have lived more fully if I had been able to rattle off more old chestnuts—just as I would have if I had made more close friends."

I take Rorty to be saying something more than that poetry and friendship provide pleasure. He is saying that they carry us across the threshold of the self into richer and stranger regions than any we have known alone. Philosophy needs the language of poetry to enter the penumbra—that force field around us, partly lit, partly in shadow, that shapes who we are yet defies our attempts to fully control or comprehend it. Whether we refer to this realm as natural, spiritual, historical, or political is less significant than its essential ambiguity. It enthralls us to the same extent that it eludes us. And though it may unsettle and even destroy us, it may become a source of generative power.

In a magisterial study of Sinhalese sorcery, Bruce Kapferer explores this ambiguity. His starting point is the "magicality" of human existence, a term he borrows from Sartre to emphasize that "human beings are at once individuals and beings who transcend and transgress the boundaries and space of their own and others' organic individuality."[8] This field of wider being in which we are immersed is "magical" because our knowledge and mastery of it always remain slippery and uncertain. Thwarted in our efforts to achieve presence, prosperity, and power through direct social and economic action, we have recourse to magical, occult, or ritual means of attaining our goals. In the Sinhalese social imaginary, this is the field of sorcery, embodied in the image of Suniyam riding a blue mare (emblematic of his power), carrying a broken pot of fire in his left hand (destructive heat) and a sword in his right (judgment and punishment), and his body covered with snakes (venomous punishment). What fascinates Kapferer is that the forces of sorcery permeate both the body politic and the individual body, so that the struggle against political anarchy implicates a psychological struggle against madness. This is compellingly shown in the life story of Lillian, a "soothsayer" (sastra karaya) able to work with demonic forces in ways that enable her to dispense medical and spiritual advice to clients.

Lillian was in her seventies and had been attending supplicants at a temple in Colombo from 1935, though she had her own shrine in the poverty and crime-racked shantytown of Slave Island where she lived.

Her father, a rickshaw man, had come to Slave Island from an equally notorious part of the southern provincial city of Galle. Lillian and her parents lived among a group of Tamil drummers, members of an outcaste community. As Lillian tells it, she would dance at their ritual occasions, and at eleven she experienced her first encounter with the goddess Bhadrakali, who possessed her. Three years later she married Liyanage, who sold tea to the dockworkers. By then her father had died, but his ghost (*preta*) maintained an attachment to her. When she became entranced by her father and danced possessed, her husband was infuriated and beat her. Her husband continued beating her as Lillian had other possession experiences. The ones she recalls in particular are her entrancements by the goddess Pattini, whose violent and punishing form she connects with Bhadrakali. In 1935, after bearing five children, she left her husband and journeyed to the main shrine of Kataragama in the southeastern corner of the island. While she was at Kataragama, her husband, who was still fighting with her, met with an accident and was killed. Lillian felt that he had been punished by the god Kataragama and by Bhadrakali for beating her and her ill-treatment. Lillian possesses the violent and punishing powers of Bhadrakali and Pattini. She has her warrant (*varam*) from the main Bhadrakali shrine at the Hindu temple of Munnesvaram (outside Chilaw, north of Colombo). Lillian also has a warrant from god Vishnu, which she achieved at the time when she first began to manifest and use her violent powers. As she describes it, she would visit the shrine to Vishnu at a local Buddhist temple and declare before the god that she had achieved knowledge, or realized the truth (*satyakriya*), and that she was pure, refusing sexual contact with her husband and having no intention to be married again. On one occasion, the eyes of Vishnu's image closed and then opened. Lillian took this as a sign that Vishnu had granted her his powers through which she could control the violent forces that she manifests. Lillian constantly renews her relationships with the gods by visiting their key shrines. She claims that she got the idea of being a *maniyo* ["mother," "soothsayer"] at the Bhadrakali shrine from her involvement in the annual festival at Kataragama, where the god is attended in procession by the six mothers (*kartikeya*) who took care of him at his birth.

Lillian expresses in her own life a personal suffering and a violence present in close ties. She also embraces in herself wider forces of violence as well as difference. She freely admits a connection with criminal elements in the city, and this is vital to her own power. Lillian represents herself as a totalization of diversity and claims a knowledge of eighteen languages (eighteen being a symbolic number of the totality of human existence). . . . Lillian, I note, is an embodiment of fragmenting force but also a potency for the control and mastery of such force. This is one significance of her warrant from Vishnu, the guardian of Buddhism on the island and a major ordering power. Lillian is pleased with her own success in business. She has controlling interest in three taxis.

Lillian's clients invoke the powers that reside in her body. Some address her directly as Bhadrakali *maniyo*. Lillian says that she has cut thousands of *huniyams* [sorcery objects], and has used her powers in the making and breaking of marriages, the settlement of court cases, and the killing of personal enemies.[9]

This powerful story reminds us that the world around us—whether conceived of in terms of supernatural or market forces, of sectarian, class, or caste identifications—is potentially a source of well-being *and* destruction. Not only must we struggle against an external world that limits our choices and circumscribes our existence; we must struggle against our *inner* fear of being crushed and erased, as well as our anger against the forces that oppress us.

I have cited Lillian's story at length because it brings into dramatic relief the complexity of the struggle to exist in a world sundered by sectarian violence, class conflict, and oppressive political power. Strategies to earn an income through business ventures coexist with tactics to avoid domestic violence and channel the powers of the gods. But Lillian's story also calls into question the appropriateness of labeling her choices as real or illusory, or asking whether it is better to struggle against injustice rather than devote oneself to "private projects of self creation."[10] There are no algorithms for answering such questions. We can neither know for certain whether a Marxist analysis of social injustices in Sri Lanka would be helpful or harmful nor know for sure whether our understanding of Lillian reflects our own Western dismay at unnecessary human suffering. For Rorty it is enough to describe and testify to the lives of others, as far as we can, on the grounds of our human solidarity with them. They are not misguided creatures, in alien worlds, but *ourselves* in other circumstances.[11] But to invoke poetry or to speak of the consolation of wild orchids may be to risk rendering the world too benign and to leave its social violence unremarked. During his first trip to India, Rorty spoke to a fellow philosophy professor who was also a politician. After thirty years of attempting to help India's poor, this man confessed that he had found no solution to the problem. "I found myself," Rorty writes, "like most Northerners in the South, not thinking about the beggars in the hot streets once I was back in my pleasantly air-conditioned hotel."[12] But back in America, recalling his experiences, Rorty's only conclusion is that all the love and talk in the world—the technological innovations, the new genetics, the power of education, the politics of diversity—"will not help."[13] Is this defeatist? A confirmation that, for us, the poor will always remain unthinkable? And where does such a conclusion leave us? Withdrawn into the safe confines of our own small world, immunized from the perils of actually entering the world with which we claim solidarity, consoled by poetry? Or inspired to return to the streets until we find one person whose life is changed, no matter how imperceptibly, by his or her encounter with us, so that the question is no longer whether solidarity can be thought into existence but how it is actually brought into existence by our everyday choices of what we do.

CHAPTER 3

Hermit in the Water of Life

And in the evening of my days
Let me remember and be remembered
By the friends that I have made . . .

—Brijen K. Gupta

If I have recourse to metaphors of water and darkness to describe myself at twenty-one, it is partly because I spent that turbulent year in a harbor city buffeted by high winds and ransacked by winter storms. In this emotional maelstrom, I knew only one person who seemed to have the knack of staying afloat. And so I clung to him as to a life raft, buoyed by his concern for my welfare, guided by his advice, secure in his example. In retrospect, I am amazed that Brijen Gupta was only ten years older than I was.[1] Yet the difference between twenty-one and thirty-one is the difference between youth and manhood, and it was magnified, in this instance, by Brijen's political savvy, breadth of experience, and formidable self-confidence.

Though he lectured in the Asian studies program at Victoria University of Wellington, he enjoyed the company of students as much as academic colleagues and presided over our small circle of leftists and would-be writers with the autocratic assuredness of a guru and the bemused detachment of a Cheshire cat. Whether in the student café or at a Ghuznee Street coffee shop, Brijen would play the avuncular roles of provocateur and sage. I remember riding in his car through rain-swept, pitch-dark Wellington streets as he, by turns, chanted Hindi lyrics or chided me for my romantic illusions about tribal societies.

Talking in the cities, longing for the earth,
Those ignorant of life will tell their neighbors

That in the country there is natural bliss
For men and women, who are nearer angels
Because they feel the wind upon their faces,
Or eat their supper sore from tramping furrows
And see the lightning scorch the prairie night.

These have not woken in the smothering dark
To listen to the clock draining away,
Second by second, the inner spring of joy;
Nor caught the smell of death that floats around
The farmhouse in the early afternoon.[2]

That I was not crushed by Brijen's criticisms may have been because I had such a dim view of myself and envied Brijen's urbanity, erudition, and forthright way of engaging with everyone he met, from gas station attendants to professors. But it irked me that he was always in the right, always calling the shots, always knowing what was best, politically, aesthetically, and intellectually, and brooked no opinion that ran counter to his own. Perhaps this was his failing, or the price of his precocious and encompassing knowledge of so many fields—that he was inclined to associate with those who would assent to his opinions and look up to him as a god. In any case, it was the absolute asymmetry of our relationship—his assumption of authority, and my willing acquiescence to it—that made me deaf or indifferent to the snippets of information he shared about his background. And it wasn't until I came to Harvard in 2005 that I rectified this and asked Brijen—who was now retired from university teaching and living in Rochester, New York—if he would agree to a conversation about his early years in India and the United States. So began a series of meetings and e-mail exchanges that gradually filled in the gaps in my knowledge of this man who had figured so importantly in my development, a man to whom, in many ways, I owed my life.

Not long before our conversations began, I had read Albert Raboteau's essay on Thomas Merton and Martin Luther King Jr., both of whom died in 1968.[3] Raboteau chronicles the events that brought these men to understand that the monastic and prophetic traditions of which they were a part were not incompatible with critical thought and social activism. Sixteen years after publishing *The Seven Storey Mountain*, in which he embraced a philosophy of world renunciation, Merton decided that this goal was illusory, and he experienced "the immense joy of being a man, a member of a race in which God Himself became incarnate." His epiphany occurred in the most pedestrian setting: a shopping district at the corner of Fourth and Walnut in Louisville, Kentucky.

> I was suddenly overwhelmed with the realization that I loved all those people, that they were mine and I theirs, that we could not be alien to one another even though we were total strangers. It was like waking from a dream of separateness, of spurious self-isolation in a special world, the world of renunciation and supposed holiness. The whole illusion of a separate holy existence is a dream. Not that I question the reality of my vocation, or of my monastic life: but the conception of "separation from the world" that we have in the monastery too easily presents itself as a complete illusion: the illusion that by making vows we become a different species of being, pseudo-angels, "spiritual men," men of interior life, what have you.[4]

Martin Luther King's transformation from church pastor to civil rights leader was triggered by the 1955 Montgomery bus boycott. Like Merton, he came to the realization that love for his fellow human beings was the way to God, and that fighting for human rights—even if it cost him his own life—was the path to righteousness.

Raboteau's insights also helped me understand that, for me, the dialectic between the outward and inward poles of being had not found expression in a rhythm of political activism and periodic retreat but in an oscillation between intellectual or literary work (which is, of necessity, solitary and silent) and a passionate engagement, as an ethnographer, in the lives of others on the margins of the Western world. This was my personal variation on the theme of being at home and being away.

Fortuitously, Brijen was not only sympathetic to Merton's paradoxical synthesis of contemplation and social commitment; he identified with the disillusionment that preceded Merton's decision to retreat from the chaos of the world in the early 1940s. Brijen drew my attention to Arthur Koestler's famous essay, "The Yogi and the Commissar," in which Koestler uses the image of the spectrum to account for "all possible human attitudes to life." At the infrared end, the figure of the commissar exemplifies a commitment to *change from without*. He is the revolutionary for whom all means, fair and foul, are justified in realizing his vision of a brave new world. At the opposite, ultraviolet, end of the spectrum, where the waves are short and of such high frequency that they cannot be seen, crouches the yogi who believes that little can be accomplished by willful striving and exterior organization. In seeking change *from within* he distances himself from the social sphere in order to make possible a mergence with the universal and cosmic all-one. "It is easy to say," writes Koestler, "that all that is wanted is a synthesis —the synthesis between saint and revolutionary—but so far this has never been achieved. What has been achieved are various motley forms of compromise . . . but not synthesis. Apparently, the two elements do not mix, and this may be one of the reasons why we have made such a mess of our History."[5]

There is, perhaps, a third way. I glimpsed it in a letter Brijen wrote me in 1965, at a time when his energies were being drained by his involvement in the American civil rights movement and protests against the war in Vietnam.[6] "I wish I could be nearer to you," he wrote. "I know that we [friends from Wellington days], could start a circle of friendship, in which sharing and creativity may bind us together. But I know now it will remain a vain dream: I dreamt of it in India when I was in college, and it was shattered; then I had a vision of success in the sixties; it has now turned into frustration." It was a utopian theme to which Brijen would return several times in his conversations with me—that a close-knit family or an intentional community offered the possibility of closing the gap between retreat and engagement, and that an intimate group of friends or kin could provide a refuge from the wider, impersonal worlds of national, academic, or corporate life yet prevent narcissistic withdrawal into oneself. Only in such contexts could one forge the bonds of mutual care, shared interest, and affection that make life worthwhile.

At first, Brijan was coy, resistant to my proposal that we retrace the course of his life. Memory was fallible, he said, and memories often painful. Even if accurate recollection were possible, and pleasurable, what was the point in returning to the past when it is the present that summons us? He then cited one of his 1952 poems in Hindi that began: *mere itihason per smriti laga gai hai tala* (Memory has placed a lock upon my histories). But my references to Merton seemed to trigger something in him, and he began recalling his childhood in the city of Dehra Dun, the present capital of Uttarakhand State in northern India. Delhi was only 140 miles away, and to the north lay the Himalayas—images, one might say, of the political and religious poles that pulled Brijen in such different directions for so many years.

"I was born into a middle-class, well-to-do family, mostly of professionals and some business executives. The household, by Indian standards, was fairly Westernized. Until I was sixteen, I lived in Dehra Dun, in the foothills of the Himalayas, home to a unit of the British brigade and a host of government agencies and institutions, which gave the town an urbane atmosphere and above-average interracial contacts. Dehra Dun was also the home of many

Anglicized schools and a refuge for boys and girls who wanted 'modern' education. At my parental home we had electricity, running water, and a flush system in the toilet. A maid washed the dishes and kept the house clean. A full-time gardener also doubled as a watchman. And there was a Brahmin cook. The most remarkable feature of our life was evening meetings when, as a rule, men congregated in one room and women in another. Children were not allowed to attend these discussions, but we stayed on the steps of a staircase and listened to the talk, which ranged from the bizarre to the profound. Moreover, I was enrolled in the American Presbyterian Mission High School from grade four to ten and made friends with my American teachers and matrons (I was a part-time boarder, though the school was less than a mile from home!). Being at a Mission school meant heavy doses of English language and literature and compulsory Bible classes. To balance my religious education, my mother had me study Sanskrit and Hinduism with a private tutor. I graduated from high school in my fourteenth year, two years earlier than the average. Thanks to my principal, Rhea McCurdy Ewing, a Princeton graduate, who was a regular at our home, I had early exposure to Western classics, not only Palgrave's collection but Wren's tome of representative European literature. The trick was to respect and stand in awe of the literatures of India at the same time as one respected the Western canon. Not an ordinary feat because, aprés Macaulay, Indian literatures were not worth studying, since the mission of the Empire was to create a class brown in color but English in outlook and tastes. Though my family observed Hindu feasts and festivals, we were not temple goers.

"My first moving encounter with the West came, I believe, in 1942. That summer, in the hills of Mussooree, in the company of my matron (and lover to be) and a couple of other boys, I visited a European cemetery. I was touched by the great number of graves of little boys and girls, children of British civilian and military officials, as well as the numerous graves of women (wives) who had died in India. The number of adult males paled in comparison. The grief that possessed me was that thousands of 'innocent' Westerners had given their lives in and to India for whatever reasons and motivations.

"I think I came of age in 1942: Gandhi had launched the Quit India movement and I had entered puberty, though did not know at that time what puberty was. But the crisis I faced was to identify which part of me was Indian (or Hindu) and which part Western. Like Nehru, I had become a curious mixture of East and West, out of place everywhere, at home nowhere. I did not have any good friends in my own age group: I solicited the company of persons much older than I was, but there was a catch. These elders generally affected a professorial manner.

"Within fifty miles of Dehra Dun was the holy city of Haridwar, and in the lofty hills of the Siwalik range nestled dozens of ashrams led by swamis, chastened by Vivekananda and Aurobindo, preaching neo-Hinduism (Sankara's Vedanta) to illiterate but English-speaking Hindus who felt uncomfortable with Hindu religious rites and temple visits. One of the women swamis was Anandmayee, to whom my parents were devoted and who became famous several years later when Nehru and his daughter, Indira Gandhi, joined the group of her acolytes. From 1942 to 1952 I would visit her almost every month either in Dehra Dun or Benares, toying with the idea that I would renounce and join her ashram.

"In 1943 I entered the local college to read English literature, physics, chemistry, and mathematics, since my parents had decided that I was to pursue engineering. But thanks to the librarian, Daulat Singh Chauhan (and what a ramshackle library he had, probably containing less than 10,000 books), I embarked on a curriculum of my own. He urged me to go through 'histories'—the history of English literature, the history of Western political thought, the history of economic ideas, the history of religion, and so forth. In one of the junk piles at the library, I found a beat-up but complete edition of the *Encyclopaedia Britannica* and I persuaded my parents to have it bound and placed on the library shelf. But one fine day, out of the blue, arrived a bundle of books from my great-uncle, Bhupal Singh, author of *A Survey of Anglo Indian Fiction*. This bundle included Hastings's *Encyclopaedia of Religion and Ethics*. So 1943–1945 became two of my most academically instructive years.

"But these were also troubled years. I was being pulled in different directions. The nationalist struggle pulled me one way, a desire to be a hermit pulled me in the opposite direction, not to mention my desire to read and reflect. I was also confused about my sexuality. Though short in height and small in weight, college girls nevertheless found me attractive and I had modest sexual encounters almost every week. I bared my life in those years to my English professor, R. L. Nigam, a wonderfully well-read man, a lecher and a renegade Marxist-Leninist, who referred me to Abelard and Heloise.

"With all these quandaries, I left home in the summer of 1945 to enroll at Benares Hindu University and train to be an engineer. But my heart was not in it."

Brijen seldom spoke of his parents, except to say he had disappointed them. But their active involvement in India's struggle for independence undoubtedly shaped his own sense of political responsibility. Though drawn to Western philosophers, particularly Karl Marx and Rosa Luxemburg, Brijen was equally intrigued by Aurobindo Ghose and Swami Vivekananda.

Sent to England at age seven to be educated, Aurobindo returned to India fourteen years later, "thoroughly denationalized," to find that his father was dead and his mother afflicted by senile dementia.[7] After many years in the vortex of the nationalist movement, Aurobindo gradually withdrew from the world. With Mira Paul Richard, a Frenchwoman who left her husband and children to join Aurobindo, he developed his philosophy of integral yoga and founded a famous ashram in Pondicherry. Vivekananda was a disciple of Ramakrishna and integrated the contemplative and quietist philosophy of his guru with the activist spirit that came from his studies of Western and Christian thinkers.

Paying lip service to high principles is one thing; realizing them in practice is another. This may be why several of Brijen's anecdotes concerned intellectual or spiritual leaders whose own lives fell far short of their ideals—Gandhi's compromised vows of celibacy and his racist remarks about Africans, John F. Kennedy's personal failings, and so on.

In early 1946, at the end of his first year of studying at Benares Hindu University, Brijen was delayed at the railroad junction of Laksar because of the derailment of an earlier train. He was obliged to spend thirty-six hours in an overcrowded waiting room.

"As providence would have it, an ochre-robed swami, Lokeshwaranand, of the Ramakrishna Vivekananda Mission, took pity on me and kept me amused, wondering why I, who had such good knowledge of his Mission and its founders, had not made any attempt to be active in the Mission.

"These were the final years of British rule in India, and I had excellent political connections with the Congress Left. I now began an active correspondence with Swami Lokeshwaranand—two or three letters a week—and his own personal story as to why he had renounced the world made a deep impact on me. At his urging I left home to spend three months at the Ramakrishna Vivekananda Mission in Mathura, where I accidentally saw a kanya, the equivalent of a Catholic nun, having oral sex with the head swami. The swami behaved as if nothing had happened. He got up, put on his robe, took me for a walk, and explained to me that such casual sex was the stuff of Indian renunciation. The swami's sex was of no consequence, as no attachment with the novice was involved. The swami, whose name I have forgotten, was a learned man. In a discussion that I vividly recall to this day, he outlined for me the key difference between India and the West. In India, spirituality and sexuality coexisted, and the more of one did not necessarily mean the less of the other. In the West, increased spirituality meant decreased sexuality. All of a sudden, a new light dawned on me, though it could not excuse the behavior of the swami. I left Mathura after three days."

As Brijen's story began to unfold, I was reminded of Leopold Fischer, who was born into an assimilated Jewish family in 1923, became enamored of India from an early age, and was inducted into the Dasnami Order as Agehananda Bharati. Though Bharati was six years older than Brijen, both were intellectually precocious in their youth. And while Bharati found himself more at home in India than Europe and Brijen "rejected the relevance of Hindu philosophies in [his] personal growth" to espouse an existential Marxism derived from European sources, both men shared a cosmopolitan vision that eschewed identification with any one nation, religion, or ethnicity. Thus, Bharati embraced a humanism exemplified by G. E. Moore, M. N. Roy, Russell, and Wittgenstein, while Brijen adhered to an ethos of friendship, family, and communitas that he had first glimpsed in an Indian ashram. Moreover, both Gupta and Bharati were fascinated by the tantric tradition, and Bharati's succinct observation that "the theme of harnessing instead of suppressing the senses for the sake of the higher life is one of the most delicate and . . . most important in the religious traditions of Asia"[8] found echoes in Brijen's discomfort with asceticism and his view that the sexual impulse was not inimical to liberation but one way of achieving it.

These themes were familiar to me from the times Brijen and I had spent together over many years—our paths crossing in London, New York, Rochester, Bloomington, and Cambridge. In times of desolation, he helped me out. In his belief that poetry, stories, myths, and art—like friendship and love—make the emptiness of existence bearable, and that "analysis makes the absurdity of life more than one can bear," I found consolation for my own attempts to integrate social science with philosophy and literature.[9] In the delight he took in Frank Harris, the Kama Sutra, and literary pornography, my own Puritanism was exorcized. But though I spent years in community development and welfare work in Australia, England, and the Congo, committed to making small improvement in the lives of the poor, the homeless, and the downtrodden, I would never find in myself the sustained devotion to the needs of others that characterized Brijen's life.

Salman Rushdie's novel *Midnight's Children* draws an analogy between the story of India's birth as an independent nation on midnight, August 15, 1947, and the story of a group of telepathic children, born at the same time and brought together by Saleem Sinai, the hero and narrator of the book. Brijen's story had similar overtones, as if India's struggle for independence coincided with his struggle to find his path.

Brijen entered DAV College in Dehra Dun in 1943, when he was fourteen. "During the following five years, I discovered myself, buried myself in Indian and European literature and philosophy, overcame my adolescence, suffered romantic agony, entered student politics, came under the influence of radical socialists Acharya Narendra Deva and Ram Manohar Lohia,[10] made friends with mighty men of my generation like S. Radhakrishnan,[11] later president of India, and Amaranatha Jha, successively vice chancellor of Allahabad and Benares Hindu Universities, and fell afoul of Govinda Malaviya, the university's acting vice chancellor, whose appointment I had bitterly opposed as a student leader. In 1948 he suspended me from the university."

Abandoning his political and social activities, breaking off his contacts with the Congress Socialist Party, and limiting his correspondence with Lohia, Brijen intensified his reading of religious and philosophical texts—Hindu, Buddhist, and European. To cover his material needs, his parents (at his grandfather's urging) paid Brijen a monthly stipend.

"As I read more and more religio-philosophical tomes, a desire came upon me to go travelling and visit various ashrams. I had the proper letters of introduction to speak directly to the leaders of the ashrams, but the results were mixed. My difficulty lay in my rejection of religious rites and rituals, temple worship, and an anthropomorphic God. Under the influence of R. L. Nigam[12] and Lohia, as well as Marxist and existentialist writings, I had become a humanist in its narrowest formulation. I found Vedanta troubling and yet scholastic and challenging. Yet I could not bring myself to accept Cārvāka's materialism as an alternative.[13] Buddhism fascinated me for its nonmonotheistic outlook, and Nigam helped me discover the Buddhist doctrine of sunyata (void), which was only a stone's throw away, as I would later discover, from Camus's notion of absurdity. Sunyavad (the doctrine of void-ness) rejected the absolutism of Vedanta, as well as nihilism, and I decided to study it further.

"In addition to Anandamayi and Lokeshwaranand, my memorable visits in 1948 were to Sri Krishnaprem, the Aurobindo ashram, and Maharishi Ramana's ashram.[14] Sri Krishnaprem, née Ronald Nixon, was a Cambridge don who had come to Lucknow University with another don, Chadwick,[15] to teach English. Both fell under the influence of Vice Chancellor Chakravarti's wife (Monika Devi, later Yashoda Ma). Chadwick left Lucknow to go to Aurobindo at Pondicherry, and Nixon, initiated by Yashoda as Krishnaprem, went to Benares and then Almore in the Himalayan foothills, where he and Yashoda Ma built a temple and ashram called Uttar Brindaban, a few miles away from the palatial home of Gertrude Emerson Sen, granddaughter of Ralph Waldo Emerson.[16]

"Sri Krishnaprem was a remarkable man, a scholar and a religious devotee rolled into one.[17] I stayed with him for about a week, found him very comforting, yet was not equal to his intense devotionalism (bhakti) and left dissatisfied. My week at Gandhi's ashram at Wardha was also unfulfilling. The devotion of his disciples to Gandhian ethical social action (karma) was admirable, but Gandhian ashrams, like most other ashrams in India and elsewhere, rejected libido.[18] This came into conflict with my firm view that woman was anodyne. My visit to Aurobindo's ashram was a failure: I could not see or speak to the master. The visit to Sri Ramana Maharishi's did not yield much: I saw the master briefly and his deputies spoke to me in clichés, reminding me that the journey to spiritual salvation was long and treacherous. My visit to a Tantric ashram in the Vindhyachal range, near Mirzapur, where I was willy-nilly introduced to hallucinogens, opened an area of inquiry that I never seriously entertained, notwithstanding encouragement some years later by Agehananda Bharati. Whenever anyone talked to me of salvation, and almost every swami did, I was reminded of Calvin. But I did not ever think that man was born into and lived in 'sin.' Yet with all these imperfections, Indian ashrams were a sight and an experience to behold. They rejected caste, they treated men and women almost equally, and all were supposedly engaged in bringing internal realization to every individual, one at a time if necessary.

"Enter Quakerism. The booklets Horace G. Alexander gave me had a profound influence.[19] Quaker commitment to pacifism was more clearheaded than Gandhi's or any Buddhist's. Suddenly I realized that the tension between agape and eros, which non-Tantric Indian religions had resolved by renouncing libido, was a creative one. Quaker references to God were, moreover, benign, and Christ was seen as neither relevant nor irrelevant. And their relief efforts were more than Boy Scout exercises."

By November 1948 Brijen was preoccupied by the need to put some distance between himself and India.

"My father thought, as usual, that I might learn something from someone, somewhere in England or Europe, and did not object. But my mother was heartbroken. She had lost her only brother when the ship on which he and his wife were returning to India had been sunk (in 1941 I think), and she was bedeviled by the idea that England was a curse on her family. She again urged that I go into retreat at an Anandamayi[20] ashram somewhere in India. Even Nigam, my peripatetic mentor, was against my leaving India. He saw it as an escape from life, and felt that 'action' was in India. He gave me newspaper accounts of how Britain in 1948 was still suffering from the ill effects of the Second World War.

"After promising my mother that I would be back within a few months, she relented. Radhakrishnan (Fellow of All Souls) arranged a visiting studentship at Balliol, while Lohia introduced me to several labor leaders. Gwen Catchpool[21] agreed to provide funds and hospitality in London.

"Early in 1949 I set sail for London. No member of my family or any friend came to see me off. Once at sea, I saw my voyage as an exile.

"The ship was almost entirely occupied by English families, returning to the motherland with sweet but mostly bitter memories of their departure from India. I thought the source of their bitterness came from their knowledge that they would never replicate their Indian lifestyle in their homeland, and many were already talking about packing up again and migrating to Canada, New Zealand, or Australia. Several opined that they would soon be back to India, to govern a country that Indians would find ungovernable. But a lot of the women were happy to be going home. Though the women my age deigned not to socialize with me, I endeared myself to the married women because of my uncanny ability to delight their children—still blissfully ignorant of racial prejudice and fear of strangers.

"The three-week journey was engrossing: I was neither particularly happy nor sad. I had ample time to meditate. And the small library had plenty of good books I had not read. I had also brought with me a few books on Indian philosophy and a couple of articles by T. R .V. Murti who, in the 1950s, would emerge as perhaps the greatest living commentator on Buddhist philosophy.[22] I had attended his lectures at Benares, where he was considered the putative heir to Radhakrishnan.

"The voyage had few ports of call. From every port I sent a postcard to my mother. I wrote to no one else, even though the steamship company offered free airmail service. I could not get over the fact that no one had come to see me off. Though this brooding was not consistent with my character, the feeling was nevertheless there."

Of his year in England and Europe, Brijen would say little except that he spent several months as a relief worker in a Quaker Center in Darmstadt, Germany, and that, in retrospect, it was a period of "withdrawal." I suspected that he had encountered, and been stunned by, the endemic racism in Britain—and when I pressed him on this point, he grudgingly admitted as much, referring to "pervasive and subtle" snobberies of class, grafted on to a deep-seated contempt for coloreds and colonials who would not accept their lowly place in the allegedly "natural" order of the world.

"I slipped back into India in May 1950 as quietly as I had slipped out of it. I had made up my mind to resume college and eventually become a teacher. After finding my Dehra Dun apartment intact, and debating whether I should return to Benares or remain in Dehra Dun, I opted for the latter. Geographically, Dehra Dun was midway between the political capital Delhi and the spiritual homes (ashrams) that dotted the Himalayan foothills, and this tension between political and spiritual yearnings still ruled my life. My life was also suddenly and deliriously complicated by love.

"Her name was Beena Banerjee. She came to DAV in July 1951. I was then in the final year of my BA, and from the very first moment I laid eyes on her, I was smitten. Whenever I saw her, she would return my glances with a mysterious but mischievous smile. Then, one rainy August afternoon, as I stood half drenched under one of the classroom verandahs, she crept up behind me. 'I am Beena, can I talk to you?'

"I froze. Though notorious for straight talking, I was speechless. Sensing victory, she smiled. 'You see, I am taking English Literature, and Professor Nigam told me that you have the best notes for the first year. Can I borrow them?'

"It was sheer flattery. She needed my notes like a hole in the head. But the ploy worked. Now, however, I was in command of myself. 'And what do I get in return?' I asked.

"'Friendship,' she said, and without waiting for any response she darted off to her philosophy class, leaving me to wonder whether she meant merely friendship or love.

"The whole conversation took less than a minute, but it transformed my life. Over the next twenty-two months we exchanged 917 letters. We walked to and from college, read books together, shared private jokes, mused on life, and loved each other intensely. With Beena, my philosophical outlook matured. Following Sartre and Heidegger, I affirmed conflict as the natural relationship between man and man, stressed the absurdity, suffering, and futility of life, and assumed the evanescence of God.

"On the political front, I resumed my contact with Lohia and assisted him in firming up his ideas about the Third Camp—equidistant from the orbits of Washington and Moscow. I had met Harris Wofford and his wife Clare (who were to become close friends of mine after 1953) and I had become fascinated by their idea of a world government—which I told them was a pipe dream. But Lohia's socialism, in which I had a great investment, was rapidly going down the tube, though he would only realize this several years later. Those he considered possible partners in an International that would rival Trotsky's Fourth International were following Tito's example and courting Nehru. And he refused to believe, despite my persistent urging, that nationalism was already on the way to eclipsing socialism. He believed the opposite would be the case. Together with Tito, Mao, and Ho Chi Minh, he envisaged a creative synthesis of humanism, agrarian socialism, and nationalism. As for me, I considered nationalism a cancer that was bound to lead to chauvinism and strengthen totalitarianism. "In 1951 India had its first general elections. My grandfather, who was a member of the Constituent Assembly, predecessor to the Lok Sabha [the directly elected lower house of the Indian Parliament], decided not to run, and he and my parents suggested that I run for a safe provincial assembly seat on the Congress (Nehru Party) ticket; Lohia made me a similar offer for a Socialist Party ticket. All agreed that though I was only twenty-two, and the election law required a minimum age of twenty-five, the age issue could be finessed by a false birth certificate. I found this repellent, but my friends and I nevertheless decided to be politically active, and we put up a close associate, Gulab Singh, as an independent candidate with covert support from my family's and Lohia's vote banks. Gulab Singh lost by one percentage point to a Congress candidate, so strong was the hold of the Congress Party over the 1951 electorate.

"While I was trying to cope with the disarray in Lohia's political thought as well as the disarray in India's everyday politics, I was also preoccupied by my own inner growth. New ashrams had sprung up in the Himalayan foothills led by gurus who hailed from what is now Pakistan. I visited a few of them and found them unappealing. With a friend of mine, Balram Khanna, who shared my spiritual yearnings and had become my close confidante, I revisited Sri Krishnaprem in the summer of 1951. He granted me a private audience, only to denounce European philosophies as the devil's handiwork, designed to lead true believers astray. In his public audiences over the next three days, he propounded on Indian and European ideas of consciousness, and I considered him ill-informed. On the last day of our visit I found a note in Hindi pinned to my pillow. Beautifully handwritten, it read: *Find God, peace without Him is not possible.* I never saw him again. But in 1965, at the Abbey of Gethsemane in Kentucky, Father Louis (Thomas Merton) said the same thing to me.

"My break with Hindu worldviews was now almost complete, though I could not ever rid myself of the Maya postulate that the world does not exist, it is merely an idea, an idea that wishes to be entertained, and once entertained forces the mind to accept it as reality.

"It was also in 1953 that I met Agehananda Bharati for the first time. He was an honorary professor of philosophy at Benares Hindu University and came to Dehra Dun to visit Nigam and Nigam's mentor, M. N. Roy, the ex-Stalinist who mentored Mao, established the Communist Party in Mexico, and was a humanitarian philosopher in his own right. It was great to see Bharati and Nigam get along so well.

"Bharati and I kept in touch thereafter. Ironically, after I had left India, Bharati and Beena became lovers, and he was expelled from Benares Hindu University when caught in a tryst with her. In May 1991 he died in my presence and in the arms of his last lover, Rita Narang. Together we had nursed him during his last days.

"In 1952 I declined a Rhodes Scholarship, mostly at the urging of my mother, who was then not well but partly because of my involvement with Beena. I was not at peace. I was smoking heavily and had begun drinking. Beena disliked both. I proposed to her, but she declined, asserting that one marries to have babies, and she was not ready for them. We also toyed with the idea of setting up an intentional community on the model of the kibbutz, as many of my Gandhian friends had done, but neither Beena nor I were the salt of the earth.

"That same year, Radhakrishnan was elected vice president of India. Since 1946 he had been my mentor and patron and had castigated me from time to time for my Left and pro-Western orientations. But he was pleased that I was aiming to be a teacher, and early in 1953, when asked by Maude Hadden, president of the Institute of World Affairs (Radhakrishnan was on its board), to nominate an Indian student to participate in a six-week-long international affairs seminar, he nominated me. Maude accepted his recommendation. Three weeks of hard bargaining followed before I secured an all expenses paid, six-week trip to the States with the added provision that Maude would help me get into an American university for graduate studies.

"In the summer of 1953 I left for the States. My mother was convinced I would never come back. All partings are partings forever. I promised annual visits and kept my bargain until she and my father died. Lohia was in mourning, but both he and I knew that there was no political future for me in India. As for Beena, she was angry that I had announced my decision without confiding in or consulting her—which was not entirely true. One day, soaking our legs in the sulphur springs near Dehra Dun, I told her of my decision. She wanted no explanation and simply said, 'All right.' When I told her that I would come back to her, and she could later join me in the States, she replied with a sense of resignation, 'We shall see.'

"In June I was on a TWA flight to Paris and New York. I had a premonition that my break with India was now final. In another few weeks, Beena left for Benares Hindu University to read philosophy. We never met again."[23]

The six-week seminar on international affairs was led by Walter Sharp of Yale. Impressed by Brijen's acumen and ambition, Sharp offered him an Overbrook Fellowship. In his year at Yale, Brijen met several key figures in the Democratic Party and began a lifelong relationship with the Dutch-born Socialist and pacifist Abraham Johannes Muste.[24]

"Almost every time I would go to New York City, I would call on him and his wonderful assistant Colette Schlatter, my first love in [the] USA, who a year or two later forsook me to join Bruderhof, an intentional, Jesus-centered community, in Rifton, New York, where she married, produced half a dozen children, and scores of grandchildren and great-grandchildren, all committed to the communal way of life. My unwillingness to accept Jesus as savior, and other Hutterite tenets (including unprotected sex) kept me from following her. Before she opted for Rifton, we had discussed Taos, and as a parting gift she had given me Witter Bynner's *Journey with the Genius*, which I treasured for more than fifty years.

"So you can see that my life was full at Yale, thanks to Maude Hadden, whose munificence helped me avoid spending too much of my time making money, though I was on the lecture circuit in and around New Haven and received honoraria for speaking on Gandhi and India.

"At the end of the 1953–1954 academic year, I decided to spend the summer in Cambridge, Massachusetts, where Russell Johnson, a Quaker, had offered me room and board. He and I had agreed that I would speak on nonviolence, Gandhi, and civil liberties on a Quaker circuit, beginning with a one-week summer camp at Avon, Connecticut, where A. J. Muste was also going to be on the faculty. This plan came in conflict with my inner yearnings, exacerbated by Colette, to discover my identity. So I left Russ in midsummer and moved to New York with the aim of spending several weeks at the Catholic Worker,[25] to which Muste and Colette had introduced me.

"The Catholic Worker was unlike any other church grouping I had known. It was committed to labor unions, and both Muste and Schachtman were friends of Dorothy Day, who they consulted when drafting their manifesto for a third camp in world affairs. One of my tasks during those eight weeks was to add my knowledge of Asia to the roundtable discussions. Through Muste and/or Dorothy Day I also met Bayard Rustin and Michael Harrington. And it was out of the Catholic Worker experience that I became interested in Thomas Merton, who I was to meet in 1965."

I was fascinated by the echoes between Brijen's and Merton's concern for the "gap between thought and action."[26] Like Brijen, Merton pondered the relationship between religious traditions, East and West, only to come up against their "essential difference." For Merton, the Christian view that Christ is at the center of all reality, "a source of grace and life," and that God is love, could not be reconciled with the Hindu view that "God is void," though he would foster interfaith dialectic with a passion that Brijen could not share.[27] Moreover, both Brijen and Merton were deeply influenced by the Catholic Worker and profoundly concerned about the pervasive violence in America, particularly its racial strife, social injustices, and the war in Vietnam. But how could one bring together a monastic life on the edge of the polis (atopos) and an active life within it?[28]

During "a year of reflection" at Pendle Hill,[29] with weekly breaks to attend a seminar on Arnold Toynbee[30] in New York City, Brijen's interest in the relationship of "withdrawal" and "return" was sharpened by Toynbee's ideas, by conversations with Dorothy Day, and by his reading of Thomas Merton's recently published *The Sign of Jonas*. Later he would fall back on Koestler's contrast between "change from without" and "change from within" and Bernard McGinn's contrast between "flight" and "commitment" to articulate this struggle to be a "hermit in the water of life."[31]

This struggle also arose from Brijen's relationship with his homeland.

"After Yale I made a quick trip to India to visit my parents and Radhakrishnan. Radhakrishnan was quite upset at my plans. He called me something of an aimless wanderer, dismissed me uncharacteristically without offering a meal, and I do not think he ever replied to my notes thereafter or agreed to see me again. His son, Sarvepalli Gopal, a distinguished historian, also grew quite hostile to me over the years, and he berated me at two conferences. I have already told you that I had lost Beena's friendship a year earlier, though had gained Bharati's.

"By the summer of 1954 I realized that my ties to India—to family, friends, politics, and philosophy—were both attenuating and changing. Muste and Scott Buchanan[32] had replaced Radhakrishnan. The Labor Action crowd of Irving Howe, Lewis Coser, Hal Draper, and Michael Harrington had replaced my socialist friends in India. Also the troubled Bayard Rustin. And in a superficial sense, Dorothy Day and Catholic Worker, Muste and Liberal Quakers had taken the place of Mother Anandamayi. Why I hung around Muste and Dorothy Day remains an unexplained mystery to me. Their mysticism was Christ-centered and their faith in Christianity unshakeable. Yet here I was, totally rejecting Christianity and Christ. Though I had utopian ideals, the Kingdom of Heaven was not my goal.

"September found me settled in a cozy little room at Pendle Hill. Henry Cadbury and Howard Brinton were also in residence; Gilbert Kilpack and Peter Docili ran the 'academic' curriculum. Every morning there was an hour of silent worship. I found these times greatly strengthening. Peter introduced me to Simone Weil and her pamphlet on the Iliad, published under the Pendle Hill imprint in 1956. My commitment to peace and pacifism grew even stronger. In the spring of 1955 Gwen Catchpool (recently widowed) and Horace Alexander came to Pendle Hill, and the three of us ran a seminar on the Gandhian tradition.

"Thanks to unlimited free postal privileges, I managed a lively correspondence with many people. The year helped me not only extend the frontiers of my knowledge but be at greater peace with myself. I felt that I was destined to establish a new Pendle Hill—not a transient but a permanent intentional community, without the academic rigors of an Institute for Advanced Study and faithful to Martin Buber's vision. In this I found an ally, pioneer, and mentor in Ralph Borsodi, whose romantic agrarianism I found compelling. A friend of Dorothy Day, he was about to close his institute in Suffern, New York, and move to Melbourne, Florida. For the next few years we kept up a lively correspondence."

I was keen to know more about the impact of Marx on Brijen's thinking, and how he reconciled his pacifism with his views on overcoming the world's social injustices, inequalities, and structural violence.

"During that critical year at Pendle Hill," Brijen replied, "I came across Marx's *Economic and Political Manuscripts of 1844*, commonly known as the Paris Manuscripts—the notebooks of a very young Marx. This volume led me to Feuerbach's *Essence of Christianity*, and both these books firmed up my view that industrial societies create an alienated man, and unless human beings returned to what Borsodi called romantic agrarianism, Gandhi called rural socialism, or Buber envisaged in the Israeli kibbutz, humanity was doomed to a culture of internecine violence. This idea I would later refine under the influence of Christopher Lasch, who taught me that family was a haven in a heartless world.

"Quakerism influenced me but did not fulfill. Even in my encounters with Muste and Day, I remained a liberal agnostic humanist at heart. The Labor Action crowd of Max Schachtman, Michael Harrington, Irving Howe, and Hal Draper firmly instilled in me the idea of social justice: that until utopia was achieved, I had the duty to do whatever I could to further human rights and social justice, but it was incumbent upon me to be a witness for nonviolence, if not pacifism. Milton Mayer's essay on Muste, 'The Christer,'[33] moved me. On several occasions, Milton and I appeared in Quaker-arranged institutes, and his opposition to the Second World War, even though he was a Jew, greatly touched my life.

"In 1954–1955 liberation movements in Asia, Latin America, and Africa were all in full swing. Cuba under Castro had appeared as a challenge. Mao reigned supreme over China. Both Tito and Ho presented challenges to Marxist orthodoxy. Suddenly I saw Marxism and nationalism intermarrying just as, in a different way, socialism and nationalism had been integrated under Hitler and Mussolini. I saw most of my Quaker activists supportive of these movements, ignoring Muste's and Mayer's ardent belief that there could be no compromise with any kind of authoritarianism, let alone totalitarianism. I was leery of the argument that Communist Russia and China and semi-Communist Cuba were authoritarian because of Western hostility toward them. Here I found Lohia, Muste, and Schachtman[34] instructive: a liberal, humanist democrat had to be equidistant from the two warring camps in world affairs. I did not budge from this position, and by 1969, which is going to be [the] terminal point of my narrative,[35] I had become totally irrelevant to the world around me.

"As far as inner growth was concerned, I think that by 1955 I had become alien to Hindu and Buddhist mysticism, though I continued to admire both Sri Krishnaprem and Anandamayi. Reading and rereading the Bhagavad Gita, I found it to be a hopeless treatise, whose central message, like the Iliad, was war, power, and greed. No amount of retelling by Gandhi or Vinobha could modify my thinking. Hardly anyone who rejects the Gita has the right to call himself a Hindu. The Judeo-Christian God did not impress me as an alternative: he was the God who commanded Abraham to sacrifice his son, Isaac. Nor could He answer the fundamental questions that Job had raised; He only rewarded him with material goods. On Christ, privately but not publicly, I took my cue from D. H. Lawrence's great fable *The Man Who Died*. Sexual fulfillment was the paramount need, and eros was more important than agape. Only through eros could man find beauty. Yet I continued to admire Muste and Day, as well as Merton, until they lay dead. I reaffirmed to myself the tenets I had worked out with Beena: that God was evanescent, that life was absurd, that Abel and Cain realistically represented the human dilemma, and that woman was the true anodyne for human suffering."

This was the second time Brijen had used the phrase "woman is anodyne," and I asked him to elaborate.

"Generally speaking, Vedic literature and the two great epics, Ramayana and Mahabharata, treat women with disdain. Manu, the great commentator on Hindu law, imposes restrictions on a woman's freedom, her right to property, education, and almost everything else. In the Ramayana, Lord Rama, God's incarnation, bemoans that it was a woman who caused not only a great war but the imminent death of his loyal brother who he loved more than his wife. The Ramayana enjoins that women should be treated like drums, idiots, animals, and outcastes, and beaten regularly. In the Mahabharata, the communal wife of the five brothers is staked by her husbands in a poker game, and though Lord Krishna throws her a lifeline in the form of a long sari as she is being stripped, the message is nevertheless clear that she can be gambled away. Not so in the non-Vedic shakta literature, which focuses on Shakti or Devi, the Hindu divine mother, as the ultimate godhead. Here Siva's consort Parvati is at all times equal to and at times superior to her husband in every respect, even though he is the rejuvenator of the universe. The divine energy of which Tantric texts speak so eloquently is essentially if not exclusively feminine. Having rejected the inferences inherent in Vedic texts, and without accepting all that goes with Tantric mysticism, very early in my life I was attracted to the concept of equality between the two sexes, a concept strengthened by my parents and, to a lesser extent, by my own association with Anandamayi. But there was also the influence of coming of age in northern India, where ties between males and their female siblings are quite strong. While traditional North Indian families do not have a Father's or Mother's Day, or even the equivalent of Valentine's Day, there is a Sister's Day, called Raksha Bandhan, when a brother affirms his vows to protect his sister or sisters, including at least first cousins. Indeed, it is quite common for boys/men to adopt sisters, and to carry on a highly charged Platonic relationship with them. Additionally, special bonds are fostered between a woman (called bhabhi in North India) and the younger brother or brothers of her husband, and a married man and his wife's sisters. In a paper I once wrote, I observed that such bonds often led to the initiation of the young into adult sexual activities. Boys/Men come to see women/girls as anodynes. When they cannot open their hearts to their mothers, they do so before their adopted sisters and sisters-in-law. True, erotic activities are frowned upon, but low-level activities within certain well-crafted limits do take place.

"Let me now merge text with context. A visit to the Meenakshi Temple—in my judgment the most beautiful Hindu temple in India—brought me face-to-face with the gentler side of Goddess Parvati, who in most other temples is depicted as a fierce goddess who can dance over the body of a prostate Siva, the First Lord of the Universe. There for the first time I heard Lalitha Sahsarnamah, which had the same calming influence on me as Gregorian chants. Sahsarnamahs are panegyrics to principal male gods but the Lalitha was to a goddess, which increased its poignancy and relevancy. All the Puranas, those wonderful, irrelevant, mini-epics written after the fourth century, are full of eroticism, and the Saivite ones particularly so, but nobody reads and admires them except perhaps Wendy Doniger, whom I have, alas, never met."

In the summer of 1955 Brijen was again in a quandary. Chester Bowles, a former U.S. ambassador in India, proposed that he spend a year at the Democratic Party headquarters. Scott Buchanan had arranged, at Brijen's request, a month at the Abbey of Gethsemane (Brijen had already been corresponding with Thomas Merton). But while teaching a summer course on India at Columbia, Brijen met Virginia Martin, a Wooster graduate he would marry in 1957. Ginny had come to New York after a "missionary" year at Piney Woods, a black school in Mississippi. She had enrolled in courses on art history before heading to Chicago in the fall. "A product of the Brethren tradition, her commitment to public service and pacifism matched mine, though she rejected all my intellectual, neo-Marxist, trappings," said Brijen.

Rather than pursue his original plan to do his doctorate at Yale, Brijen followed Ginny to Chicago, where he graduated in 1958. There followed two years teaching at the Southern Illinois University, Carbondale, during which Brijen's and Ginny's second child, Sunita, was born. But social life in Carbondale was as dull as it was politically conservative.

"I was denied a haircut by a barber in town because I was not white, but decided it was not worth making a fuss when a black barber welcomed me with open arms and scissors. Whenever we went out to eat at a fancy restaurant, we made sure that they served blacks. There was no cultural life, not even beer bashes. It was still the McCarthy era, though ebbing. There were no Quakers in the area. Though Ginny and I had each other, and our children, I was restless, and craved intellectual companionship.

"During my Chicago years, the civil rights struggle had picked up steam. Almost all my New York friends were banking upon a Democratic victory. Bayard Rustin urged me to join the struggle, and when I declined he declared me an AWOL Gandhian. Harris Wofford, as early as November 1959, had predicted a Kennedy victory and had left his law practice to join the campaign; he invited me to follow. But I had promised myself and Ginny that I was going to sit this one out. One of my mentors at Chicago was Hans Morgenthau, and since 1955, if not earlier, he had been predicting looming disaster for American foreign policy, and he was no peacenik. His devastating piece on the Kennedys—I believe it came out in *The New York Review of Books*—shattered any faith I had in the Democratic Party. So I began shopping for a small college. Bert Hoselitz, my academic advisor at Chicago, worked overtime to recommend me. I was interviewed at several places and pleased to receive several offers. Then one day Ginny saw an ad in the *Times Educational Supplement* for a teaching position in the newly inaugurated Asian studies program at Victoria University of Wellington.

"The decision to move to New Zealand was made very quickly. Contrary to my general style, I did not consult anyone about it, not even Hoselitz. Mercifully, I didn't have to ask for recommendations because Chicago maintained a placement file, and this sufficed. Victoria University's academic bureaucracy was courteous and efficient. The registrar made me an offer; I asked him to improve it; he did, and advanced the money to travel. In Wellington, Leslie Palmier, head of Asian studies, was exceptionally warm, helping us find a house in Koro Koro and offering other aid. Ginny had hastily read up on New Zealand and opined that it was going to be the agriculture-based paradise I was longing for. She was surprised that New Zealand did not welcome Asian immigrants but realized that Australia was even stricter. Indeed, there were job opportunities in Perth and Adelaide, but I had not applied. Once I accepted the offer, postcards went out to my mailing list that had, by 1960, grown to about four hundred. I had already resigned from Carbondale and had also notified the dean at Bucknell—a beautiful small university in Lewisburg, Pennsylvania, overlooking the famous penitentiary— that I would not be accepting his offer. Several of the recipients of my postcards wrote back to say that they found my decision unbelievable. Borsodi asked me to benefit from my New Zealand sojourn and help him upon my 'return.'

"Toward the end of my Carbondale years I had worn several masks. I did not discourage my parents and friends in India from believing that in a year or so I would be returning, even though I had made up my mind long ago to seek my notoriety and poverty in the West. Notwithstanding Carbondale's intellectual and cultural isolation, my New York friends continued to see me as one of their own in their march for civil rights, nuclear disarmament, and economic intervention in third world societies, though I had grown weary of them. My love for A. J. Muste and Scott Buchanan continued unabated.

"As far as my academic future was concerned, I was making a bad move. Under Eisenhower and the challenge of Sputnik, America had embarked upon strengthening Asian and European studies, though African studies lagged. Jobs were opening up in almost all major universities, and I was bound to land an offer sooner or later to start a South Asia center. From day one, when I landed in [the] USA in 1953, I had cultivated potential donors, and my access to them was bound to be a plus. Hoselitz had visions of getting me back to Chicago if the reviews of my first book[36] were good. But I had powerful foes too. I had alienated Dan Ingalls (Harvard), and he was one of the godfathers certain to be asked for an opinion on any major appointment. The world had lost Robert Redfield, and I did not expect any support from McKim Marriott, his putative successor.

"Politically it was also a bad move. Rosa Parks and the Little Rock Nine had ushered in a new era in civil rights, and the Warren Court was busy dismantling all the legal underpinnings of racial discrimination. With the passage of the Civil Rights Act of 1960, Jim Crow had found himself shot in the leg. Though not entirely visible at that time, a cultural revolution in the West was in the offing. Old-fashioned colonial empires were crumbling though new imperialisms were on the horizon, needing to be challenged. The revolution of rising expectations provided new opportunities, both creative and destructive, to the old imperial masters.

"Cliff Dancer, my son Martin's godfather and a dear friend, was peeved that I had made the decision to go to New Zealand secretively and expressed the strong opinion that I was escaping, and that action lay in New York, not New Zealand. Yet Ginny was deliriously happy. She wanted a break and was completely unconcerned that my Victoria salary was going to be about one-half of what Bucknell had offered. Her parents' poignant comment was 'Come back soon.' Though I assured Leslie Palmier that we were moving to New Zealand for good, in 1960 I saw New Zealand as a temporary refuge, a Toynbeean withdrawal. Little did I know that we would fall hopelessly in love with the country.

"We fitted at Victoria fairly well. I cannot recall any on the faculty who crossed me. Ties with Peter Munz [professor of history] and Keith Buchanan [professor of geography] were particularly strong, though the two were not the best of friends. Val Maxwell[37] and Margaret Clark were my earliest students and friends, and they introduced me to several other students whose cosmopolitanism (not internationalism) I found refreshing. Outside Victoria, the Friends House and Sunday meetings filled a great void. Literally dozens of Friends befriended us, and we quickly melted into Wellington society.

"During my New Zealand years I met you, and our friendship has endured. For years my ties with Margaret Clark remained strong: I helped her get a Rotary Fellowship to Malaya, and she was grateful. Two other women continued to be in touch long after: Narena Oliver Randall and the future Janet Macdonald. Like you, they had [an] ambivalent relationship with New Zealand, largely because they found the country too confining, which Ginny and I did not.

"Early in 1962 Ginny and I, with Marty and Sunita, moved to Canberra for several months. While in Canberra I received feelers from John Hope Franklin, then chairman of the history department at Brooklyn College, and a job offer materialized. I asked Victoria to give me a year's leave of absence, but the request was made at the wrong time, because Palmier had resigned to take up a UNESCO posting in India, and it was declined. Pissed off, I resigned, and we were back in the States. Soon after we returned, we felt the desire to go back to New Zealand. I applied for a position at Auckland, was selected, but before I could accept the offer it was withdrawn, without explanation. I knew then that something had gone awry, and a return to New Zealand was never going to take place. For almost half a century now I have felt that resigning from Victoria was the worst academic decision in my life."

As our conversations drew to an end, I was struck by the extent to which Brijen's life had oscillated between disenchantment with the world and engagement with it. This "dialectic between withdrawal and return, flight and commitment," has always been, as Bernard McGinn observes, "an essential element in the history of the monastic movement,"[38] and so I asked Brijen if he could help me understand why he had been so attracted by ashrams, Quaker retreats, and places of peaceable community yet had thrown himself so vigorously into the struggle for civil rights and social justice. "Would it be true to say," I asked, "that the polis often proved exhausting, corrupting, and disillusioning, and that, despite your commitment to improving the state of the world, you have recoiled at times, and sought refuge in a more manageable microcosm?" Brijen did not give a direct reply but agreed that my observation was "correct."

Perhaps all one can say is that every person must make his or her own way through this world, seeking a path through trial and error but hoping for occasional sustenance or guidance from other travellers. One's journey is always improvised, a work in progress. On the one hand, the world itself offers possible openings—more for some than for others. On the other hand, we come into the world with personal predilections and dispositions that draw us to certain ideas, people, and places but not others. Hammering out a rough amalgam between our inner persuasions and what the world provides defines the work of a lifetime. Nor is any path or position, once discovered, something we can settle for, sufficient for all time and every exigency. We change, as do our circumstances. The path we took yesterday may prove an impasse today, obliging us to retrace our steps or strike out into the wilderness again, seeking another route. Accordingly, no map, no way, no experience, no precursor is intrinsically superior to any other. Each must be tested against the situations we encounter and the inner yearnings that compel our steps. And even when some exemplar, met along the way, suggests a shortcut or gives us a light to cut through the darkness ahead, we quickly learn that their retrospective accounts of their journeys cannot be used to chart our own. Map is not territory.

Yet everything is potentially grist to our mill. One needs silence in order to think or write. But one needs the noise of the world to have something to write about. One needs routine to make a family life run smoothly. But without confusion and argument, order is not necessary. Whether we must also accept that there is a time for peace and a time for war, a world for the rich and a world for the poor, I cannot say. I only know that striking a permanent balance, or organizing such disparate elements into a coherent whole—politically, aesthetically, theologically, or intellectually—is an absurd task. Better to accept the incoherence of the world than try to render it intelligible.

Teaching in a divinity school, I meet students who are passionate about being of some use in the world, doing some good, changing things for the better, yet whose ambitions never clearly differentiate political goals from religious ethics. Many see in interfaith dialogue between East and West a way toward peaceful coexistence. All play down the incommensurability of traditions, as well as the practical impossibility of the heroic ideal that one *can* change the world. Wisdom seems to lie in scaling down such ambitions, in what Bharati calls a "fastidious humanism,"[39] that while tolerant of human differences focuses on those with whom one has something in common. Thankfully, one finds such people everywhere, despite the dogmatists who assert that men and women, Christians and Muslims, and old and young are essentially unalike and best left to their own devices. Like Brijen, I am grateful for the friends I have made and mindful of the mystery of elective affinities, the widely scattered, intentional community to which I now belong—a symbolic kindred[40] centered on myself, yet not assembled out of self-centeredness. While such a community, when freely chosen, can be a haven in a heartless world, coercive communities like prisons, ghettos, refugee camps, and tribal reservations represent some of the most abhorrent examples of man's inhumanity to man. Nor is a chosen community, familial or national, immune to the self-satisfied belief that its charter myths and way of life are superior to all others. As Hannah Arendt observed, the political refers primarily to relations among human beings, and only derivatively to relations among nations, polities, and abstractions. It is by recovering this original sense of the political (and the ethical) that we best avoid the hubris that comes from extending our ambitions too far, and seeing the world as an arena on which our particular will or worldview must be stamped.

Indeed, there were moments in Brijen's narrative when the lists of significant others grew so compendious that I had the impression that his personal genealogy had metamorphosed into a political history. It was as if his life encapsulated the theme of my book—the oscillation between identifying as a singular individual and identifying as a member of a collectivity, cultural or human. As with Walt Whitman's *Song of Myself*, the celebration of life begins with an author who "dotes" on himself, but almost immediately this author proposes that "every atom belonging to me as good belongs to you." His thoughts "are really the thoughts of all men in all ages and lands, they are not original with me." "Do I contradict myself?" he asks. "Very well, then, I contradict myself, I am large, I contain multitudes."

Brijen Gupta contained multitudes. The individual elements did not always coexist easily within him. But he refused to suppress any one. I like to think that when Brijen was honored with the India Community Center of Rochester's first award for lifetime achievement in 1997, it was not only for his financial and personal gifts to this community, or even for his efforts as a social activist over many years, but for a humanitarianism that was realized through adversity and vitality rather than spelled out as a set of precepts to which lip service alone was due—a humanism born of a struggle to reconcile spiritual and political passions—the hermit and the water of life made one.

CHAPTER 4

Writing Workshop

The conscious mind always wants to be liked and wants to be interesting. The conscious mind is going to suggest the obvious, the cliché, because these things offer the security of having succeeded in the past. Only the mind that has been taken off itself and put on a task is allowed true creativity.

—David Mamet

In his much-cited Letter of Lord Chandos, the fin de siècle Viennese poet Hugo Von Hofmannsthal describes the despair of a writer who has become so disenchanted with language that he can no longer write. In the winter of 2009, something akin to Von Hofmannsthal's "inexplicable condition" afflicted me. At first I suspected that my inability to write stemmed from a disenchantment with language that had been deepening for many years—a doubt that words could ever capture or convey a sense of the life one lived or the world one lived in but only gesture pathetically and longingly toward experiences that remained forever beyond one's grasp. Most writers are all too familiar with the sense of disillusionment and disgust that overwhelms them when they return to passages that they believed to have captured the vitality of an event, only to find no trace of what had been so vividly in mind during the act of writing. Some, like T. S. Eliot, have likened the poet's "intolerable wrestle with words and meanings" to the existential plight of humanity, waiting for God to reveal Himself, to illuminate the "dark cold and the empty desolation" of life on earth. The fictitious Lord Chandos, whose "inner stagnation" imposed on him "a life of barely believable vacuity," admits to being able to keep his despair from his wife and servants, going about his business as if nothing untoward had occurred, "rebuilding a wing of his house and conversing occasionally with the architect."

I was not sure how long I could pretend that I had not lost my way in Dante's *selva oscura*. Rescue came in the form of an e-mail from two Irish anthropologists, inviting me to lead an ethnographic writing workshop in County Wicklow that spring. Rather than confide to Keith and Fiona my current difficulties, I accepted their invitation in the hope that my inability to resolve my own quandary would not prevent me from offering useful advice to others. Certainly I had more to gain by travelling to a country where I had never set foot than sitting at my desk, staring at an empty screen or out the window, waiting for my ice-bound creativity to thaw. Even if my crisis continued, I might stumble on some other form of self-expression and even reinvent myself in the process.

I was lodged in a thatched cottage that adjoined a cemetery and a ruined chapel. Though picturesque from the outside, with its whitewashed walls and wooden doors, the cottage was dank and musty, with cold flagstones underfoot. After depositing my rucksack in a room under the rafters, I set off for the commune at Slí na Bande where our workshops would take place. There was a cool wind blowing, with snatches of sunlight between banks of cumulus cloud, and as I trudged up the narrow road, I felt sudden relief at having escaped the university office where I had sat deadlocked and uninspired for so many months. The flowering gorse had a coconut scent. Or was it better described as biscuity? The roadside was a tangle of nettle, sorrel, brambles, and buttercup. A missel thrush whistled in a hedgerow. And when I looked east across the indelibly green landscape, the Irish Sea was visible as a slate-gray slab under the suddenly cloudless sky.

Over the next two days, I listened and responded to a series of research papers on topics that were as diverse as they were arresting—the lives of sex workers in Dublin, children's games in Northern Ireland that bore traces of "the Troubles," the struggles of classically trained musicians to find work in Athens, evocations of deceased loved ones through touching their photographs or objects and clothing that preserved their memories, stories of pilgrims climbing Croagh Patrick in County Mayo, the preoccupations of people in the Shankill and Falls Road areas of Belfast, the vexed situation of an ethnic minority on the Sino-Burmese frontier, the "archives of sorrow" in Australia, in which the stories of the stolen generation are stored. How trivial my own impasse seemed by comparison with those described with such sensitivity, in such detail, and in such searching ways by these students—determined to do justice to their interlocutors, constrained by academic protocols, yet hoping to communicate their findings to audiences beyond the academy and in some small way ameliorate the lives of others.

That night I woke from a dream that recalled a disconcerting moment in the life of Andrés Segovia. Toward the end of a recital in Berlin, Segovia's guitar developed a crack, and he was forced to abandon the stage. A few weeks later, Segovia learned that a friend, who had made the guitar, had died in Madrid at the precise moment that the instrument split and became unplayable. Worried that my dream signalled an oblique connection between my inability to write and some remote disaster of which I was as yet unaware, I crawled out from under the heavy duvet and in pitch darkness felt my way to the hole in the loft floor where a short flight of wooden steps led down to the kitchen. One had to stand on the third step in order to reach the light switch. However, the 40-watt bulb that hung unshaded from the rafters gave insufficient light to read by, and so I blindly made my way back to bed where my thoughts turned to Glenn Kurtz's book, *Practicing*, which I had read some weeks before. A child prodigy who took his first guitar lessons at the age of eight, appeared on national television backing Dizzy Gillespie, and was accepted into the elite New England Conservatory of Music, Kurtz had his heart set on becoming the next Segovia. But after suffering a crisis of confidence at the age of twenty-five, he gave up the instrument that he describes in the language one might use of an unrequited love. "Only a very few loves can disappoint you so fundamentally that you feel you've lost yourself when they're gone. Quitting music wounded me as deeply as any relationship in my life. It was my first great loss, this innocent, awkward failure to live with what I heard and felt."[1] Kurtz avoided music for more than ten years, lost touch with friends from his Conservatory days, and worked in a publishing house in New York City before migrating to California, "land of the reinvented self." Throughout these years he struggled with the pain of losing the skills and sensibilities he had worked so hard to develop, finding little compensation in his new employment. Then, on a cold March day, after sorting through some old notebooks and journals that his parents had shipped to him in San Francisco, Kurtz remembered the passion he had once felt for music. Taking his guitar from his closet, he opened his music books, "like a long-lost cache of love letters,"[2] and began to play. His return to music was not easy. Periods of regret and humiliating incompetence were punctuated with minor breakthroughs as he recovered techniques that lay "concealed in his hands."[3] No longer did he hope to build the fabulous career he had once mapped out for himself in his imagination, but perhaps he could again enjoy practicing the music of which he and his guitar were capable, carried away by the sense of an instrument perfectly in tune, its strings and body resonating in sympathetic vibration, player and guitar becoming one. This sympathetic vibration, Kurtz writes, "reaches across centuries and languages, binding us together like with like."[4] And there his memoir ends, with the last lines of "Weeping Willow Blues" still ringing in one's ears.

The following afternoon we piled into several cars for an excursion to Glendalough, the site of an early medieval monastic settlement whose founder, Saint Cóemgen (Saint Kevin), spent seven years as a hermit in a nearby cave, living on wild herbs and fish brought to him by the otters in the lake. Legend has it that a local farmer became curious as to why his cow began producing copious amounts of milk, and he followed the animal to Kevin's retreat, where he watched as it licked the anchorite's feet and clothing as he knelt in prayer. Converted to Kevin's Christian faith, the farmer then persuaded the hermit to return to society and spread the Gospel.

Keith told me that Glendalough flourished for several centuries. People came from far and wide to consult the monk, who possessed oracular powers and could perform miracles. If a penitent travelled seven times to the Glen of Two Lakes, this journey would be considered the equivalent of a pilgrimage to Rome.

Keith went on to tell me about his own journey to Santiago de Compostela in Galicia, northern Spain, where the bones of St. James are thought to be interred. Along this medieval pilgrimage route, Keith got to know individuals from as many walks of life as the sorrows they carried in their hearts. While some sought closeness to God, others saw the pilgrimage as a pretext for a vacation, while others hoped for some alleviation of personal suffering. One man had been walking parts of the road for several years, grief-stricken over the death of his beloved daughter. A young woman had chosen the Camino as a way of overcoming the numbness and immobility that had oppressed her since her father's death. An elderly Norwegian couple joyfully drank their way through each day, marking "their third and final Camino, and the reality that they would not be able to walk it again."[5] An American man in his forties, whom Keith got to know particularly well, confessed to feelings of failure, unfinished business, and aimlessness. The Camino, Keith said, offered all these people a way of leaving themselves behind. Through the rhythms and routines of the pilgrimage they hoped to experience themselves anew. As for Keith, he was not only seeking an anthropological understanding of pilgrimage, he was searching for new insights into his fluctuating relationship with the Roman Catholic Church.

I was so affected by Keith's account of these pilgrims, and his allusions to how deeply our biographies are embedded in whatever work we do, even as ethnographers, that when we reached Glendalough I wandered off on my own, scarcely aware of the wooded glacial valley that now held me in its hands, or the oaks, holly, hazel, and mountain ash that encroached on the ruined settlement. Only gradually did I take in the reconstruction that had begun there in the late nineteenth century, including the priest's house, the cathedral, four churches, and the six-storey granite and slate tower where, according to Keith, relics and treasures were stored for pilgrims to venerate.

It was not until much later that day that I realized the common thread that connected the seminar papers I had heard that morning, the anecdotes Keith had shared with me on the road to Glendalough, the restoration of the old monastic city, destroyed by the English in 1398, and W. B. Yeats's preoccupation with towers, including the round tower at Glendalough that conjured, for him, images of "winding, gyring, spiring"[6] stairs that led in one direction to ancestral figures and in the other to close friends like Major Robert Gregory, killed on the western front in 1918, his artistic promise unfulfilled. Given the losses we sustain in life, how on earth do we begin again? One can readily understand the traveller who seeks to "walk out of a depression,"[7] and the perennial hope that when stuck, blocked, or stagnating we can get back on our feet and walk out into the world again, recovering our lives.

Much later I tracked down a dimly remembered poem by Yeats and discovered that his thoughts at Glendalough had also turned to the possibility of redemption. Speaking of "some stupid thing that he had done that made his attention stray,"[8] Yeats questions the temerity of even thinking that one can change one's ways and be born anew. No doubt Yeats was thinking of Saint Kevin as he wrote these lines, not only the life-transforming miracles attributed to the Irish saint, but his harmonious relationship with all wild things. It is said, for example, that as a seven-year-old child, sent by his well-heeled Irish parents to St. Petroc's Monastery in Cornwall, Kevin was kneeling in prayer on the first day of Lent when a blackbird alighted on his up-turned hand and commenced to build its nest there. In return for this secure nesting place, the blackbird fed the boy berries and nuts. Like Seamus Heaney, who has written of this episode, I was amused by the irony that, having offered his hand as a sanctuary for the blackbird and "finding himself linked into the network of eternal life,"[9] the devoted boy had to remain in physical agony until the fledglings had hatched and flown. So it is that we wait for a resolution to our difficulties, the reconciliation of our competing desires, and an amelioration of our pains. If the anecdote of the blackbird calls to mind the dark night of the soul in which the believer waits for God to appear, or appear again, then it also speaks to more secular hopes, such as a break in the weather, a broken relationship repaired, a change in one's fortunes, an error forgiven, the recovery of something lost. And I wondered if my resistance to the idea of perfection, either artistic or moral, as well as my repudiation of certainty as an attainable intellectual goal, was simply another way of walking the Camino.

One of the students who had made a presentation that morning was suffering from what she called writer's block. She needed what she variously called a framework, an overview, a coherent map, before she could write. I suggested she set aside these abstract considerations and focus on a specific event or particular observation, allowing her mind to become deeply absorbed in a detailed description of something very concrete. Gradually, I said, an interpretation of this episode will dawn on you, and connections will be revealed with other episodes that at first sight seemed unrelated. In this way your thesis will emerge like a seedling from the black loam of empirical particulars.

By the time we got back to Slí na Bande that evening, I was wondering whether I might well take the advice I had given my student and whether I had somehow lost the Zen technique for writing that I had developed in my early thirties, allowing *it*, the writing, to eclipse *myself*, the writer, whose thoughts, anxieties, and expectations could only be obstacles in my path. My routine was to write for two or three hours each morning before the distractions of the day intruded. Even if I had more time, I would not use it, for I had always had a strong sense of having a finite amount of writing to do each day and that this quantum had been prepared overnight in my unconscious. As soon as I had exhausted this small fund of events, ideas, and images, I would give myself over to e-mails, lecture writing, student consultations, committee meetings, and the other matters that make up the everyday life of an academic. But by late afternoon I was always home or walking in the woods, resting my mind, allowing it to fill again with what would become my next few pages of prose narrative. That walking loosens the mind, opening it up to the possibility of unbidden and illuminating thoughts, is a mystery that many authors have remarked on, and there were echoes of this refrain in Keith's reflections on pilgrimage. For it is when the physical rhythms of walking occlude the workings of the discursive mind that new understandings tend to arise. Yet how difficult many of us find this yielding to the road, giving up the desire to comprehend our condition or search for God, even though we know that such resignation is a precondition for the very transformations we crave. As Thoreau observed, in suggesting the need to let things lie fallow, "a man is rich in proportion to the number of things which he can afford to let alone."[10]

The following morning we met for a final workshop in which Keith and Fiona led a discussion about Irish anthropology. Several participants expressed a concern that a country that had endured six hundred years of occupation and won its independence at the cost of so many lives should not nurture a colonial form of anthropology that exploited the cultural knowledge of ordinary people for academic ends. How could one move from an anthropology *done to us* to an anthropology *done by us?* How could ethnographers keep faith with those who opened their hearts and homes to them? How best could that debt of hospitality be repaid? Within minutes, the case of "The Yank in the Corner" was raised, and students recalled local reactions to the American ethnographer Nancy Scheper-Hughes who did fieldwork in a village on the Dingle Peninsular, County Kerry, in 1974–1975. To the criticism that she, an interloper, had not consulted local people before publishing intimate details of their lives, Scheper-Hughes countered that she had divulged no "personal" secrets and had written only of what was common knowledge: "the depressions and drinking associated with the lonely winter months, the difficulty of keeping an heir on the land, the old people sent off to die in institutions, and the distance and alienation between the sexes."[11]

There was, the locals admitted, "a lot of truth in what she said, you can't deny that. But did she have the right to say it, so?"[12] And people spoke of the shame they felt, their lifeworld intruded upon, "bits and pieces" of themselves severed and strewn about with no consideration of the consequences.

I saw no point in taking sides. As Joan Didion observed, "writers are always selling someone out."[13] But it was clear why a people whose history had given them every reason to be wary of outsiders, and whose isolation had only increased their sense of vulnerability, should see the preoccupations of this anthropologist as both alien and condescending. Admitting her "brashness,"

Scheper-Hughes asserts that "anthropology is by nature intrusive, entailing a certain amount of symbolic and interpretive violence to the 'native' peoples' own intuitive, though still partial, understanding of their part of the world."[14] But does this entitle us to ride roughshod over the interests and wishes of others, even though they might seem misguided and self-defeating? Rather than persuade others that our values and worldviews might be advantageous for them to adopt, we would do well to find ways of expressing solidarity with others, despite the differences between us. Surely forging a bond with others is more valuable than possessing knowledge of them. Scheper-Hughes shows sympathy and gratitude to those who offered her and her young family hospitality in "Ballybran," but she is not prepared to place her way of seeing them on a par with their way of seeing themselves, or for that matter of seeing her. "You wrote a book to please yourself at our expense," one man tells her when she comes back to Ballybran twenty years after the publication of her book. "You ran us down, girl, you ran us down. You never wrote about our strengths. You never said what a beautiful and a safe place our village is. You said nothing about our fine musicians and poets, and our step dancers who move through the air with the grace of a silk thread. You wrote about our troubles, all right, but not about our strengths. Look, girl, the fact is that ya just didn't give us credit."[15] In the closing pages of the 2000 edition of her book, Scheper-Hughes attempts to address the complaints and make amends. But like so many anthropologists, she needs to have the last word, to privilege her voice over the voices raised against her. "In the end perhaps we deserve each other—well matched and well met, tougher than nails, both of us. Proud and stubborn, too. *Unrepentant* meets *Unforgiving*. And in a way villagers were right to say, 'We don't believe you are really sorry.' For in their view this would mean nothing less than a renunciation of self and my vexed profession, a move I could not make."

I have far fewer qualms about renouncing myself and my profession, particularly if it comes to a showdown between the jargon of the human sciences and the idioms of those we subject to our analytical gaze. For me, what matters most are the ways in which the anthropological project can make possible and mediate forms of coexistence. These social considerations may so completely eclipse our ambition to interpret, explain, or change the lives of others that some anthropologists refrain from publishing the results of their research, not wanting to build a career on the knowledge acquired during fieldwork. Although I have experienced these doubts, they have been allayed by Kuranko friends who see my work as an affirmation of their worth and not a betrayal of their trust, and this has reinforced my resolve to find ways of writing ethnography that respects the Kantian imperative that one act in such a way that one always treats humanity, whether in one's own person or in the person of another, never simply as a means but always at the same time as an end.[16]

What then had stayed my hand? Brought my writing to a standstill?

On our last night together, we were sitting around the dinner table in the farmhouse, warming to one another's company, our tongues loosened by red wine, when someone suggested we take turns to recount an embarrassing anecdote from our fieldwork, a mistake or faux pas that had made us ashamed to be an anthropologist.

My story went back to 1970, when my wife and I were living in a town in northern Sierra Leone. Our daughter Heidi had been born at the beginning of the rains, and after many months of exhausting fieldwork in remote villages I was desperately in need of a break. One night, after closing the shutters and doors of our house, my wife and I fell to talking about Cambridge and the life we would return to when my work in West Africa was done. When we heard voices approaching the house, we stopped talking and waited for the inevitable knock on the door. It was my field assistant Noah and his wives. They had come to greet us. I shouted that we were in bed, hoping that Noah would take this to mean that we did not want to be disturbed. But among the Kuranko, as in many other societies, deafness is a metaphor for social insensitivity, if not madness, and so our visitors sat on the porch, talking softly and rapping on the door from time to time as if waiting for us to come to our senses and invite them in. Half an hour passed before they finally drifted off into the night. And though I apologized to Noah the next day, the shameful memory of my churlishness has never left me.

As we went on in this confessional vein, Marlene, our hostess, moved between the kitchen and dining room, bringing out bowls of homegrown vegetables, tofu burgers, and salads and clearing away our dirty plates. But she was also listening to our stories.

When a lull came in the conversation, Marlene announced that she too had a story. "I am not an anthropologist," she said, "but I know what it is like to be an outsider, to invade another person's space and feel shame at one's insensitivity." Marlene met her Irish husband, Douglas, when she was nineteen and backpacking through Ireland. They shared a dream of buying a piece of land and establishing an alternative community. Marlene would practice meditation and psychotherapy. They would generate power from wind and sun, grow organic vegetables, and achieve a sustainable lifestyle. When they first visited the property, however, they thought it gloomy and uninspiring. But they returned for a second look on a sunny day and decided to buy. That first year they suffered several mysterious setbacks: their vegetable crop was stolen, their car was gutted by fire, and the chalet they had built had its windows broken. One night Marlene witnessed a Victorian funeral cortege making its way across their land toward the ruined church and grave-yard that lay on the side-fall of the hill. The coffin lay on a horse-drawn car-riage. The men wore top hats. The women wore black veils. Marlene had been told that faeries once used this route; now she realized they still did. It had been the spirits of the place that had resisted Marlene and Douglas, remind-ing them that they were interlopers. Marlene arranged a ritual. Eight friends stood at the cardinal points as she addressed the genii loci, asking if they could live side by side in peace, the faerie path protected, and one part of the farm left uncultivated for their use. The "other crowd" did not trouble her again.

This would not be the last time I was made aware of the Celtic twilight, and of how history haunts and sometimes hounds the living, interfering with our efforts to create lives on our own terms in the here and now. In Dublin, for example, I stayed in a hotel opposite Kilmainham Gaol, now a museum, where the British imprisoned, court-martialled, and executed the leaders of the Easter Rising in 1916, including James Connolly, whose ankle had been shattered by a bullet during the siege of the General Post Office. Connolly had to be strapped to a chair in order for the firing squad to accurately aim at his heart. During my rambles around the city in the company of Keith and Fiona, visiting the General Post Office on O'Connell Street, the house at 82 Merrion Square, where Yeats lived, or crossing the Liffey and recalling the figure of Anna Livia Plurabelle, I was mindful of the eternal recapitulations of time and history and the ways in which our stories are drawn into the same vortex, their leitmotifs combining and recombining in ceaseless repeti-tions and cycles—what is one's own entangled with what belongs to the wider realm of one another.

CHAPTER 5

How Much Home Does a Person Need?

Every migrant knows in his heart of hearts, that it is impossible to return . . . because he has been so deeply changed by his emigration. It is equally impossible to return to that historical state in which every village was the center of the world. The one hope of recreating a center now is to make it the entire earth. Only worldwide solidarity can transcend modern homelessness.

—John Berger

At the heart of contemporary anthropology lies a dilemma: How can we do justice to what is at stake for people in their "local moral worlds"[1] and *at the same time* strive to broaden our analytical horizons to encompass the general and global conditions of human life on earth? This dilemma is at once methodological and empirical. As Michael Herzfeld has shown,[2] the discursive tension between a localizing ethnographic gaze and a generalizing theoretical perspective echoes the social and political tensions between societies at the margins of the modern nation-state and the centralized, bureaucratized structures of the state. Moreover, there is probably no human society in which people have not wrestled with the ethical question of how one can reconcile a sense of shared humanity with the essentialized distinctions between gender, age, birthright, caste, and class on which social structures are typically built. These questions are fundamental to existential anthropology and exercised me throughout my years in Denmark, provoked undoubtedly by the curious experience of feeling increasingly at home in a place where I was culturally, linguistically, and officially an outsider. That my reflections on the paradoxes of human plurality were inspired by Hannah Arendt's incisive comments on the ambiguity of what it means to be human may have had something to do with the fact that Arendt herself was also an expatriate,[3] and that my work on the politics of storytelling[4] evolved as a set of variations on a central theme in her book *The Human Condition*.

I first visited Denmark in 1969 with my first wife, Pauline, who had been learning Danish at Cambridge with Elias Bredsdorff as part of her PhD work on the Icelandic family sagas. In Copenhagen, Pauline would spend four weeks in a "language-intensive" program, improving her spoken Danish while I hung out at Bellahoj, where we were camped, writing an essay on Malcolm Lowry, whose eye for uncanny connections and natural symbols seemed to me, at the time, worth imitating as an ethnographic skill. After our month in Copenhagen we planned to drive to Paris and wait for a sailing from Le Havre to Sierra Leone, where I would begin my PhD fieldwork and put into practice the same attentiveness to detail that characterized Lowry's writing but had, ironically, brought him to the point of madness.

At Cambridge, Pauline had become good friends with Elias Bredsdorff's daughter, Kristine, and in our free time we explored Copenhagen together. Elias had been active in the wartime resistance and was editor of its underground newspaper, so the Resistance Museum was one of the first places we visited. Reading my notebook from that time, I am reminded of how preoccupied I became by the problem of trust, for under occupation one's life is often in the hands of strangers. Is it then safer to keep to oneself, to withdraw into a small circle of family and trusted friends, or does one's duty to compatriots in peril compel one to risk one's life to help them? Elias Bredsdorff ran these risks and survived the war. But within months of the war ending, he left Denmark to take up a lecturership in Danish at University of College London. Though Kristine was born in London, the family moved to Cambridge in 1949, when Elias was appointed head of the Scandinavian studies department. His magnum opus, published in 1975, was a critical biography of Hans Christian Andersen.

Kristine was also eager to have us experience the Copenhagen jazz scene, and one night she took us to the famous Jazzhus Montmartre. We probably didn't hear Ben Webster on tenor sax and Teddy Wilson on piano (they were touring in Norway that August), but I learned a little about the importance of cities like Paris, Amsterdam, Helsinki, Stockholm, and Copenhagen in a global diaspora of jazz music and musicians that dated from the 1930s. By the early sixties, Copenhagen rivaled New York for its musical energy and new-wave innovations. African American expatriates and touring stars improvised with local Danish jazzmen in settings that Dexter Gordon spoke of as "conducive to [his] well-being [and] peace of mind."[5] In Copenhagen, he felt "relaxed and comfortable," considering it "a second home." Here, according to Dexter's widow Maxine, musicians could count on longer engagements and better pay than in the United States, and get informed and sympathetic reviews. But just as important as regular paid employment was the absence of racism,[6] and many black musicians settled in Denmark for this reason, including—for various periods—Dexter Gordon, Ben Webster, Kenny Drew, Stuff Smith, Sahib Shihab, Idrees Sulieman, Ray Pitts, Oscar Pettiford, Duke Jordan, Mercer Ellington, Horace Parlan, Brew Moore, Albert Heath, and Ed Thigpen.

Thirty years after my first visit to Copenhagen, I returned with my second wife and our two children. Unable to find work in my own country, I had accepted a temporary appointment in the Institute of Anthropology at the University of Copenhagen. We ended up living in Denmark for six years, three of them in an apartment on the corner of Åhornsgade and Nørre Allé, only a few blocks from the Assistens Cemetery, where Hans Christian Andersen, Niels Bohr, Søren Kierkegaard, and several African American jazzmen—Ben Webster, Kenny Drew, and Richard B. Boone—were buried.

I visited the cemetery often. It was a quiet place to stroll or even take a picnic lunch. Whenever I passed the section reserved for the black jazzmen who had died so far from home, I would reflect on the irony that while the United States had become a tolerably better place for African Americans since the early sixties, Copenhagen had ceased to be the haven for expatriates it had been back then. Even though I was treated hospitably, I was always mindful, during my annual visit to Immigration for a new work permit, that I was more welcome than the refugees and asylum seekers among whom I waited my turn for an interview. And hardly a week passed that I was not made aware when talking to Iraqi, Somali, Palestinian, and Kurdish neighbors in Nørrebro that they felt ghettoized and stigmatized in a country that had granted them legal residency only to socially shun them.

I used to think anthropology might share the spirit of Paul Gilroy's *The Black Atlantic*, embracing the view that essential distinctions between different ethnicities have long been complicated and transgressed as people travelled, traded, interacted, and intermarried across the globe. More significant than the hard-line sense of difference that perpetuates racial stereotypes and prejudices are the forms of conversation, civility, and coexistence that have made hybrids of us all. While anthropology today acknowledges these global processes of transnational mobility, media dissemination, and cosmopolitanism,[7] it continues to document the countervailing presence of local worldviews, nationalisms, religions, and ways of life, suggesting that no matter how universal the public sphere becomes, the private sphere is never eclipsed but, on the contrary, often works as a corrective or subversion. My own work took this thesis even further by arguing that the lived experience of any one person, though conditioned by the sociohistorical milieu in which he or she has come of age, is never reducible to that milieu, and that an indeterminate relationship exists between imperatives felt to be one's own and equally strong imperatives that are felt to be external or other. It was this relational perspective, with its emphasis on the inner life of human subjects in relation to other subjects, and not merely in relation to global spheres of climate change, market processes, genetic transfers, international politics, pandemic illnesses, communication technologies, media, migration, and mobility, that gave some of my colleagues the impression that I was out of touch with contemporary politico-economic realities and engaged in some kind of solipsistic philosophical anthropology. But I was never sure whether it was my intellectual work that made me anomalous, or my expatriate and impermanent status, my failure to acquire fluency in Danish, and my tendency to keep to myself.

Twice a year Henny Pedersen and her colleagues at the Institute would organize a mystery tour. We would meet for drinks before being ushered onto a bus and spirited to a location in the city or countryside, or along the coast, where we would visit some story-worthy site and afterward enjoy a restaurant meal in one another's company. The intimacy and conviviality of these occasions was something one rarely encounters in institutional settings outside of Denmark. Personal differences were set aside, candles lit, beer consumed, food passed around, songs sung, stories told, toasts made, bonds formed. But while the art of creating this cozy and familial ambiance (*hyggeligt*) impresses the outsider, it can also leave one feeling that one could never be entirely a part of it. On one excursion to an offshore island a few miles south of the city, we wandered in small groups along a rutted farm track, and thence across water meadows to a shingle beach, where we stopped for lunch. As we were unpacking our rucksacks, it began to rain. It was obvious from the bruised and lowering clouds now rolling in from the sea and the sound of distant thunder that the storm would be upon us within minutes. Though my colleagues acknowledged the dangers of being caught out in the open during an electrical storm, no one made a move. Without a second thought, I now climbed to my feet and announced that I was going to seek shelter in the farmhouse we had passed only minutes before. No one approved or disapproved my proposal, and it was with some dismay that I looked back, not long after leaving the group, to see everyone still sitting in the water meadow, as solid as stones, even though the rain was now falling heavily and lightning was tearing open the darkened sky. Ignoring a No Trespassers sign, I clambered over a padlocked gate to the farmstead, which was deserted, and took refuge in the canopied back of a cattle truck. It was only then, with torrential rain drumming on the canvas and thunder crashing around me, that I realized I had broken an unspoken rule, acting on my initiative rather than in concert with others, and that I had exposed myself as incorrigibly *uhyggeligt* and un-Danish. Not only had I ignored a padlocked gate and a notice declaring the farm to be private property, but *I had acted alone*. In due course, some of my colleagues, drenched to the skin, joined me under the leaking canopy. But most trudged back to the landing stage in the rain.

This sense of never quite fitting in made me understandably sympathetic to the African American jazzmen who had escaped the insupportable and everyday humiliations of racism on one side of the Atlantic only to find themselves experiencing the loneliness of exile on the other. Ben Webster was treated with respect, but he often missed the company of kindred spirits and American friends and drank heavily to drown his sorrows.[8] It is not that there is no place like home but, rather, that there is nowhere one can feel entirely at home. To be cosmopolitan is supposedly to find compensation for this lack of any specific place where one truly belongs. But the word is an abstraction that does not resonate emotionally with the experience of living as an expatriate or exile. What one struggles for is not a word[9] with which to name this condition of being a part of the world while feeling apart from it; one seeks a way of *living* betwixt and between.

It is the impossibility of reconciling our inward and outward senses of self that renders existence absurd. One may give one's all to others, embrace a cause, or seek fusion with a transcendent power, be it a nation, a moral principle, or a god. But the more one tries to eclipse oneself, to submerge one's passions and particularities in one's relations with others, with absolutes or something greater than the self, the more one is brought back to the indissolubly singular truth of who one is. George Orwell, borrowing a phrase from Mahatma Gandhi, referred to this as "the unregenerate part of life," including the side of a saint's life that is suppressed, devalued, and disavowed in order to pursue a higher moral calling.[10] The reverse is also true, for the more one reflects on one's individuality, the more one discovers in oneself evidence of one's ancestry, habits that reveal one's social conditioning, dispositions that reveal one's history, and intimations of one's own mortality. This is Søren Kierkegaard's "paradox of existence."[11] One can no more achieve fusion with one's family, one's ethnicity, one's lover, or one's God than sustain for very long the illusion of one's own uniqueness. To sink one's consciousness in the sea or sky is perfectly possible, but sea and sky are like anesthetics from which one inevitably comes round. One may have hoped that they would bear one away, into another space, another sphere of consciousness, but they turn out to be mirrors in which you discover your own face again.

En route to South America, and with less than a year to live, Albert Camus spent hours alone gazing at the sea. In the moonlight, the ocean seemed like a summons to life, but in the tarnished darkness of its depths it was an invitation to death.[12] One night, saddened by how few stars there were in the southern sky, he found himself thinking of "our Algerian nights, swarming with stars."[13] The Algerian War of Independence had been raging for five years, and Camus's noncommittal public statements on where he stood no doubt reflected his inability to disentangle his political and personal thoughts. If he could see no political solution to the crisis in Algeria, it was because he could see no resolution of his own personal dilemmas—an intellectual who was skeptical of philosophical systems and political ideologies, a natural solitary who had become a celebrity. "I don't love Algeria in the same way a soldier or colonist does, but can I love it other than as a Frenchman? What most Arabs don't understand is that I love it as a Frenchman who loves Arabs and wants them to be at home in Algeria, but I don't want to feel like a foreigner there myself."[14]

Camus's deepest struggle, however, was to transcend identity thinking, to live outside the terms that history dictated to him and the social contradictions into which he was born. Two months before he sailed for South America, he confided to his diary: "For years I've tried to live according to everyone else's morality and I forced myself to live like everyone else and to resemble everyone else. I said what was needed to unite people, even when I myself felt estranged from them, and in the end the catastrophe came. Now I wander amid the debris as an outlaw, drawn and quartered, alone and accepting to be so, resigned to my singularities and weaknesses. And I must reconstruct a truth after having lived a sort of lie all my life."[15]

Is it possible to strike a balance between being true to oneself and meeting the demands placed upon one by one's children, one's friends, one's country? The expatriate possibly feels the tug of these competing imperatives even more than the exile, for while the exile is morally recused from allegiance to the country that has forced him to live abroad, the expatriate must remain loyal to his homeland as well as conform to the rules of the country in which he lives as a resident alien. As a result, the expatriate finds fulfillment neither in his country of origin (because his life there has been placed on hold) nor in the country of adoption (because his life there lacks the depth and warmth that come from being in a familiar place). One's mind is always wandering— worrying where one properly belongs, where one really should be; wondering about the life that one passed up in order to improve one's chances elsewhere; preoccupied by what is missing in the life one has made when compared to the life one was born into.

At sea, en route to Denmark, Helga Crane is momentarily liberated from having to be the person others want her to be, from conforming to the persona that others impose upon her. Helga Crane is the key figure in Nella Larsen's novel *Quicksand*, and it is hard not to imagine that Helga's thoughts are also the author's: "But even the two rough days found her on deck, reveling like a released bird in her returned feeling of happiness and freedom, that blessed sense of belonging to herself alone and not to a race."[16]

Larsen's mother was a Danish immigrant in the United States; her father hailed from the Danish West Indies. Did this make her a "Negro," or was this identity foist upon her by a society so deeply divided along color lines that many people were never free to decide their identities for themselves?

Larsen was born in Chicago in 1891, at a time when the city was beginning to divide along racial lines. Her father soon disappeared from her life, and her mother married another Dane with whom she had a second daughter. Reviled by her stepfather and stepsister, Larsen also became a victim of the city's segregation laws that made it impossible for a "black" person to live in a "white" neighborhood. Destined "to live a life apart,"[17] yet resisting a world premised on a crude and fundamentalist division between black and white, Larsen's life would become an unending struggle to find a place that transcended such divisions, a place between. If her fiction is anything to go by, Larsen hardly ever experienced the feeling of release that she attributes to Helga Crane. In her first few months in Copenhagen, Helga's dream is realized, of "the things which money could give, leisure, attention, beautiful surroundings," the kinds of things that being black in America doomed one to admire at a distance but never possess. But after two years in the Danish capital, subjected to the gaze of people for whom blacks were exotic and alluring animals, she began to wonder whether the more malign stereotypes of North America might be more bearable. It was the kind of thought that passed through the minds of some of the black jazzmen who settled in Copenhagen in the 1960s. That Danes embraced black music so enthusiastically was not only because it offered something beyond the exhausted European systems of harmony, melody, pitch, and timbre; it allegedly aroused a more libidinal, sexually energized mode of being. Ornette Coleman objected to this stereotype of the music and the musicians. James Baldwin was not surprised. Prejudice was prejudice, whether it categorized you as naturally stupid or naturally rhythmic. In 1965 he passed through Denmark on his way to Sweden and paid a visit to Hamlet's "castle" at Elsinore. In a letter to his brother, David, Baldwin mentions a pond near Elsinore, "invented" by Shakespeare. On this pond he had observed a family of black swans being "ignored" by a lone white one.[18]

After two years in Denmark, Helga Crane is only too glad to get back to Harlem's "dirty streets [and] "dark, gay humanity."[19] But she has discovered that race, in one form or another, will follow her wherever she goes. It is so deeply and indelibly inscribed in the consciousness of both whites and blacks that it cannot be waived or written off. Against every attempt to make yourself the person *you* want to be, and to find acceptance as this person, the false consciousness of essentialism does its insidious and corrosive work, reminding you that you have only created a façade, a pretense, and that beneath your sophisticated airs, stylish clothes, educated manner, and brilliant writing you remain incorrigibly Other. You are nothing but a poor copy, a plagiarized version, of an Other that is beyond you. Under all this pressure, is it any wonder that you doubt yourself, your intelligence, your writing, your determination to be *more* than merely black or white, or some indescribable mixture of the two? And if black intellectuals conspire to exaggerate the significance of racial identity, to inadvertently perpetuate the essentialisms that underwrote slavery and segregation by making "passing" the ultimate betrayal of one's history and identity, then you have no allies, no place to go.

Henry Louis Gates's essay on Anatole Broyard exemplifies the dilemma. His essay is a sustained condemnation of the sin of passing. Broyard's efforts to transcend his origins are seen as denials of those origins, even as Gates recognizes that Broyard's options were impossible ones—like the Scylla and

Charybdis of being true or false to one's ethnicity that made Nella Larsen's life so vexed.

> So here was a man who passed for white because he wanted to be a writer, and he did not want to be a Negro writer. It is a crass disjunction, but it is not his crassness or his disjunction. His perception was perfectly correct. He *would* have to be a Negro writer, which was something he did not want to be. In his terms, he did not want to write about black love, black passion, black suffering, black joy; he wanted to write about love and passion and suffering and joy. We give lip service to the idea of the writer who happens to be black, but had anyone, in the postwar era, ever seen such a thing?[20]

The tension between how we think of ourselves and how others think about us is a variation on the theme of how we adjust our sense of our own projects, our own needs, our own interests, our own sense of self to the conventional ways in which our humanity is identified for us. How difficult it must be to a Muslim in a time and place that polarizes Sunni and Shia identities, making them mutually antithetical. How impossible it must be to live in countries where sectarian divisions have become so entrenched and self-perpetuating that violence is seen as the only way in which one way of life can be defended against the other. One is left with no middle ground, nowhere to stand if one refuses the dreadful logic of essentialist reason—that if you are not for us, then you are against us. Like Nella Larsen and Anatole Broyard, Zora Neale Hurston avoided harnessing her writing to an explicitly political agenda. Her priority was testifying to the "helter skelter skirmish"[21] that was life for the people she knew best, even if this meant sharing their distance from the political agendas of black urban intellectuals. She therefore laid herself open to censure and accusations of selling out from politicized black writers like Ralph Ellison and Richard Wright. And it would take another generation, and the appearance of Alice Walker's notable essay "In Search of Zora Neale Hurston,"[22] before the quality of Hurston's work ceased to be measured against some ideological yardstick but recognized and celebrated as literature. By this time, Hurston, like Larsen, had died, penurious and forgotten.

Hurston once wrote: "At certain times I have no race. I am *me* . . . I have no separate feeling about being an American citizen and colored. I am merely a fragment of the Great Soul that surges within boundaries."[23] James Baldwin also wanted to be free to broaden his experience beyond the cage in which identity politics had confined it. Growing up, he had fought against being a figment of the white imagination.[24] He left the United States for France because "I wanted to prevent myself from becoming *merely* a Negro; or merely a Negro writer. I wanted to find out in what way the *specialness* of my experience could be made to connect me with other people instead of dividing me from them."[25] The trouble is that the expatriate may expand his or her horizons and even become, as Baldwin did, an internationally admired figure, but this comes at the cost of losing touch with the specific world, however limiting and oppressive, in which one grew up and in which one's core sense of self was formed. One cannot have it both ways. Becoming a public figure is always going to make it difficult to protect one's private life, just as going abroad is always going to estrange one from one's homeland.

CHAPTER 6

Clearings in the Bush

There are three conditions which often look alike
Yet differ completely, flourish in the same hedgerow:
Attachment to self and to things and to persons, detachment
From self and from things and from persons; and, growing between
   them, indifference
Which resembles the others as death resembles life,
Being between two lives . . .

—T. S. Eliot

A recurring preoccupation of Arthur Schopenhauer was the impossibility of finding happiness in the company of others. Insisting that "no man can be in *perfect accord* with any one but himself"[1] and extolling the virtues of self-sufficiency, Schopenhauer nevertheless acknowledges that, for many people, the inner life is so empty and unsatisfying that they are driven "to the company of others which consists of men like themselves, for *similis simili gaudet*" (Birds of a feather flock together).[2] Elsewhere, he makes this point with a parable. A number of porcupines huddle together against the winter's cold, only to find that they cannot avoid pricking one another with their quills. They therefore disperse, only to be driven back together for warmth. It seems there is no middle way whereby the porcupines can draw comfort from being with others and avoid the discomfort of close proximity.[3]

It is tempting to read this parable as an oblique commentary on Schopenhauer himself, by all accounts a reclusive and misanthropic individual who felt more affection for dogs than people and found greater consolation in philosophy than friendship. But as Freud would remark in 1921,[4] Schopenhauer's parable of the porcupine discloses something fundamental about intimate human relationships: that they are characterized by both attraction and repulsion, and that our desire to be with others is always accompanied by a countervailing search for autonomy, to *not* lose oneself in the other, to define oneself against convention, to *not* follow the crowd. This ambivalence toward social life is echoed in the West Sudanese view that sociality "is not an ideal; it is a necessity to which men must adapt and adjust themselves." Social life is often compared to a bulb of garlic. "The cloves continue to cling to each other although all are equally evil smelling. It is the same with men and their communities."[5]

The history of colonialism is replete with examples of the tragic dimensions of this quandary of how to strike a balance between losing one's autonomy in a foreign and possibly repugnant lifeworld and retaining one's independence from it. But this history is also marked by a terrible forgetting. Writes Schopenhauer: "Almost all are for ever thinking that they are such and such a man, together with the corollaries resulting therefrom. On the other hand, it hardly ever occurs to them that they are in general a human being with all the corollaries following from this; and yet this is the vital question."[6] Colonialism, it can be argued, suppresses this vital question; it censors it out; it forgets its corollaries.

In Australia, Aboriginal people quickly saw advantages in trade relations with whites. In exchange for sex, food, information, and labor, they could acquire glass to make spearheads, iron axes, sugar, flour, and tea. But relations between indigene and invader quickly degenerated. Assuming cattle to be game animals like kangaroos, Aboriginals hunted them. In turn, white pastoralists hunted down Aboriginals as though they were animals. And assuming that the land was unowned, if not unoccupied, white settlers seized it without a second thought.

Initially, Aboriginal people stood their ground, fighting to retain their lands and livelihoods. But as they were overwhelmed, they either submitted to a marginal and dependent existence on the fringes of white settlements or withdrew into remote areas where whites were less willing to venture. Though avoiding the quills of the invader meant great hardship, avoidance strategies ensured survival, or at least staved off the evil day when the invader would discover in even the most inhospitable deserts, mountains, and forests minerals to mine and resources to exploit. It was then that the invader decided that the people it had treated so atrociously were fated not to survive. But if extinction was inevitable for the "race," then perhaps an afterlife might be found for the children born of mixed parentage. And so began the government policy of forcibly removing "half-caste" children from their Aboriginal mothers, making them wards of the state, placing them in institutional care, and preparing them for menial work in white households.

Aboriginal people did not die out. They were rounded up and herded into missions and settlements. For a nomadic people, accustomed to living in small, mobile family groups, these overcrowded communities were demoralizing and destructive. Unlike the porcupines, it was impossible to keep one's distance, to follow customary protocols for avoiding in-laws or marrying "wrong-way," or to act on one's own initiative, in one's own time, in one's own place. Of Wujal Wujal on southeast Cape York, a Kuku Yalanji man said that there was so little room to move that one felt "like a crane standing on one leg on a little island." And because social distance was an index of respect, people described their lives in these concentration camps as pervaded by a sense of profound shame.

Only in moving away from such unintentional communities, only by returning to one's traditional land, could one hope to recover a viable existence. This is what the Salt family achieved in 1992, resettling a parcel of ancestral land purchased for them through an Aboriginal and Torres Strait Island Commission grant.

In 1994 my wife Francine and our small son, Joshua, spent a year living with the Salts in their rainforest camp, fishing each evening on the nearby beach and constantly negotiating, like the porcupines in Schopenhauer's parable, a viable distance between our families, as well as between the Salt's camp and the many "blow-ins" (mostly affines or distant kin) whose presence sometimes caused such mayhem that our hosts would simply move away to a temporary, separate camp on the beach.

A CLEARING IN THE BUSH

Peter Fisher moved away but did not return. He elected to make his home in the forested watersheds of the Daintree and Bloomfield Rivers. According to Mabel and McGinty, he rarely visited the mission.

"Does that mean he doesn't want visitors?" I asked.

"I dunno," McGinty said.

I was used to McGinty's noncommittal way of responding to a direct question, this characteristically Aboriginal strategy for ensuring that no advice was ever given that might be later used against you. Better to say nothing than say something that might have negative repercussions.

Francine and I decided to make the trip anyway.

The road from the coast rose steeply, little more than a rain-gouged track. It took us through partly cleared grazing land, past the site of China Camp (named for the Chinese, Javanese, and Malay "wages men" who mined alluvial tin in the area from the mid-1890s to the period around the First World War), past Roaring Meg Falls, and across boulder-obstructed streams.

At last we came to a grassy clearing, cropped by a couple of untethered horses. I parked our Toyota near a barbed wire fence and gate. Beyond was a garden filled with citrus trees, pawpaws, and banana palms.

The old man, stiff in the hips, came hobbling through the pawpaws to the gate, but it was apparent from the relaxed and open expression on his face that he was happy to receive visitors.

After my wife and I had made our introductions, we sat in the small, open-sided shed with a dirt floor where Peter slept and cooked. I noticed some onions, chili peppers, salt, and plates on a makeshift counter. "I don't eat much," Peter said. "Tea and damper mostly, like when I was a boy." He said he felt guilty that he had no *maiyi* (food) to offer us.

Francine said no apologies were needed; we had brought something to eat.

Peter had been living in the wilderness for fifteen months. It was the site of the old Collins homestead, he explained. He had had to clear the lantana and scrub before making his garden. The river ran nearby, so he had plenty of water. And the horses kept the grass down. I expressed amazement that he had accomplished so much in a little over a year.

Francine explained to Peter that we had visited the falls on our way up. "Kijanka," Peter said, using the *bama* (Aboriginal) word for the locality (literally "moon place"). "You have to be careful when you approach the falls," Peter warned. The falls had the power to draw a person over the edge. He also mentioned a rock at the top of the falls that could move to the bottom of the falls of its own accord, and back to the top. But when white miners began blasting with gelignite at China Camp, they killed the stone, which now lies immobile at the foot of the walls, bereft of life. "Same thing happened at Daintree," Peter said. "There was a stone. No matter how many times *bama* rolled it to the bottom of the waterfall, it would find its way back to the top. But you know how pig-headed Europeans can be? Well, some policemen wanted to roll the stone down to the bottom. *Bama* said, 'No, don't touch it, don't go near it'. But they rolled it anyway. After that it stayed there at the bottom, dead."

I thought, *when stone was in the hands of* bama, *it was not stone, it was an enchanted thing, animated by the respect it was given, the songs that perennially brought it back to life. When it was taken from them, it lost its meaning and died, like the alienated land itself, now untended and untravelled. And as one's connection with the ancestral world atrophied, so time stood still as if turned to stone.*

"I can tell you some terrible stories about this place in the early days," Peter said. "Europeans were very bad to Aboriginal people. *Bama* would try to help them, but they were always repaid with unkindness."

Peter's biological father was a part-Aboriginal man called Dick Fischer, the son of a German immigrant, who mined tin for a while at China Camp. Peter never met his father because when his mother became pregnant she was sent away. When Peter was a very small boy, the police came to his mother's camp looking for "half-castes." He hid in the bush, but his friend and age-mate Oglevie was caught and taken to the Mission Station at Yarrabah, south of Cairns, where he died two months later, Peter said, "of homesickness and a broken heart." As for Peter, his mother disappeared when he was seven, leaving him in the care of his maternal grandmother. "My granny was very good to me. She looked after me better than my own mother. When I was starving, she fed me wild yams. She is buried near here. That is why I came here to live and to die. I have had this place in mind all my life. I wanted to be close to her."

Peter made us mugs of tea, and we shared the food we had brought with us, even though Peter's garden contained enough food to feed a small community.

After eating, we strolled along the grassy paths, Peter showing us his yams and taro, string beans, cabbage, tomatoes, cassava, and tropical fruit, while Francine plied him with questions about the changes he had witnessed in his seventy-six years of tin-mining, of working on pearl luggers and in the cane fields of northern Queensland, of living in places like Daintree, Mossman, Wujal Wujal, and Wonga Beach.

Peter wryly observed that if you visited another camp in the old days, as we had visited his today, you would sit and wait beyond the perimeter with eyes downcast, saying nothing, until the hosts approached you with food. But the worst infractions of traditional protocol centered, in Peter's view, on marriage. "These days, everything is mixed up. People marry just anyone, like dogs. Cousins, even in-laws. I can tell you about one man, he married his mother-in-law. When he had a daughter, that means he was supposed to marry her. The old people had it the right way. Just like with cattle. You keep a bull in the pen. You don't let it in with the cows just anytime, anyhow. The breeding would be too close."

Peter also spoke of young people's disrespect toward elders, their shameful indifference to the rules of in-law avoidance, and the various taboos that helped control the exploitation of natural resources. His twenty-something grandson had come and spent a few weeks with him. Peter had tried to teach him the names and uses of various trees—the *wumburru* (bull oak) that was good for making furniture, the *gujiguji* that was good for fence posts, the *galkanji* (spiky bark) that burned easily and cleanly—but the young man was uninterested and did not want to learn.

I asked Peter if he ever felt isolated and alone up there in the middle of nowhere.

"I am never afraid or alone," he said. "I have seen God with my own eyes. He is with me. I pride myself in owning nothing. A storm could blow away this camp. It's nothing. I wouldn't worry. Not like those houses people build. I'm nothing. I was never cut out to be a boss over anyone. I'm just a storyteller."

When it was time for us to return to the coast, Peter said: "I wouldn't want to live at Wujal. All that drinking, smoking dope, that confusion. I worked all my life. I couldn't just sit around like the people at the mission. I don't need money. I never smoked. I never drank. I can buy my flour and tea at Mareeba every three or four months. If my family come and visit, that's all right. But I never feel the need to leave here. Never."

I felt drawn to Peter Fisher for reasons I could not, at first, fully fathom. His life in his rain forest clearing, midway between a tragic past and an uncertain future, came as close as any life I had ever known to absolute acceptance, to the peace that passes all understanding. At once anchorite and sage, he seemed more than reconciled to his lot; he appeared entirely at one with it. Here was a man whose freedom was defined by the confines of his clearing—a clearing I could not help but see, metaphorically, not as an Eden recreated on earth but as a form of enlightenment (Heidegger's *lichtung*). Here was a man who was avowedly "nothing" yet whose story was the story of "everyman."

One might also say that Peter Fisher lived in a penumbral zone between the living and the dead, a place of ghosts. In ongoing conversations with Peter, and in the course of everyday life in our camp, Francine and I were constantly made aware of the ways that Queensland's violent past impinges on the consciousness of Aboriginal people in the here and now, perpetuating fears of further injustices, clouding the possibility of a future. During one of his reminiscences, Peter described what happened after the death of an old man known as Sandy.

When Peter was a small boy, Sandy would carry him everywhere and, at night, allow him to sleep close by for protection. When Sandy died in his sleep one night, the small boy was unaware that his protector had passed away.

"I'll tell you something that'll be hard for you to believe," Peter said, "but I saw it with my own eyes when I was a child. People had come from Wujal, Daintree, Mossman, from everywhere, for Sandy's funeral. We all sat in a line so the spirit in the body could get out. It came out like a firefly. It stopped at the doorway. Then people spoke to him. It then brightened up, so we could see our shadows. They said, 'All right now. You leavin' us now. You gotta go see father. Before you go, you see our people at Banabila [a large Aboriginal camp near the mouth of the Bloomfield River]. There was a big mob there. It was a bright light. He flew down that way. And they said, 'Oh, he came down and visit us now.' I don't know if anyone else still remembers. You might ask."

It was impossible to ignore this numberless and nebulous community of lost souls. They were like the afterimages of loved ones lost, semi-embodied memories. And, like the past, they were ever-present, hovering in the penumbra of consciousness, shadowy and repining.

Dubu, or ghosts, most often appear to the living as strange lights—a trail of fireflies moving in the darkness, a torch that mysteriously switches itself on in the middle of the night, a bright light that for several hours uncannily follows the car in which one is driving home after a funeral in another settlement, a blue light hovering in the sky like a UFO, or lights flitting among the trees. In almost every case, ghosts are spirits of the dead made manifest— unquiet shades that torment and haunt the living who have abandoned them, or spirits that are reluctantly making their way to the land of the dead. But ghosts are not only external phenomena, haunting the living. They are also projections of the inner distress of those who have lost loved ones. Ghosts are, to use Winnicott's term, "transitional phenomena." They make their appearance in the "potential space" between intrapsychic and external worlds, and are important means whereby people undertake the difficult passage from attachment to separation. It is in this "potential space" that people disclose their fears and feelings, review the troubling phenomena they have just witnessed, and reach agreement as to its cause, its possible consequences, and what course of action may best deal with it. In other words, standardized cultural notions about the spirits of the dead and subjective feelings toward an individual who has recently passed away come together to produce a provisional understanding that then serves as the basis for dealing with one's confusion and dismay. Among the Kuku Yalanji, this involves sticking together (since ghosts don't trouble people in company), ensuring that proper mortuary rites are performed (notably, "smoking" the deceased's possessions by passing them over a fire and thereby decontaminating them), and reinforcing an avoidance relationship with the dead by not speaking their name or otherwise remembering them in public. Often, Francine and I would be enjoined not to leave water standing around our tent when we were away, as it might attract some errant ghost.

Kuku Yalanji responses to strange lights and inner grief demonstrate the healing power of shared experience. To be witness to unusual phenomena, or subject to disorienting thoughts and feelings, is to risk feeling different, isolated, and even crazy. But as soon as an experience is brought from the private into the public realm and shared, its character is instantly changed. Assimilated to the collective wisdom of the tribe, and subject to conventional actions, it is literally made common; it is brought within the familiar bounds of what is recognized and within reason. It is like bringing an outsider back within the social pale, or releasing a prisoner from solitary confinement—restorations of the sociality that alone provides security and sanity.

Primo Levi once observed that "If one lives in a compact, seried group, as bees and sheep do in the winter, there are advantages; one can defend oneself better from the cold and from attacks."[7] But in extolling the virtues of living "at the margins of the group, or in fact isolated," he goes on to say that one may thereby enjoy the freedom of leaving when one wants to and getting "a better view of the landscape." Levi would, for this reason, have admired Peter Fisher, though there is in Levi's life story and tragic end evidence of an ambivalent attitude toward the loner who chooses "a winding path, forming for [himself] a haphazard culture; full of gaps, a smattering of knowledge." If Levi's reflections on other people's trades permit no resolution of these opposing life courses, it may be because they can never be fully separated, the one privileged over the other as a permanent ontological possibility.

A few weeks after our visit to Peter Fisher's camp, McGinty confided to me that his sister-in-law's daughter, Kimmy, was frightened to sleep alone in the house when her husband Algin was away. When kinsmen go away, it is as if they have died. And just as the spirit of a dead person will hang around the camp of its living kin, craving their company, yet vengeful because it has been abandoned, so something of an absent kinsman remains behind, a haunting presence, an afterimage, a ghost. I could not help but relate these anecdotes of lost souls to Aboriginal experiences of dispossession and loss. It was not simply the absence of a kinsman or spouse that preyed on one's mind; it was the violent history one had endured, of separation from the land from which one drew sustenance, separation from one's own children, separation from a dominant culture that treated one like shit. But ghosts won't trouble people when they stick together, I was told; they won't bother you as long as you are with others.

These themes of safety in numbers, the importance of solidarity with others, and the dangers of being on one's own and setting oneself apart or standing out were replayed day after day as our relationships with Aboriginal people developed. Driving back from Cooktown, through country to which Mabel and McGinty had no kinship or affinity, we passed a Land Rover in dark camouflage colors, parked on the side of the road. Hearing a beep-beep, I slowed down, thinking someone was in trouble. But our travelling companions knew that this was not a *bama* (Aboriginal) way of signalling for help, and nothing about this vehicle suggested that it belonged to any *bama*. As I reversed to see if help was needed, Mabel and her sister Lizzie crouched down to avoid being seen. When McGinty said we should drive on, and I did so, everyone collapsed in laughter. Relief at a narrow escape? Embarrassment at their overreaction?

I recalled other incidents in which people had recourse to strategies of avoidance and joking in dealing with the unknown and the strange: McGinty not asking in Cooktown if he could fill his plastic bottles with water, but waiting until we had crossed a river well away from town before laboriously clambering down the riverbank to fill the bottles; McGinty explaining that there was only one fast-food shop in Cooktown that *bama* felt comfortable about entering; *bama* sitting impassively outside the Reef Café, eyes averted, lest one accidentally look a stranger in the eye and suffer the consequences; Sonny telling me that "tourists bring sickness"; Louie telling me that Adelaide should not walk alone on the road because a "whitefella" will rape her; Mabel accompanying Adelaide (her daughter) into the scrub when she needed to pee, "to keep her company" and ensure no harm came to her.

We drove to Port Stewart on Princess Charlotte Bay, the area where McGinty spent his first years of life. It was a preliminary meeting of dispersed Lawa Lawa people, to prepare a legal case for reclaiming their traditional lands. For the first time in his life, McGinty spoke into a microphone, addressing the crowd. "I had a little bit of a hard time too, on cattle stations [another old ringer had just spoken of how Aboriginal boys were beaten and abused by white bosses]. When I was young, you couldn't leave the job on the station. Couldn't go back home. Anyway, no one was there. All the Lawa Lawa got rounded up, deported to Bamago Mission."

McGinty was suddenly at a loss for words. He handed the microphone to a white lawyer.

That evening, McGinty told me that he went back to Lilyfield Station last year. The station owner gave him permission to visit his old camp. "There's nothing there," McGinty said. "Only wild pigs. That made me real sad, you know. I left my country a long time ago."

I thought of asking McGinty if getting land back was a case of too little, too late, but I knew that this process must be worked through, and that it might take several generations for something to come of it.

That night we woke to a hoarse keening in a nearby camp—ascending and descending scales, an alien melodic line, a sound as if from deeply disturbed sleep or possession. McGinty's brother, Alan, thought that someone had died. He followed the keening to its source and reported back to McGinty. One of the old Lawa Lawa men's daughters had just arrived from Bamago. He had not seen her in a long time. The keening was a *bama* way of showing one's feelings, McGinty said. "Fair dinkum. The tears are real. But not many people do it any more. People use grog now to let their feelings out."

Drinking may enable a person to vent his or her feelings, even to gain a sense of substantiality and invincibility in a world that seems to conspire in making him or her feel worthless and small. But the aftermath of binge drinking is something else, particularly if one wakes up alone in a police cell with the dry horrors.

"After heavy drinking, you know, you get paralytic drunk and get the shakes, you can hear voices, voices saying 'I'll kill you.'[8] I've been through that, hearing voices and things. It makes you feel you want to commit suicide. Makes you think people coming to get you, makes you think that before they get you you'll kill yourself. . . . When you're locked up and going through that thing, you need people around, you should have the lights on. In the light you're safe, but in the darkness you think that person [is] going to come and kill you."[9]

AFTER FIELDWORK

Back in Sydney, after a year in the company of *bama*, it took time to readjust. I experienced the strangeness of having been away and having returned, changed, of being in possession of experiences that no one was particularly interested in or could understand. This was painfully familiar to our friend Peter Herbst.

Peter was born in Heidelberg, Germany, in 1919. Shortly after Hitler came to power in 1933, Nazi storm troopers broke into the Herbst home and threatened Peter's father with internment in a concentration camp. Seeing no future for his intellectually gifted son in an anti-Semitic National Socialist Germany, Herbst sent his son to England to complete his education at Haileybury College. After graduating, Peter lived cheaply in London for a while, but after Dunkirk and the fall of France, it was widely rumored that German citizens living in England were enemy agents, planted to assist the planned invasion of Britain. Peter was arrested and sent to an internment camp in Liverpool. On July 10, 1940, he left England with 2,036 other Jewish refugees from Austria and Germany, on HMT Dunera.[10] The voyage to Australia would become notorious for the overcrowded conditions on the ship (whose capacity was only 1,500 people, including crew, not 2,542) and the inhumane treatment the internees suffered at the hands of the British guards on board. Many were physically assaulted; others had their few possessions stolen; all endured the indignity of verbal abuse and nonkosher food. At first the refugees fared little better in Australia. While some Australian religious and political leaders had expressed outrage, as early as 1933, over the persecution of Jews in Germany, most Australians either turned a blind eye to events in Europe or argued that too many educated migrants would take jobs from Australians. At the Évian Conference, convened by Franklin D. Roosevelt in July 1938 to discuss the issue of increasing numbers of Jewish refugees fleeing Nazi persecution, the Australian minister for trade and customs argued that Australia was "predominantly British" and should remain so. It was agreed that 15,000 Jewish refugees would be accepted over a period of three years.

Peter was interned at Hays in New South Wales and enrolled in the unofficial university that the well-educated refugees quickly established at the camp. As the fortunes of war changed and local attitudes toward the internees softened, many of the refugees were allowed to leave the Hays camp in

1941. Some returned to Britain; others, including Peter, volunteered for service with one of the employment companies of the Australian Military Forces.[11] In 1942 Peter met the family of the painter Arthur Boyd and resumed his study of philosophy at the University of Melbourne.

Reflecting forty years later on this period of his life, Peter remembered how drawn he was to this Australian family. Perhaps it reminded him of the family he had lost. "I was delighted to find an environment in which contact with literature and creative art was perceived as a joy in itself, without the dingy carrot of academic advancement or the puritan remorselessness of high-minded self betterment."[12] But even as he admires this close-knit group, he betrays reservations about its self-sufficiency, its contentedness with domestic life, its seeming lack of any "need for outside involvement."[13]

I have often pondered Peter's ambivalence and wondered if the experience of losing his own family and fatherland found expression in a disenchanted view of both parenthood and patriotism, not to mention philosophers who lose the common touch.[14] I find the following passage painful to read because of its thinly disguised autobiographic allusions, its poignant evidence that a child who has suffered abandonment will find it difficult, as an adult, to become a loving parent and an intellectual raised in the European tradition will find it hard to be accepted, let alone respected, in his country of adoption.

> I admire the Boyds, but I do not regard myself as committed to the nuclear family as an ideal social unit. I lack religious and political reasons for doing so. On the contrary, I think that in our acquisitive society the family is often an instrument of torture. It subverts authenticity and encourages evasiveness and moral cowardice. All too frequently the family is a haven for mindless mediocrity. As for nationalism, we have had as much of it as we can bear. . . . [It] takes the form of pommybashing, xenophobia, obsessional preoccupation with an allegedly distinctive popular national culture. The ancient cultures of other countries, aesthetic, philosophical, and literary, are relegated. The attitude of those who favour the exclusion of un-Australian or "irrelevant" cultural strands is often offensive and aggressive. "Multiculturalism" is basically a political idea. The level at which the survival of foreign cultures is encouraged is superficial. Migrants are induced to play-act at being themselves.[15]

There is so much in Peter's veiled autobiography that speaks to the plight of marginalized people, dispossessed on one continent and obliged to begin again on another, that when his book on the Boyds appeared in 1990 I began, despite myself, to see him differently. Indeed, Peter's references to Arthur

Boyd's "habit of setting biblical subjects in the Australian bush,"[16] his "attempts to locate European archetypes in the Australia landscape,"[17] and the "expressionist, angst-ridden inclination of Arthur's imagination from the war years onward"[18] seem to echo Peter's own struggles to reconcile the world he had lost with the world into which he had been cast. And in Peter's account of Arthur Boyd's life, "divided between two hemispheres,"[19] I discern the Faustian pact that weighs on every exile's mind—whether, in one's desire to exchange hell for paradise, one ends up with the poorer side of the bargain.

We stayed with Peter and his wife Valerie at Bell's Creek, an old gold mining town near Araluen. Since finishing *The Art of the Boyds*, Peter had been working on a book about the Faust legend and devoting his spare energy to conserving the environment. But my own research on home was never far from my mind, and over lunch I asked Valerie where home was, for her.

"Here."

"Bell's Creek, you mean?"

"Mmhm."

Francine asked Peter where he called home.

"Nowhere, really."

Val looked shocked.

"Well, perhaps, geographically speaking, this is my home," Peter said.

"I guess home is somewhere you're recognized," Francine said.

Valerie agreed. "My mother used to say, when she lived with us, I feel like a cabbage. She had no identity anymore. No one really knew her. No one recognized her."

"Ubi bene, ibi patria," Peter said, quoting the Latin proverb. "Your home is where they treat you well."

After lunch, Peter walked us over the farm. He carried a machete, an adze, and a trowel for grubbing thistles. His asthmatic fox terrier raced ahead of us through the wet grass. Peter turned over cowpats, looking for dung beetles to show Joshua. He bemoaned the blackberry that was getting away from him. And he told us about the gold rush in the late nineteenth century and the Chinese who flocked to the diggings. There were still rusting pipes in the long grass and a collapsed water race. But almost all traces of the miner's camp had disappeared.

"What became of the Chinese?" I asked.

Peter recounted the story of one young man called Quong Tart (Méi Guangdá) who immigrated to Australia with his uncle in 1859. Only nine at the time, Guangdá found his way to the goldfields around Araluen, where he lived for a while in the store of a Scottish immigrant called Thomas Forsyth. Guangdá was then informally adopted by the wealthy family of Robert Percy Simpson, whose wife Alice was charmed by the boy's Scots accent. Under the tutelage of the Simpsons, Guangdá converted to Christianity and prospered by investing in gold claims. At twenty-one, he built a cottage at Bell's Creek and became a naturalized British subject. After a trip to China, he went into the tea and silk trade in Sydney, and married a young English schoolteacher in 1886. Though Chinese, he dressed and behaved like a Victorian gentleman, played the bagpipes, and had his five children baptized in different denominations to avoid charges of prejudice. "In his dotage," Peter said, "Quong Tart became quite autocratic. Everyone at Gallop House, family as well as servants, had to race around, doing his bidding. Then the old man was murdered for his money." He was assaulted with an iron bar in his office in the Queen Victoria Building in downtown Sydney, and never recovered. He died, almost a year after the bashing, at age fifty-three. Gallop House became a heritage building, and after the passing of many years was expanded as a home for elderly Chinese.

"A few years ago," Peter continued, "Quong Tart's elderly granddaughter turned up at Bell's Creek, wanting to see the site of her grandfather's cottage, and be guided around the Chinese diggings. She had some old maps. I don't know who made the maps, but they were all ridiculously inconsistent. Some reminded me of childlike treasure maps, and the cardinal points were all in the wrong place. Val and I wondered if she was looking for buried gold. She stayed with us for a year. She drove a majestic Mercedes Benz. She'd drive into Braidwood for supplies, cultivate friendships in Araluen, and spend days wandering around the farm. A year after she first turned up, she erected a tent on the hill where she thought her grandfather's cottage must have stood. She worked out a way of weatherproofing it. But the big Mercedes sat out in the paddock, neglected and exposed to the elements. One day she turned up at the house with some tattered legal documents and explained they were the deeds to Bell's Creek, including our land. I had to trick her into moving away. She pitched her tent across the road. Then she got bitten by an insect, the bite became infected, and she died. Lonely and dispossessed, looking for the past, her imagination [was] fed by her need of the place that was once home."

In central Australia, Warlpiri do not speak of life and death as poles apart. Rather, they speak of an oscillation between absence and presence.

"Palka" means embodied in present time (*jalanguju palkalku*). "Lawa" means just the opposite. These words capture the perpetual comings and goings in Warlpiri life. Anything that has "body" is palka—a rock hole or river with water in it, the trunk of a tree, a person whose belly is full, a country where game is plentiful, the desert blooming after rain, anyone who is in your presence. But if a rock hole is dry, a stomach empty, tracks erased, the desert devoid of game, or a person faints, falls asleep, or goes away, then there is lawa, nothing. Palka is that which is existent and life-giving. By contrast, lawa connotes the loss of the persons and things that sustain one's life. But just as the cycle of nomadic life necessitates the periodic dispersal *and* reunion of kin, so ceremony can bring the ancestral order back into being, fleshing it out in the painting, song, and mimetic dance of the living. Giving birth to a child, naming him or her after a kinsman or kinswoman who has passed away, having a dream in which ancestral motifs are revealed, visiting a sacred site, or singing and dancing the Dreaming into life are all modes of "bringing into being" (*palka jarrimi*) that which was temporarily absent, latent, or hidden. They are ways of "drawing out" the Dreaming from pastness and potentiality and realizing it as an actively embodied presence. All these modes of transformative activity are "signs," "prints," "marks," or "traces" (*yirdi*) of the circumambient Dreaming as well as ways of reanimating it.

I like to think of writing as a way of bringing something that has passed away back to life.

CHAPTER 7

The Gulf of Corinth

... in bed lying quiet under kisses
Without signature, with all my debts unpaid
I shall recall nights of squinting rain,
Like pig-iron on the hills: bruised
Landscapes of drumming cloud and everywhere
The lack of someone spreading like a stain ...

—Lawrence Durrell

A recurring critique of the ethos of modernism is that it fosters alienation from and indifference to the world and a regressive absorption into one's own personal situation. Faced with a macrocosm that is too overwhelming to contemplate and too complex to control, people take refuge in a narcissistic concern for their own survival and the emotional imperatives of the self.[1] "To live for the moment is the prevailing passion—to live for yourself, not for your predecessors or posterity."[2] While it may be argued that being self-fulfilled is the best guarantee of being able to give support to others, one tends to encounter *either* the "modern" view that one's "main task in life is to give birth to [oneself], to become what [one] potentially is"[3] (the corollary being that submergence in the social is a flight from the self), *or* the antithetical "traditional' view that self-sacrifice is our highest calling—the sublimation of personal desires and interests in order to serve God, raise a happy family, or save humankind.

While I do not share Erich Fromm's view that we seek relatedness and union with others because we cannot stand "being alone and separated," I think he is right in claiming that our own potential unfolds only "*in the process of being related.*"[4] Fromm speaks of this process as a "productive" relationship to the world, and of love as its moral essence. But selfless love is as unproductive as selfish love. "Not only others, but we ourselves are the 'object' of our feelings and attitudes; the attitudes toward others and toward ourselves, far from being contradictory, are basically *conjunctive.*"[5]

Such heady deliberations were far from my thoughts when I travelled to Greece in the early summer of 2009, but in the weeks that followed they came to speak to the mystery of a long-distance friendship as well as my relationship with my fourteen-year-old daughter Freya. For just as no one exists outside of his or her relations with others, so no time in our lives is separable from other times. "The past is never dead. It's not even past."[6]

The south of France, May 1983: It was dusk. I stood for a moment on the stone step while my eyes grew used to the darkness that had already laid claim to the garden. Gnarled wisteria held the portico in its grip. Cypresses along the driveway impaled the sky. I had broken off my conversation with a young woman who was studying anthropology at Cambridge and explained to William Waterfield, our host, that my wife was unwell and that I needed to get back to her. After locating my daughter Heidi,[7] who had become attached to William's fox terrier, we set off down the drive. But the anthropology student ran after us. Scribbling her Cambridge address on a scrap of paper, she invited me to write to her and perhaps finish our conversation that way. So began a long-distance friendship that we have sustained to this day. In all this time we met only once, in New York City in 1990. After strolling around Greenwich Village for a couple of hours, we had lunch, then went our separate ways without having overcome the disparity between the intimacy of our letters and the awkwardness we felt in each other's company. That our correspondence continued was, I suspect, not because of any compulsion to "really" get acquainted but because we both felt the need for a trusted stranger with whom confidences could be shared and anxieties confessed without the risk of real-life repercussions. And so we found in letter writing a place to which we could repair, an imaginary companion in whom we could confide, and a mirror in which we could see ourselves more clearly.

In the early summer of 2009, all this changed. Having promised my youngest daughter a trip to a country of her choosing when she graduated from middle school, I found myself on my way to Greece, where Sofka had been living for eight years. When I told Sofka of my plans to take Freya on a tour of the Peloponnese, she insisted we stay a couple of days with her and her family in Athens. It would give us a chance to get to know each other, a litmus test that might finally determine whether our long correspondence was born of a real or an illusory affinity. As I later discovered, Sofka felt as much trepidation about our meeting as I did, for if we found ourselves indifferent to each other, or in deep disagreement, then this would surely spell the end of our letter writing, and we would part, disenchanted and deeply embarrassed to have spent so many years in an epistolary folie à deux, assuming an empathy that had no basis in reality.

At Athens airport, my mind was immediately set at ease by the warmth of Sofka's welcome, her attentiveness to Freya, and her lighthearted attitude toward the strange experiment to which we had decided to subject our friendship.

At first we kept to the safety of small talk. How was our flight? Did we get any sleep? How long had we had to wait in Madrid for our connecting flight to Athens? Freya wanted to know about Sofka's daughters, Anna and Lara, how old they were and whether they lived near the sea. As for me, I found it hard to believe that a mere ten hours had passed since leaving Boston. The offshore islands were swallowed up by mist and cloud as we ascended. We slept through the night and awoke to the new day breaking over the sun-baked, biscuit-colored landscape of central Spain, smudged with slate-gray pools of cloud shadow. But what was most astonishing was the sense that I had passed, like Alice, through a looking glass and entered a world where what had been imagined was suddenly there, before my eyes, and that what had been so vivid yesterday now seemed vague and remote.

Sofka served a late lunch on the terrace. The artistry that came through in her writing, paintings, and driftwood mobiles was evident in the dishes she placed on the table—an oval plate of feta, sprinkled with oregano and interspersed with glistening black Kalamata olives, ceramic bowls of fried aubergine and courgette, juicy tomatoes stuffed with savory rice and pine nuts, snap peas drenched in olive oil, slices of country bread, and tumblers of clear water. How strange to be sitting under the pergola she had described in her letters, in the midst of the rosemary, sage, and thyme she had planted among the rocks and the olive, fig, loquat, and orange trees, with jasmine climbing a dry stone wall. Listening to Sofka's husband Vassilis talk about the recent EU elections or Sofka negotiating with her daughters over household chores, music practice, and how long they could stay out that evening, the uncanny similarity between this household and mine began to sink in, and I felt at home.

That evening, with the sun setting over the Saronic Gulf, Sofka and I finally found time to talk. She asked me what I was writing. It was, perhaps, too early to say. But I already sensed that my visit to Greece would form part of the mosaic, and speak to the theme, I had in mind. I explained this theme as the struggle to strike a balance between one's relationships with others and one's relationship with oneself, of how one may become so absorbed in the lives of others that one's own identity is eclipsed, or so preoccupied by one's own work that one grows negligent of others. "Perhaps you sometimes felt this about our correspondence," I said. "I know I did—wondering whether, without any face-to-face contact, we risked lapsing into solipsism, each of us construing the other solely from our own perspective."

"But the amazing thing," Sofka said, "is that we *are* face-to-face, and I have absolutely no sense that you are anyone other than the person I have been writing to for all these years."

I confessed to Sofka that I had always felt anxious about meeting her because of our class difference. Her paternal forebears were Russian aristocrats; mine were English working-class emigrants. Sofka was both irked and amused. "Isn't this an example of what you were just saying? Making me a figment of your imagination, rather than seeing me as I am? Whether or not I was born into a family with relative material wealth, I find that element so much less relevant to my identity than dozens of other factors that affected my childhood. The fact that both my parents battled with depression and alcoholism, for example. In any case, I refuse to think that who we are is decided by our family backgrounds or income. I hate it when people assume that the rich are somehow less human than the poor, and the poor possess moral virtue simply because they are materially impoverished. Why can't we see one another as individuals, as human beings, and not reduce people to abstractions like class, culture, or nationality? These labels only ever seem to apply to the other, and never to oneself! If only people actually met, they would see the artificiality of their constructions. But they don't meet, or won't, and so the constructions are never tested, and become more and more out of touch with reality."

I had to admit that the problem was mine. As a child I had felt gauche and inferior. I had a dread of appearing foolish, of not measuring up, of being rejected. In writing, I felt in control of my situation. Though I might not be accepted as a person, perhaps my literary creations would be. I could hide behind them. They would circulate in the world, but I would not. I could remain apart, safe and unscathed.

Sofka found this hard to believe.

"But what of your fieldwork, your travels. You're always venturing out into the world. No one could be less reclusive than you."

"I have pushed myself hard. I still do. But, at heart, there is always this small boy, shaking in his shoes, not sure whether or for how long he's going to be able to sustain the conversation, continue the lecture, or go on returning to the field."

"But everyone's like this, deep down. Everyone gets cold feet. Stage fright. Writer's block. Just look at me!" Sofka asked if I had read Patrick Leigh Fermor. I knew the name but had not read his books.

He was an old friend of Sofka's family. When Sofka's first book was launched in Athens, Leigh Fermor attended, fortified with whiskey and fulminating against the dying of the light.

In 1933, at the age of eighteen and with only a few pounds in his pocket, he had walked from the Hook of Holland to Istanbul. Having completed this remarkable journey, he settled in Greece, became fluent in the language, and mastered several of its dialects. But before his fame as a travel writer, he was known for his exploits on Crete as a Special Operations Executive officer during the war. Disguised as a shepherd, he lived for two years with a band of Cretan guerillas, holed up in the mountains and leading raids against the occupying Germans. He was awarded the Distinguished Service Order for his role in capturing the commander of German forces on Crete, General Heinrich Kreipe, in 1944.

Leigh Fermor's longtime friend and correspondent, Lady Deborah Devonshire (née Mitford), recalls the event with admiration and affection:

Their prize was bundled into the back of the German official car: Moss[8] drove them through a town in the blackout, Paddy sitting on the front seat wearing the general's cap, in case anyone should glance at the occupants. After a four-hour climb on foot to the comparative safety of a cave in the mountains, they spent eighteen days together, moving from one hiding place to another and sharing the only blanket during the freezing nights. When the sun rose on the first morning and lit up the snow on the summit of Mount Ida, the general gazed at the scene and quoted a verse of an ode by Horace. His captor completed the next six stanzas.[9]

When Leigh Fermor had finished, there was a long silence. Then the general said, "Ach so, Herr Major!" "It was very strange," Leigh Fermor would write years later, "as though, for a long moment, the war had ceased to exist. We had both drunk at the same fountains long before; and things were different between us for [the] rest of our time together."[10]

Yet this man of the world—this bon vivant and formidable raconteur, fluent in so many languages, fearless and gregarious—was also a man who would periodically retreat to his study "for unusually long and uninterrupted spells"[11] and chose to build his house on the isolated southern coast of the Peloponnese. Sofka spoke of his "time of silence," when Leigh Fermor retreated from the world—to the Abbey of Saint Wandrille, to the monasteries at Solesmes, La Grande Trappe, and Cappadocia. "In the seclusion of a cell—an existence whose quietness is only varied by the silent meals, the solemnity of ritual and long solitary walks in the woods—the troubled waters of the mind grow still and clear, and much that is hidden away and all that clouds it floats to the surface and can be skimmed away; and after a time one reaches a state of peace that is unthought of in the ordinary world."[12]

I told Sofka that Leigh Fermor reminded me strongly of Blaise Cendrars, another man who lived life to the limit yet valued solitude.

"How hard it is, though," Sofka said, "to find the right balance between time to oneself and time for others.

Within days of our departure, she and Vassilis would retreat to Patmos for a few weeks. But already Sofka's list of things to do was growing at an alarming rate—collecting school reports, attending to the terrace plants, fixing the automatic watering system, seeing the girls off to England, and buying dog food. "Thankfully, Patmos always restores some equilibrium," she said. And she described an austerely beautiful landscape of bare, rocky hills and of small stony beaches, buffeted by summer winds. Simple routines. Life pared down to the essentials. Lying in the shade with a book, and occasionally plucking a plump fig from the trees. Evenings with friends in a beach taverna. And lying at night under the stars, until you felt you were floating free, suspended in space over a dark bowl.[13]

The next morning Sofka took us to see the Parthenon. I told her that when I lived briefly in Athens, in 1965, I formed a romantic attachment to one of the caryatids on the Erechtheion. Sofka wanted me to show her which one. Though it was only a copy of the original figure (which had been moved to the Acropolis Museum), she was still as beautiful to me as when I first set eyes on her. Her arms and feet had been amputated, perhaps when a Turkish shell almost destroyed the building in 1827. Her face was ruined. But the erosion that had scarred her nose and upper lip had imparted to her a beauty more compelling than if she had remained perfectly unblemished—her supple shoulders, her relaxed stance, the left knee slightly bent, breasts and belly sensuous beneath the folds of an Ionian tunic. Years later I discovered that my experience at the Erechtheion had a literary precedent in Virginia Woolf's *Jacob's Room*:

> Jacob strolled over to the Erechtheum and looked rather furtively at the goddess on the left-hand side holding the roof on her head. She reminded him of Sandra Wentworth Williams. He looked at her, then looked away. He was extraordinarily moved, and with the battered Greek nose in his head . . . off he started to walk right up to the top of Mount Hymettus, alone, in the heat.[14]

I told Sofka that I had often wondered whether Virginia Woolf was writing about an event that actually occurred, which in turn had made me wonder whether it is art that imitates life or life that aspires to the example of art. I suppose I was telling her, obliquely and ineptly, that our letters had, like history, fostered idealizations, and that meeting each other had brought us down to earth, enabling us to recognize each other's flaws and foibles. Just as *our* humanity had been restored, so the marmoreal perfection of the caryatid had taken on the time-worn features of a human face.

The next day Freya and I left for Delphi. But rather than have us rent a car, Vassilis generously insisted we take his car. He wouldn't need it that week, and it would make getting around much easier for us. So with Google directions and lots of last-minute advice from Sofka and Vassilis, Freya and I found our way onto the highway north, before turning west across the Boeotian plain.

After Livadia the road became more tortuous and I began to wonder whether it would be possible to identify the crossroads where Oedipus, having consulted the oracle at Delphi and learned his terrible fate, found his way blocked by a chariot and in a fit of temper slew the old man who had crossed his path. But I missed the turnoff to Daulia and found instead the road to Distomo.

In the stony landscape of Judas trees and summer calm, it was hard to come to terms with what had happened here in 1944 after a company of Waffen SS was ambushed by partisans. Although the ambush took place several miles from Distomo, the retreating Germans passed some farmers working in their fields. After identifying their village, the German commander ordered his troops into Distomo. Over sixty years later, a survivor recounted to Neni Panourgiá what then came to pass.

> They gathered us all in the square across from your father's house. First, through an interpreter, the German asked our names. I don't know how they sorted us, because it wasn't alphabetical, it wasn't by age, it wasn't by height—all of us were there, every boy and man of the district. I was fifteen at the time, but my father was there, too, your uncle Tassos, Spyros, Odysseas, Nikos (both of them, actually), everybody. And then the hooded-one [the baker's apprentice] came and started pointing, without saying anything, not a word.[15]

Writing of the German reprisals, in which almost all the inhabitants of Distomo were murdered, Neni Panourgiá finds uncanny echoes of the tragedy of Oedipus—another accidental meeting that had fateful consequences, another placid backdrop to barbarism, another occasion for asking how, in the face of such violent events, we may salvage our humanity.[16]

Though Freya and I were travelling to Delphi, we had planned to stay that night at Galaxidi on the Gulf of Corinth. Galaxidi was Neni's hometown, and since I had not seen her since 1995, when we both worked at Indiana University Bloomington, I was eager to discuss her recently published book on the Greek Left and the terror of the state. But just before leaving Athens, Neni had e-mailed to say that she and her son had arrived from New York feeling unwell and had been diagnosed with swine flu. They were quarantined in their summer house and unable to travel. Given that Neni's book documented the terrible practices of incarceration, isolation, and ostracism that had marked the "fratricidal history"[17] of the twentieth century in Greece, I thought it ironic that my friend should be forcibly sequestered, and I pondered the strange parallelism between the concentration camps on the barren and wind-racked islands of Makrónisos and Yarós and the monastic forms of retreat that Sofka had spoken of in Athens.

What one finds most unbearable in life is not exclusion and deprivation as such but being denied any choice in the matter of when and to what extent one keeps to oneself or reduces one's life to the bare necessities. To be called a traitor, a cancer in the body politic, a contaminant, or a vermin is to be transformed into a pathology and one's difference turned into a disease. Accordingly, the violent exclusion of the Left under right-wing governments and military juntas in Greece echoes the extermination of Jews and Gypsies in Nazi camps, the purging of undesirable elements in Stalin's Gulag archipelagos, and the ostracism of Reds and blacks in postwar America. The all-encompassing notion of the human becomes a segmentary model, divided into those who are with us and those who are against us. And since this apartheid, in its most reductive form, deploys the antinomy of persons versus things, it must work tirelessly to police these boundaries and ensure that everything and everyone knows its place. A perverse logic then generates the punishments that best fit the crime of transgression. On Makrónisos and Yarós, as in Dachau, men are made to break and carry stone until they became as insensible as the stone they lug up and down hill from daybreak to dark.

> The order was always very clear: take those rocks from up there and bring them down here. When the transport was done, the order was reversed: take the stones from down here and move them up there. This would take place all day long, in the heat of summer or the cold of winter, always under a relentless wind, without water, without rest, without shoes, in tattered clothes, on tattered bodies.[18]

Neni shows how classical myths speak to more recent history. The age-old struggle of city-states to defend themselves against enemies within is echoed in current resistance to foreigners infiltrating the country in search of asylum and work. Similarly, in the myth of Oedipus, we discern contemporary anxieties about whom we may trust and whom we cannot, who is one of us and who is not.[19] Neni's reflections spoke directly to the theme of my own book and made me even more sorry that we would not be able to meet in Galaxidi. For her work had given my own a sharper focus, raising anew the question as to whether we can ever know ourselves through reflection, or whether our only knowledge of ourselves is mediated by the responses of others to us, in which case all autobiography is disguised autre-biography.[20]

Nor was Sisyphus very far from my mind. For who can look at those perched villages, stone walls, and terraces along the Mediterranean littoral without wondering about the lives lost in building them? Even Delphi, for all its bucolic calm, is haunted by such questions—the temples built by the labor of slaves, the heights from which Aesop was thrown to his death.[21]

We came to Delphi just as the afternoon heat was wearing off. And no less than the first time I came there, the ancient site overwhelmed me. Below me, in the gorge of the Pleistos, a vast olive grove flowed like a river toward the Amphissa plain. Looking up at the craggy, eroded rock face of the Phaedriades and at the handfuls of fleecy cloud that were drifting slowly over the summit, I grew dizzy and had to look down. Thrown by the emotions of returning to a place that meant so much to me, I wanted only to sit still. But Freya had found a stray cat and wanted to find food for it. And so we loitered in the shade of some cypresses while I assured Freya that the cat had chosen Delphi because it was a source of scraps and shelter, and I waited until she was ready to move on.

We climbed to the stadium where a cool breeze stirred in the pines. Freya's sandals scuffed the gravelly ground. My heartbeat slowed. I could hear the murmur of traffic on the mountain road, the lisp of a bird, the stitch of cicadas—and then, silence.

I told Freya that I had come there many years ago with Pauline (my first wife) and Heidi (my firstborn daughter), and that it meant a lot to me to have returned with her. Freya said she would also come back, but not until she had seen lots of others places in the world. But when she did return, it would be with her own daughter, perhaps, and she would tell her daughter how she once came to Delphi with me.

Such is one's afterlife, I thought. We think of it as something for ourselves—some form of personal immortality. But why should we assume that the question of the hereafter must always be answered with reference to ourselves? For what really matters is what we give to others, what they feel about us, and how their lives are made more fulfilling, perhaps, because of us. Only in them do we live on.[22]

At the museum, I stood before the stone omphalos with its bas-relief of navelwort like a knotted enclosing net. This was the stone that Rhea wrapped in swaddling clothes so that her brother Cronus would eat the stone instead of their son Zeus, whose siblings had all been eaten alive by their father. Zeus later set up at Delphi the stone that Cronus had swallowed and disgorged, where it was anointed with oil and strands of unwoven wool offered upon it.[23] But if Delphi is associated with the birth of time—the intercourse of men and women, the cycle of the seasons, the succession of human generations, and the passage of history—then it is also a place of nostalgic longing for the body of a land or a loved one from which we have been separated by aging, exile, or death. In returning to Delphi, was I unconsciously echoing an age-old pilgrimage through the labyrinth of this world to a place where one might overcome one's sense of solitude and the oppression of chronometric time?[24]

From Delphi, we drove to Galaxidi, where we found a guesthouse a mile from town, overlooking the Gulf of Corinth. That evening, in a small backstreet taverna, we shared a simple meal of Greek salad, country bread, tzatziki, and marinated octopus that Freya naturally wanted me to share with the street cats, all of whom resembled the stray at Delphi. Back at Zoe's Guest House, our hostess spoke of her tearful departure from Galaxidi when she was eight, and of years in Minnesota repining for Greece. From the day she returned home, she has never wanted to be anywhere else, she said. And as if her early childhood and the historical heyday of Galaxidi were intimately connected, she described the transformation of the port into a tourist town. When steamships took over the seas, Galaxidi fell into decline. But now the oaks, which were felled for the building and for the repair of ships, are regenerating everywhere, Zoe said, with evident satisfaction. And as she pointed them out to me on the surrounding hills, it was clear that she was telling me something of her own life story.

We remained at Zoe's for two days, and in that time I was constantly reminded of my own homeland—the sea-battered shingle beaches near Wellington, the Seaward Kaikouras on the southern horizon, the dark, wind-adzed ocean glimpsed through pines, the dun-colored hills of Makara, Banks Peninsular, the Cardrona Valley—and I wondered whether the Greeks who wound up in Wellington ever recognized these same affinities and felt less homesick because of them.

All day observing the altering light,
the different depths of blue, the sea's
dependency on sky for how it seems,
and remembering you as an island
I confused with "thought," where
the stiff wind turns the olive leaves,
silvering the drab green river of the grove.

There's a village across the gulf from me,
high on the mountainside, as if
rough dice have been roughly thrown.
The church is a doubtful sanctuary.
At night it is a dying fire, or visits us
in ashen dreams—the places
we were born but cast out from.

like stones down a hill that proved
to be stonier. So in old age find

ourselves like Sisyphus lugging them back
to the uphill shuttered houses
we started from, iron kettles, wooden
stirring spoons, sieves and scales
hanging where our mothers left off work
to worry themselves to death

over what would become of us,
while our fathers played backgammon
and sipped the dregs of coffee in a local bar,
inhaling the smell of fig and jasmine for the final time,
or felt the breeze across the gulf, dry
with sage and pine and wild anemone,
those same hills that now revive

the thought of forests,
though no white barquentines enter
Galaxidi now, nor mules haul
the hard green harvest to the olive press.
Only I seem blessed, a stranger
who does not need to work, watching
cloud shadow move on the arid hill,
or watering a red geranium in a jar
on a whitewashed windowsill.[25]

On the ferry from Agios Nicholaos to Aegio, Freya plugged into her iPod
while I scribbled notes. There was only a handful of passengers. As the boat
juddered and rattled its way across the gulf, I wrote of the sea lacerated by a
dry, blustering wind from the west and of headlands studded with hardy
plants, reaching for metaphors for my own liminal life.

To travel is to come as close to utopia as is humanly possible, for you never
really arrive at the place you set out for, but pass through indeterminate zones
of which you have no real knowledge and in which you have no real place.
Leaving Boston, my American life had been instantly eclipsed. Within hours
it seemed like a previous incarnation. Greece claimed me utterly, but like my
friendship with Sofka it was a transitory possession that, I feared, would become a blur as swiftly as the headland behind us had dropped into the sea.
Sofka had spoken of her own uncertainties in the first few years after she
made Athens her home: feeling "out of kilter, floundering between the different versions of 'my' Greece, and looking suspiciously (and humiliatingly) like
the foreign wives I used to pity with condescension in my student days." And

then, movingly, she describes the moment when the balance shifted and she felt a sea change. It was her birthday. Her daughters surprised her by singing "Happy Birthday" in Greek. "It marked a change of gear," she said. "The children were sweeping me along with them as they became Greek. I realized that this would change me too."[26]

I admired Sofka's ability to allow this metamorphosis to happen, her openness to being swept away from herself into the dark-blue Aegean of a new life. And I thought of her on a day when the wind had whipped up the sea off the cove where she swam every day. Torn by which way to go, frustrated and furious, the broken swell swept into the cove in a foment of foam. But Sofka walked into the maelstrom with Freya, undaunted, beside her, and both struck out strongly into the turbulent waters, leaving me fainthearted on the beach.

When I later broached with Sofka the question of risk, she reminded me that she would never take risks with the children. This was why she chose to swim in "her" small bay rather than along the coast. "But haven't we taken a risk, gambling on having something to say to each other after years of letter writing? Anyway, what would life be if we took no chances? My father took lots of risks, with himself and his family—taking us out in boats in treacherous Hebridean weather, letting us hitchhike, leaving us to fend for ourselves, dragging us up mountains until we wept. Yet I wouldn't be without those experiences. And I took a huge risk when I went to live with Vassilis in Moscow after what could have been just a summer romance. The potential for humiliation was enormous—arriving with my suitcases to start a new life in a new country with a man I'd only known for four weeks."

Though I agreed with Sofka about nothing ventured, nothing gained, I was ill-prepared for the risks one runs on the highways of Greece, with cars crossing the double line and coming toward you at 90 mph, or honking impatiently until you pull over and let them pass. It was on such a road, lined with oleanders, that Vassilis's father had been killed by a driver veering onto the wrong side of the road. And every few miles I passed roadside shrines containing icons, oil lamps, incense, and plastic flowers—intimations of a view of freedom in which one refuses to buckle up or treats central government with scorn, as if the gods alone determine our fate.

When I saw signs for Nemea, I left the highway, hoping to find the valley of which Lawrence Durrell had written so lyrically, and perhaps a quiet place to stay. But we ended the day in a windowless hotel in Nafplion, where I tried to lift Freya's spirits by telling her of the Argonauts who sailed from there, and I promised her that we would find a "really nice hotel" in Epidauros.

When Henry Miller came to Epidauros in the late spring of 1940, Europe was at war. Yet Miller experienced here a peace that passed all understanding, "the peace of the heart, which comes with surrender."[27] As Miller was recounting his epiphany in the Peloponnese, George Orwell was writing his critique of Miller's passivism, asking how anyone in his right mind could celebrate quietism in the face of fascism. And he likened Miller to Jonah, whose refuge in the belly of a whale was a kind of infantile or narcissistic regression.[28] Yet despite his activism, Orwell begrudged Miller his equanimity in the face of the dark age that was threatening to engulf Europe, his refusal to participate in the madness around him. "To be free," writes Miller, "as I knew myself to be, is to realize that all conquest is in vain, even the conquest of self, which is the last act of egoism."[29]

As I climbed the worn stone steps of the theatre with my daughter, spots of rain fell from the clear-blue sky, like tears for someone I loved, who came here once in the secret hope that she might be healed. Sitting with Freya in one of the upper rows, looking out over a distant olive grove and intersecting hills, I mentioned to her my last visit with Pauline, and told her that people had come to Epidauros for centuries to be cured of their afflictions. Though the excavated temple of Asclepius, the hospice, and therapeutic facilities were, for Freya, "just stones," they reminded me of the poignancy of our struggle to shore ourselves up against ruin. Given that everyone dies, every civilization sinks, and every good work gets forgotten, is it any wonder that we waver between fighting for our lives or fatalistically giving in to death? When Pauline first fell ill with cancer, she did everything possible to seek remission. Stricken with an unrelated cancer ten years later, she placed her faith not in a medical cure but in attaining inner peace. I have lost count of the times I have, since her death, gone back to the last entries in her journal, trying to divine what moved her to make the decision she did. In nine mantras she summed up her vision, and perhaps left her loved ones a key to how they might understand her death.

> The truth shall set you free.
> Look on all things with an equal eye.
> Make of pain a koan.
> The real you is spirit. The other you is an aberration—*not to be given credence!*

So all one has to do is walk in the spirit.
To become strong, you must be filled with strength—do this by opening
   up constantly.
Enjoy the world aright! Come into your birthright.
No change without suffering.
Forget the self—it is the cause of all one's ills. Look above—BE FREE!

Though I have doubted the wisdom of some of these lines, they helped
restore me to life. And I still wrestle with the question of when one should
yield and when one should fight, and how one decides between a time to keep
silence and a time to speak.

When I first came to Epidauros, I didn't know what to expect. I remember walking through a row of pines and suddenly it was there, outstretched
before me like open arms. Now I felt the same yielding, as if I were one
with the stone bowl and its surrounding landscape of pines and cypresses.
How is it that a place can heal, like the touch of hands? In Athens, Sofka
had told me of a physiotherapist who helped her regain movement in her
wrist after she broke it in a fall and suffered ancillary nerve damage. Even
before the therapist touched her, she trusted him; she placed herself in his
hands. But how can one give oneself up to a landscape? How can it inspire
trust or wreak changes in our bodies and our minds? Is it that our encounters with the human world have been so bruising that withdrawal from
this world is our only hope of restoration? Or is it that we find in the eternal round of the seasons, the flowering of perennial plants, a natural spring,
or a snake's ability to shed and renew its skin chthonic metaphors for our
own renewal?

At our hotel that afternoon, we learned that Michael Jackson had died of a
heart attack. Freya was deeply saddened. She wanted to know why I was not
also filled with sorrow at the death of my namesake. I thought of time as an
echo chamber, a hall of distorting mirrors. I remembered my hand clap in the
ancient amphitheatre, magnified, almost metallically, around the stone bowl.

Next morning I set off alone to the small theatre of Demos. The crowing
of a rooster took me back to a village in Sierra Leone, the muffled cor coro
coo recalled a ring-dove in Menton, the sound of water flowing down through
the orange grove made me remember Mexico, and the ching of a cold chisel
brought back to mind lines I wrote when I visited Epidauros in 1980. So unavoidable were these associations that I wondered whether, as one ages, life
becomes a succession of faded repetitions. But then I returned to the hotel

and to Freya, who was now awake and ready for breakfast at a harborside café. We sat there for the best part of an hour, enjoying our English toast and espresso coffee, planning our day. But Freya was far ahead of me. She wanted her bedroom redecorated in preparation for her freshman year at high school. She had been thinking about it a lot. "I want a complete makeover," she said. "Not only my room, but my hair. Everything."

And so began the new day.

CHAPTER 8

It's Other People Who Are My Old Age

Since the lived is . . . never entirely comprehensible, what I understand never quite
tallies with my living experience, in short, I am never quite at one with myself.
—Maurice Merleau-Ponty

In a series of interviews with Benny Levy in 1980, Jean-Paul Sartre—then
seventy-five and in the last year of his life—asserted that he did not experience himself as an old man. Everyone treated him as an old man. But for
himself, he was not old. "It's other people that are my old age," he said.[1]

The moment is poignant, because in the eyes of others Sartre *was* old—
blind, unable to write, unable to be alone, almost completely dependent, and
not always lucid in speech or in thought. But those who spoke of Sartre in
this way seem not to have realized that even in dying a person's humanity is
still alive, and their remarks suggest how difficult it is for us to accommodate
the view that a person's identity is as various as the people who encounter or
purport to know that person, including *herself* or *himself*. "We live . . . lives based
upon selected fictions," writes Lawrence Durrell. "Our view of reality is conditioned by our position in space and time—not by our personalities as we like to
think."[2]

This relativity of viewpoints was complicated, in Sartre's case, by the
quarrel that followed the publication of the Levy interviews—debates over
whether Levy had imposed his own views on the older writer, over who knew
Sartre best, the man and the thinker, and over who should be allowed the
last word on what he thought in his dying days.

One of the arresting facts of growing old is that the young see us, as we in
turn see them, as inhabiting absolutely different worlds. If aging is a process
of forgetting, then the first symptom of this amnesia is forgetting what it was
like to be young. The converse is more forgivable, for the young cannot be

blamed for having little inkling of what it is like to be old. Still, I have been haunted for many years by my inability to see past the superficial appearance of age, and my failure to ask my elders to share with me the fruit of their accumulated experience. Did it remain true for Sartre to the end of his life that a human being "is characterized above all by his going beyond a situation, and by what he succeeds in making of what he has been made"?[3] Is it as true of the old as of the young, of men and of women, that one never simply conserves or straightforwardly reproduces the world in which one finds oneself thrown, that we surpass, in some small measure and in often indiscernible ways, the situation that is visited upon us as a result of the accident of our birth, our history, our biology? For Sartre, understanding a person or a life requires a double perspective—a regressive movement in which we examine the cards we are dealt; a progressive moment in which we see how we play our hand. "This is the limit I would today accord to freedom," Sartre said in a 1969 interview, "the small movement which makes a totally conditioned social being someone who does not render back completely what his conditioning has given him."[4]

These questions haunted me during the hours I spent in the Piddington Reading Room at the University of Auckland, leafing through old anthropology theses in the hope of deepening my understanding of "the people of the four winds."[5] Though I had gone there to research the trope of firstness in the social imaginaries of Māori, what claimed my attention was the room itself, the views it afforded of Auckland harbor, the islands in the gulf, and memories of my freshman year, particularly the classes I took with Professor Ralph O'Reilly Piddington.

Though only fifty-two, Piddington seemed ancient to me—rather as Sartre was described in the last years of his life.[6] With his thinning hair, rheumy eyes, and palsied hands, I found it impossible to believe my professor had ever been young, yet alone as idealistic and adventurous as I imagined myself to be. His dogged defense of Malinowski's functionalism, and the rumors that circulated about his parkinsonism and fondness for whiskey, only added to my blighted and unsympathetic view. And though his textbook *An Introduction to Social Anthropology*, already in its second edition, contained abundant evidence of his fieldwork in Aboriginal Australia, I was blind to it. All I could see was the frail, florid-faced man who, week after week, stood behind the lectern in a faded academic gown and conducted us on a Cook's tour, as he called it, of primitive peoples, reciting his litany of ethnographic facts, native terms, and formal definitions.

Yet had I possessed even a modicum of discernment, I might have read between the lines of his text and divined a hidden biography. I might even have seen that his Malinowskian preoccupation with needs and functions referred not only to remote societies but obliquely and intimately to himself.

In his first volume he observes that "it is easy enough, on the basis of superficial and one-sided observation, to caricature primitive man as a fiend or as a saint. It requires the discipline of patient scientific observation to see him as a human being not essentially different from ourselves, capable of brutality and kindness, of greed or altruism, of obedience or defiance toward the social order, according to the culture in which he is born, his individual temperament and the particular circumstances in which he finds himself."[7]

This view is reiterated in his second volume, where Piddington reminds us that "the anthropologist in the field is a human being dealing with other human beings, and that the personal relations which he establishes and maintains with his informants are vital."[8] But instead of advocating closeness and collaboration between ethnographer and informant, Piddington suggests that the "personal bias and distortion" entailed by such intimacy should be circumvented by "a thorough training in the scientific methods of social anthropology."[9] One safeguard, he avers, is to avoid interviews and to place greater emphasis on observation, though there are dangers even here, he adds, for participant observation risks identifying the observer "too closely . . . with a particular social class," embroiling him in factional disputes, and creating bias in his data. "At all costs, the field-worker must retain his objectivity,"[10] Piddington concludes, underscoring the power of *stranger value* to maximize neutrality, maintain distance, and guarantee access to restricted knowledge.

The irony is that, despite these caveats against engagement, this lip service to objectivity, Ralph Piddington's nine months of fieldwork among the Karadjeri in 1930 and 1931 were characterized by a passionate concern for the plight of Aboriginal people and fervent advocacy on their behalf.

There are other contradictions. Piddington confides that during most of his stay in the Kimberleys, he "resided at the telegraph station at Lagrange Bay, though . . . made trips to various parts of Karadjeri country to witness ceremonies." Yet apart from one or two hunts and fishing trips, he "did not participate in economic life," and most of his ethnographic information was "obtained by interview," the very technique in which the ethnographer is, allegedly, most likely to influence "behaviour by the nature of the questions which he asks and the comments which he makes."[11] Moreover, Piddington gathered three-quarters of all his data from a single informant, Yuari—allegedly a "deviant personality"—and much of his remaining data from Yuari's brother Nirmbdi.

While Piddington admits "serious defects" in his fieldwork when it is measured against the general principles he lays down in his text, the fault lies not with the author but with both the functionalist and structuralist assumptions that informed the anthropology of his time, including, as he himself notes, the quest for a conceptually "consistent system" of kinship and the notion that deviations from a norm reflect psychological aberrations rather than quotidian strategizing and variation. But the most compelling omission is his own personal and political involvement in the Karadjeri situation—something of which he makes no mention in his text.

Though considered a distraction in Piddington's time, engagement is now central to the ethics and practice of anthropology. And it was the very thing I was hungry to hear about as a student.

And herein lies a tale.

Shortly after graduating with an MA from A. R. Radcliffe-Brown's Department of Anthropology at the University of Sydney, Piddington was awarded a Rockefeller Fellowship by the Australian National Research Committee to carry out his fieldwork among the Karadjeri.[12]

Some three months after completing his second stint of fieldwork, Piddington did an interview with a journalist from the Sydney newspaper *The World*. Given his prejudice against interviews, it is ironic that this interview should have such dramatic repercussions. In the interview, Piddington made no bones about the racial discrimination and appalling living conditions that Aboriginal people had to endure in the Kimberleys. "The system of employing aborigines on cattle stations in the North and North-west Australia virtually amounts to slavery," he observed, and he proceeded to give details of "trafficking in lubras" and the flogging and murder of blacks by whites.[13] A few months later, Piddington took his indictment of the police and pastoralists to the London press and, on the editorial page of *The World*, repeated his polemic against the maltreatment of Aboriginals.[14] This time he brought the ire of the Western Australian chief protector of Aborigines down on his head.[15]

As a member of the committee that had approved Rockefeller funding for Piddington's fieldwork, the chief protector was in a powerful position, and in

September 1932, Raymond Firth, then acting head of the Sydney University Department of Anthropology (following Radcliffe-Brown's departure for Chicago), rebuked Piddington and sought an assurance that he would make no further public statements that questioned government "control and care of Aboriginal people."[16] After reflecting on this policy of "cautious silence," Piddington elected to defend and reiterate his views in a detailed statement. The Australia National Research Council (ANRC) then terminated his funding, with Elkin, the new head of the Sydney department, approving the action.

The ANRC dossier on Piddington is revealing. It shows an anthropologist much more involved with the Karadjeri on a day-to-day, face-to-face basis than appears from his textbook account of his life in the field, leaving one to wonder whether he felt embarrassed to admit that he was among Karadjeri on a cattle station and not living nomadically in the desert. At the same time, the dossier inadvertently documents the very racist assumptions against which Piddington was campaigning. D. J. Mulvaney summarizes the file as follows:

> Piddington was observed to drive female Aborigines in his vehicle; he was seen to transport liquor; he was "said to be addicted to drink"; he took informants away without consulting authorities; his conduct was "hardly in keeping with the position held." Generally the tenor of those accusations was petty. For any Broome resident of those times to criticise alcohol consumption was sheer hypocrisy. It also revealed complete ignorance of the nature of anthropological fieldwork, while incidentally illuminating local racial attitudes towards Aboriginal people. One witness even seemed critical that Piddington travelled with his wife. However, his most heinous offense, commented on by two officials, was Piddington's presence in Broome "at a convivial evening when the Red Flag and Communist songs were sung."[17]

Six years after writing his first letters in defense of Aboriginal rights, Piddington completed his PhD in London under Bronislaw Malinowski. Apart from war service, he would return to Australia, his country of birth, only once. And his field of interest would move to action anthropology and to French Canada.

Looking back, I am left with many unanswered questions. Given the brutal realities that Piddington encountered in the field, why did he never challenge Malinowski's tendency to analyze social systems in equilibrium, ignoring the historical stresses and strains that often brought them to the breaking point? And what analogies might he have drawn between the injustices he witnessed in the Kimberleys and the injustices he himself suffered in Sydney? Half a century after taking my first classes at the University of Auckland, I am struck by the coincidence between the rejection Ralph Piddington suffered in his homeland and the case of Vere Gordon Childe, the Australian-born and internationally acclaimed prehistorian and archaeologist, who died on October 19, 1957, after falling from a cliff in the Blue Mountains, in all probability a deliberate act, provoked by failing health and a fear of intellectual debilitation.

I have left it too long to express my sense of kinship with these men. For though I too sang "The Red Flag," marched with a banner for some great cause, and struggled to reconcile the academy with the world, I now ask myself whether I ever risked as much as they did, and I imagine a kind of poetic justice in the possibility that today, in one of my classes, a student will see me as I once so mistakenly saw Ralph Piddington, as past his prime and out of touch with reality.

CHAPTER 9

Objects in Mirror Are Closer Than They Appear

"Szhivat" is a derivative from the verb *"zhit,"* to live. There are two verbs with this root that connote gradual retreat from life, the stealthy approach of "non-life," contrived through someone's care. One can be squeezed out of the living space of one's apartment or one's workplace . . . [or one can be] squeezed or edged out, not only of one's dwelling place, but of life itself.

—Galina Lindquist

In 1999 the anthropologist Galina Lindquist returned to Moscow after ten years away. She walked around the city as a revenant, finding it familiar yet utterly strange. This was not only because she had changed; Russia itself was no longer the country she had known during the years of perestroika. The late 1980s had been a time of jubilant expectation; the despised Soviet *sistema* had collapsed, you could buy books in subway kiosks that only recently you could have been sent to the Gulag for possessing, and you were ostensibly free. Ten years later, this mood of abundant possibility had vanished, replaced by a sense of anarchic limitlessness (*bespredel*) that called to mind the savage ruthlessness of the jungle. "Faith in the new institutions of the market and banking [was] crushed; people lost the money they had been saving for decades, the numerous businesses that had sprung up in the preceding years went to the wall, and the tokens of plenty that started to appear on the store shelves after the emptiness of the early 1990s became unaffordable for most of the people."[1] The prevailing mood of disillusionment and despair deepened as evidence emerged with every passing day of corruption at all levels of government, criminality in business, growing unemployment, and the atrophy of state welfare for the old, the sick, and the disabled. In this desperate situation, Galina became fascinated by the strategies people adopted to cope with the dire predicament in which they found themselves. She observed, both in her old friends and in herself, a longing for a lost time, a kind of aphasia in which one lacked a language to articulate one's sense of a vanishing life, and with it the eclipse of one's own sense of self. At the same time, Galina noticed how this space of dissolution and absence was being filled with pornography, pulp fiction, escapist videos, and cheap magazines, as well as New Age paraphernalia that offered magical, paranormal, and occult possibilities of healing and renewal. Working closely with an occult practitioner (magus) and one of her clients, Galina began to see that magic was a way in which people sought to regain a sense of control over their own lives in circumstances where normal socioeconomic avenues had been blocked.

In her first account of her fieldwork in Moscow,[2] Galina emphasizes the complementarity of markets and magic. When the market (or banking system) becomes a place of danger that one can no longer trust, "business magic" becomes an alternative strategy for making money, obtaining a loan, succeeding in business, or keeping a job. This switch from the material to the ethereal—from market to magic—is predicated upon a Western New Age cosmology that imagines the physical body to be surrounded by a "biofield" that holds information about a person's past, present, and future life and connects a human being to higher realms of astral power and divine influence. When one's physical or financial situation seems hopeless, channeling this mysterious biofield may bring a windfall or begin a flow of regenerative power.

Six years later, in her monograph *Conjuring Hope*, Galina's emphasis is less on business magic per se than the occult search for the "lost sense of tomorrow," and for increased hope.[3] Objective transformations are less significant than subjective transformations in which a person's confidence is bolstered, despair is assuaged, and hope is restored. Rather than being stuck, a person is able to feel that he or she is getting somewhere. This emphasis on magical action as a transformation in the way the world *appears* to a person echoes Sartre's famous essay on the emotions and is evidence of Galina's attempt to reconcile her early attachment to Peirce's semiology with a growing interest in phenomenology. At the same time, she seems to be seeking a mode of analysis that can encompass both the macropolitics of the state and the micropolitics of individual lifeworlds at the margins of state power. This search for a rapprochement between models of secular and sacred power— politics and religion, market and magic—preoccupied Galina as well as me, and in the course of numerous conversations in Stockholm and Copenhagen between 2000 and 2005, Galina pressed me to explain how phenomenology could possibly speak to issues of political economy. She found some answers to this quandary in Bourdieu's later work, where he argues that forms of symbolic capital (well-being, hope, and recognition), though unequally distributed in any social system, never derive entirely from external sources but reflect inner resources that are difficult to pin down and cannot be explained sociologically. Galina's determination to do justice to the mysteries of subjectivity and intersubjectivity helps us understand why, in *Conjuring Hope*, she often suspends the question of diagnostic or analytical meaning in order to explore an "indexical mode of transformation" in which a person is changed, or healed, through direct sensory experience rather than objective knowledge and through ritual rather than political action.[4] In such instances, the charismatic power and caring presence of a healer may count for more than his or her medical qualifications, just as a client's faith in a healer's power counts for more than his or her understanding of how a séance or healing session actually works. What is at stake is not so much a cure—for we cannot be cured of being-in-the-world—but an uplifting of the spirit, a replenishment of the will, a resuscitation of hope. "For the people I talked to, hope was an existential doorway out of the deadliest of deadlocks, the light at the end of the longest of tunnels; a tool for expanding the horizons of the lifeworld, for intentionality to unfold, for will to return: the will to life, no matter what."[5]

A few months before *Conjuring Hope* was published, in 2006, I attended a conference in Oxford on "The Anthropology and Psychology of Fieldwork Experience." Galina was also there, and we spent time together, over lunch and during breaks between sessions, catching up on news. But Galina was under a cloud, waiting for the results of medical tests and fearing the worst. Although she had little appetite for food, she talked passionately about her recent stint of fieldwork in Tuva, southern Siberia, where she had been working closely with Tuvan healers since 2001, studying the shifting balance of religious power between Tibetan Buddhism and traditional shamanism. In the course of her fieldwork in Moscow, Galina had become very close to her key informants. This involvement seemed to me even more intense with her Tuvan collaborators. Drawn deeply into their religious life, she had become unsettled, like many ethnographers before her, by the impossibility of drawing a line between participation and observation. But Galina's ability to dwell in the ambiguity of the ethnographic method reflected a personal disposition as well as an intellectual commitment to joining "objective analysis to lived experience." Indeed, she shared Merleau-Ponty's view that this process was "the most proper task of anthropology, the one which distinguishes it from other social sciences."[6] It was her refusal to assimilate instant experience to extant knowledge that made her skeptical of institutional religion, biomedicine, and academic fashions. Perhaps this was why, when she first fell ill, she relied on homeopathy and acupuncture and travelled to Tuva in the summer of 2006 not only for further fieldwork but for healing.

Back in Sweden, she submitted to chemotherapy, and for a while it appeared to be working. Then the blow fell. "I am ill again," she wrote to me in November 2007. "It all came very quickly and in a month developed into an inoperable tumor. They are now giving me more chemotherapy, hoping it will shrink, but i can neither eat nor move, almost. I'm not sure what will happen to me; the optimistic prognosis is that i'll remain chronically ill, for whatever length of time, living on chemos. Whatever else it means, one thing is that i can no longer make any plans and can't have people depending on me. My teaching this and next semester was cancelled; a conference on 'institutional transformations of suffering' that i have been working on organizing for three years is now going on without me."

Galina had roped me into organizing a workshop at the European Association of Social Anthropologists' conference at Ljubliana, scheduled for the summer of 2008. It was a way of addressing some of the personal issues of fieldwork that we had discussed at length during our occasional meetings. One of our concerns was to broach the question of putting other people's epistemologies on a par with our own, of breaking the historical habit of privileging European worldviews. In our draft proposal we wrote:

> Despite the fact that ethnographers often spend many years in societies other than their own, acquiring conversancy in local languages, becoming familiar with very different ways of understanding the world, sometimes advocating politically on behalf of their host society and espousing respect and affection for individual collaborators, it is rare that an anthropologist adopts a non-western epistemology in his or her work or even places such an epistemology on the same footing as theories derived from his or her own intellectual traditions. Invidious distinctions between "scientific" and "folk" models or reason and faith continue to hold sway over our thinking, so that while we may venture to speak, say, of African "philosophy" or "religion," these Eurocentric and logocentric rubrics determine which phenomenon we will include under or exclude from such headings and how we will approach the subject we define in these ways. Assumptions

drawn from classical Greek thought, or Judeo-Christian teleology and soteriology, or from Euro-American preoccupations with politico-economic power and instrumental rationality continue to constitute the dominant paradigms whereby we decide meaning, assign cause, and explain human behavior. But if we are going to critique the power inequalities between West and East, North and South, we must also critique the discursive inequalities associated with these geopolitical divisions, and this means taking other worldviews seriously, and seeing our own epistemologies from the vantage point of the other. This does not mean, however, that we cease to be skeptical of the epistemological claims and pretensions of the views of the world that various people espouse. It simply means abandoning the notion that the veracity of any worldview lies in its correspondence to objective reality or its logical coherence, and exploring, instead, the real entailments of any worldview for human lives. A corollary of this pragmatist turn is that we see beliefs and worldviews not as scripts that actors faithfully follow or principles that guide their actions but as ways that people give legitimacy to their actions or rationalize, after the event, the often unforeseen and unintended consequences of what they have done. *Moreover, in a reflexive vein, we want to explore our own familiar experience of physical and social reality from the standpoint of unfamiliar philosophies, to see what aspects of our social existence they might illuminate, and what alternative solutions to our existential quandaries and political dilemmas they might offer.*

In italicizing the last sentence, I remind myself how deeply Galina's experiences in Siberia, and her own consultations with shamans, influenced her attitude to her cancer, delaying her reliance on orthodox medical treatment.[7] And in retaining her quirky use of the lowercase "i" in her e-mail, I remind myself of how her personal world shrank as her tumor grew, and how the hope she ascribes to her Swedish doctors was something she could not share.

Three months passed before I found the time and means to travel to Sweden, and as I waited at our agreed-upon rendezvous in the concourse of Stockholm-Arlanda Airport, I felt nervous and fearful, expecting to face a diminished and unrecognizable version of my friend. But Galina looked her old self, and confident enough to drive to a nearby lake, where we strolled for an hour before finding a lakeside restaurant for lunch. It was like old times, though we now talked of mortality rather than anthropology. I remember Galina commenting on the unseasonal thaw, the unpredictability of our times, and her own experience of reaching a point where there is no future. "One lives from day to day, not knowing whether there will be two more weeks, two more months, two more years," she said. "But I no longer cling to life, and therefore I do not suffer. Suffering is resistance, not wanting to die, not wanting the pain. But I have let go, and in this yielding I have found peace."

Paradoxically, it is more often the living than the dying who cannot bear the thought of death. And I had to tread carefully as I pressed Galina for details of her treatment, lest I appear unsympathetic to the course of action she had decided upon. There was an alternative therapy, Galina said, but as a result of the lack of communication between hospitals and laboratories, she had had to do all the hard work liaising with the lab and working with the doctors who could administer the experimental drugs. It was too much to ask of a patient, and she had reached the point where the effort was costing her what little energy she had. Besides, she was feeling better than she had in many months, miraculously so.

I confessed surprise at how well she looked. But Galina set no store by appearances. Nor did she hold out any hope of a medical breakthrough or divine intervention. "Unfortunately, none of my family or friends can accept this," she said. "Nobility lies in fighting the cancer, not giving in to it. My mother tells me not to be selfish. My friends urge me to seek treatment abroad. My ex-husband, who is devoutly Russian Orthodox, implores me to embrace the faith. But God is indifferent to me, and I will live without God, though still believing God exists, His ways beyond our understanding."

In Galina's "reckoning with life" I was reminded of Gillian Rose's memoir, written during her dying days,[8] the co-presence of a profound vulnerability and an extraordinary strength. "I am dying," Galina said. Her voice quavered for a second, and then she recovered. And I saw that she had attained a state of grace where death and life cancelled each other out, and the ego has been transcended.

I went to Uppsala for a few days and then returned to Stockholm to see Galina one last time. There were no good-byes, though we both knew we would not see each other again.

OTHER EPISTEMOLOGIES / OTHER ONTOLOGIES

To face the prospect of life in a world abruptly bereft of someone whose presence sustained the very reality of that world is also to be confronted by the question as to whether one really *knew* the person whose absence one now mourns. Clearly, our knowledge of other people is unlike our knowledge of things. It can be neither fathomed nor summarized, for this "cloude of unknowyng"[9] encompasses senses, emotions, and intuitions that lie on the outskirts of consciousness. One may readily list a person's deeds or describe her appearance. One may recount the story of her life, dating critical moments, naming places where she lived and worked, mentioning significant others. But one is left with the mystery of what it was that made her presence felt. Her aura and influence slip away from the substantives with which one compiles a resume, writes an obituary, or charts a career. A death sharpens, often unbearably, one's sense of being deeply a part of another person's existence while remaining a stranger to it.

It is all too easy at such times to doubt that one can know others at all and to conclude that one's own life runs parallel to the lives of others with only the illusion of overlap, interplay, or empathy. What one thinks one knows of the other seems as unstable as memory, a mere approximation, or a single arrested moment, like a snapshot, that one wishfully believes to have captured the whole.

D. W. Winnicott coins the term "potential space"[10] to describe a hypothetical area between the infant and the mother at a stage when the infant is exploring the existential difference between being apart from and being a part of the world of another. In bereavement, one's sense of separateness is not chosen, but traumatically thrust upon one. To lose someone you love is to pass from a space in which you and the other *coexisted* to one in which you exist in relation to a memory, an afterimage, a shadow, a simulacrum. Insofar as being-in-potentia implies a reaching out for another that is reciprocated by the other's openness and responsiveness, the experience of bereavement is one of unrequited and unconsummated longing, analogous to the phantom limb phenomenon of the amputee.

Curiously enough, the experience of separation and loss may shock one into realizing how deeply human existence is intersubjective—the being of another comprehended through one's own being, and vice versa. "In reality," writes Merleau-Ponty, "the other is not shut up inside my perspective of the world, because this perspective itself has no definite limits, because it slips spontaneously into the other's, and because both are brought together in the one single world in which we all participate as anonymous subjects of perception."[11] Accordingly, solitude and sociality are not the two horns of a dilemma, "but two 'moments' of one phenomenon"[12] in which self and other are always co-present, even though the other is reduced to an object, or momentarily disappears from sight and mind. Bereavement is traumatic because the significant other now appears to us as a being *in-itself* rather than *for-itself*. Since it is no longer *for-itself*, it cannot be there for us, connected to us as a collaborator in "consummate reciprocity."[13]

This brings us to the alarming thought that positivist social science addresses the world as if it were dead, since it is only in this guise that we can presume to have knowledge of it, as it is *in-itself*.

What writers like Winnicott and Merleau-Ponty are persuading us to do is move away from constituting the other as an object of knowledge and, as a corollary, from constituting ourselves as possessing superior skills for acquiring knowledge of others. This means placing both oneself and the other on the same existential footing, and seeing all worldviews not as theories of knowledge *about* the world but as existential means of achieving viable ways of living *in and with* the world.

In the months after Galina's death, I sought a way of furthering her fascination with non-Western ontologies, and addressing the question as to how we might evaluate radically different worldviews without invoking the pejorative dichotomies of premodern versus modern, religious versus scientific, mythic versus real. Moreover, how far could one follow Heidegger in speaking of a "fundamental ontology"[14] rather than focus, as Husserl had done, on the numerous "regional ontologies" that appeared to preclude the possibility of postulating "being-in-the-world" as a universal human condition? Could one argue that all the variant forms of cultural or personal experience, belief and action, were simply alternative means of addressing existential questions and quandaries that were shared by all humanity—aspects of what might be called "the human condition"?

For an ethnographer, context is crucial. The truth value of a belief has to be measured not against some abstract standard such as rationality or logical coherence but in terms of how the belief is put to use, what sensible effects it has, and what practical transformations it enables. Without such detailed descriptions of how our ideas about the world emerge in the course of our interactions in the world, we are likely to fall into the fallacy of inferring experience from codified beliefs and failing to see the extent to which beliefs follow from what we do—stepchildren rather than parents of the activity in which they figure.[15] It was such considerations that drew Galina to Levinas, for whom life is to be lived and enjoyed before it is a matter to be understood.[16] In other words, the alleged rationality or irrationality of a practice is beside the point; what matters is the positive difference it makes to our lives, personal and collective. Consider the Christian doctrine of Virgin Birth and the Australian Aboriginal denial of paternity—beliefs that contradict our scientific knowledge of the facts of human procreation. In both cases, a logical problem is posed: how to simultaneously stress Christ's humanity *and* divinity in the first example, and how to simultaneously stress that one's human identity is determined by where you are conceived and born as well as who physically nurtures you in the womb and brings you into the world. In the Christian example, God displaces Joseph as genitor; in the Aboriginal case, patrilineal country is genitor, though in both cases, the pater is the person who provides for the child and helps raise him or her to adulthood. Let us consider another example, in which ontological assumptions that we might consider irrational nonetheless do better justice to lived experience than assumptions regarded as scientific. Such is the case of karma—which succeeds in capturing the experience with which most human beings are familiar, of life's radical discontinuities.[17] To speak of these ruptures, passages, or critical events in terms of death and rebirth may be scientifically unwarranted, yet it is symbolically appropriate, for it answers the human need to give voice to how things appear to be, even though our metaphors may fail the test of analytical adequacy. While sympathetic to such edifying descriptions of life as lived, Richard Rorty wants to reject the epistemological claims that tend to be made for them. But can we sustain such a hard and fast distinction between "edifying" worldviews that don't have to correspond to the facts or obey the rules of Aristotelian logic and "systematizing" worldviews that do? And is it not the case that even the systematic language of science is steeped in metaphor?

Let us explore the existential commonalities that underlie very different formulations of belief in very different societies by considering, first, the sense of being a part of what Norbert Elias calls "a pre-existing knowledge stream"[18] rather than existing apart from it, and, second, the sense that our fates are determined from without yet are also the outcomes of our own independent choices.

Such existential dilemmas have figured in West African thought for a long time.

Among the Tallensi, the tension between being an actor and being acted upon finds expression in the dialectic between chosen and preordained destinies. "Life—symbolized for the Tallensi in the breath (*novor*)—is only the raw material for living," writes Meyer Fortes. "What one makes of it depends on other spiritual agencies."[19] These "other spiritual agencies" include the influences of one's mother, father, or other kin (strictly speaking, "the prenatal destiny" of such significant others) and the influence of the prenatal destiny that one chooses for oneself before being born. This prenatal decision may be made against having a spouse, bearing children, or being a farmer—in effect, rejecting a normal moral life. Fortes calls this "Oedipal fate," contrasting it with the "Jobian fulfillment" that comes from recognizing the superior powers of the ancestors and seeking redemption through them. But just as a bad prenatal choice can be revoked by setting up a shrine and making sacrifices to one's ancestors—ritually submitting to and complying with "the norms and customs instituted by them"[20]—a person's positive dispositions may be undermined should he or she neglect or ignore the lineage ancestors.

How can such opposed imperatives and competing dispositions be reconciled?

In answering this question from a West African point of view, one must consider in more detail the kinds of complementary forces that may offset or countermand one's prenatal destiny, providing room for intelligent purpose and conscious control in the actual working out of one's social destiny on earth. The Kalabari Ijo of Nigeria recognize that a conflict or division often exists between a side of the personality that is decided before birth and a side of the personality that emerges in the course of a person's social existence. Rather than use Fortes's allusions to Oedipus and Job to describe the tension between the dual aspects of the personality that Kalabari call *biomgbo* and *teme*, Robin Horton prefers the Freudian concepts of conscious and unconscious. While the *teme* refers to prenatal choices, and innate dispositions of which the *biomgbo* is unaware, it is possible for divination to bring to light the unconscious forces governing a person's fate and suggest a ritual action whereby the wishes of the *teme* may be resisted.

But why not place Sophocles's drama of Oedipus, Freud's model of the psyche, and Kalabari or Tallensi myths on a par? Why should we translate "their" idioms into "ours" unless we feel that "they" are epistemologically inferior, in the same way that myth is often alleged to be an infantile attempt to create history?[21] Why not see myth, as Ricoeur suggests, as "always-already-there" in what we call history or the human condition, in the same way that stories of beginnings are haunted by a sense of the origin—the precursive reality that makes the very idea of beginnings possible, and that calls into question the discursive cuts we customarily make between religion and reason, myth and science, orality and literacy, tradition and modernity?

My preference is a pragmatist conception of truth, where truth is not evaluated primarily in terms of its logical coherence or its correspondence to objective reality but, rather, in terms of the degree to which it is conducive to life, particularly the fulfillment of our collective capacity for creating some form of community that meets the needs of everyone to roughly the same degree. One of the most compelling recent ethnographies from West Africa not only provides such a perspective; it shows how this entails a critique of Western epistemology.

For the Beng of Côte d'Ivoire, infants are said to "lead profoundly spiritual lives,"[22] in part because they are reincarnations of someone who has died, in part because they come into this world not from a void, but "from a rich, social existence in a place that adults call *wrugbe*."[23] What is remarkable about Alma Gottlieb's commentary on Beng thought is that rather than simply describe it as a "belief," she asks a pragmatist question: What "implications" does such a belief have "for how infants and young children are cared for?"[24]

First, it underscores the importance of reciprocal interactions between the world of one's predecessors and the world of the here and now, emphasizing that if one's present life is to flourish, then one's connections with the afterlife—which is, in Beng thought, the ancestral realm "where we come from"—must be kept alive. Second, if human lives are perpetually moving between this world and *wrugbe*, then the tragic repercussions of infant mortality are reduced, since children who die early will almost certainly be reborn.[25] In recognition of this continuity between contemporaries and predecessors, the names of the dead are recycled. Third, Beng beliefs imply that infants are not incipient or lesser human beings but worthy of the same respect and attention one would accord any adult. Thus, parents are exhorted by diviners to give their crying child jewelry or coins. "At the psychological level," Gottlieb writes, "the diviner is communicating to the parents the message that the infant needs to be valued more . . . respected as a fellow person rather than viewed as a suffering, wordless creature. 'I miss my other home,' a Beng baby might be trying to communicate while crying wordlessly, 'please give me something to remind me of home.'"[26] In other words, infants have memories, desires, multilingual skills, and a capacity for understanding that adults ignore at their peril.

The proposition that residents of *wrugbe* represent all the ethnic groups in the world, and have full comprehension of all the world's languages, might seem absurd unless one took into consideration the worldview it underwrites. Here is how Alma Gottlieb makes this point:

> One day I was playing This Little Piggy with the toes of Amenan's then six-month-old daughter, Amwe. As the last little piggy went home, I laughed aloud at myself, acknowledging that baby Amwe couldn't possibly understand the words of the ditty, all the more because they were in English. To my amazement, Amenan objected strongly to my remark, which she took as an insult to babies. In fact, she insisted that Amwe understood perfectly well all that I was singing. When I asked skeptically "You think so?" Amenan explained her answer by invoking the linguistic situation of *wrugbe*. Unlike in this world, she pointed out, in the afterlife different ethnic groups do not live apart from one another. Rather, in *wrugbe* members of all the world's ethnic groups live together harmoniously. Associated with this ethnic mixture is a striking degree of linguistic ecumenism: when the residents of *wrugbe* speak to each other in their own languages, everyone understands; they have full mutual comprehension.[27]

Elsewhere, Gottlieb argues for seeing *wrugbe* as "political allegory"— evoking a place where people enjoy greater well-being, health, and humanity.[28] A nostalgic image, perhaps, of the precolonial past, and a reminder to we who extol the virtues of modernity that it is never possible to say that the gains it brings outweigh its losses. One thing is sure, however: our persistent lack of regard for the lifeworlds and worldviews of those we see as being outside the pale of modernity. If we are to take seriously the proposition that beyond cultural difference lies a common humanity, then we have to place our own worldviews on the same footing as all others, even if this means abandoning the antinomies with which we have distinguished "us" from "them"—reason versus faith, science versus religion, modernity versus tradition, knowledge versus belief. We can best do this by not seeing alternative views as epistemologies whose truth may be decided by asking whether or not they cohere logically or mirror reality, but as ways of serving our interests and defining our values. If truth is a matter of whether or not a "belief" enhances the life of a community, then an obsession with identifying it gives ground to a concern for humanizing it.

It is probably true that no human society, no human being, is bereft of some notion of humanity transcending one's own particular humanity. Deliberately masked and distorted though this idea of a common humanity may be, the best evidence of its hold over us is the length we have to go to when we try to deny it. Privileging a conception of the other as oneself in other circumstances rather than as an essentially different kind of being implies, as Terence put it, "being human, nothing human is alien to me" (*humani nil a me alienum puto*). No matter how different, how abhorrent, how admirable, the other always represents a potentiality in oneself.

Discontinuities within West Africa are small, and echoes of the same mythemes are found throughout the region. As one goes further afield, the discontinuities become greater until the lifeworlds of Africa, Asia, Europe, and Polynesia seem far apart. Yet significant continuities conjoin these worlds of thought, just as they unite the people who claim them as their own, and suggest a proto-narrative, a proto-ethic, a prototypical humanity. This common humanity does not simply consist in unconscious structures of the human mind, as Lévi-Strauss suggests; it is grounded in such existential aporias as the incompatible destinies and power struggles between the generations, between men and women, between siblings, and between those within a community and those without. Every new society, like every new beginning, conserves traces of the origin, of the abiding human dilemmas to which those new social formations are a response. Which is why, as Sartre noted, our analytic method must be progressive-regressive—fully recognizing that while every event, every experience, is in one sense a new departure, a rebirth, it conserves the ancient, inert, and inescapable conditions that bind us all to a shared humanity and makes each of us a being who carries within ourself "the project of all possible being."[29]

It goes without saying that the truth of this view is one thing; living it is another. It is often too daunting to recognize that what we consider unique to ourselves is part of a common human heritage, or that what is foregrounded in one society lies in the background of another, much as our egos are simply the visible aspects of personalities whose depths contain potentialities we prefer not to acknowledge. Against this balkanization of being, the most an intellectual or artist can accomplish is a kind of subversive irony that strips away the masks whereby people lay claim to singular or pure identities, that reveals the illusion of bounded selves or polities, and that indicates how intermingled all human beings have been, from their origins, whether they like it or not.

In 2004 Bulgarian filmmaker Adela Peeva released a documentary entitled *Whose Is This Song?* about her travels through Macedonia, Turkey, Greece, Albania, Bosnia, Serbia, and Bulgaria, tracing the social biography of a Balkan ballad. In most places, the ballad is known as a love song, though the lyrics vary. In Turkey and Bosnia it is, however, a call to arms. Despite the ubiquity of the ballad and its ancient, untraceable origins, Peeva was confronted by shocked, angry, and incredulous reactions wherever she travelled, as people laid claim to the song as their own. "The Turks took it from us," cried an Albanian in Tirana. In Vranje, a town in southern Serbia, Peeva's Serbian hosts stormed out of a restaurant when she played a Bosnian version of the song. "This is theft!" one man shouted as he rushed away.

"We tend not to accept we have a common identity," Peeva later commented, with disarming understatement.[30] But Peeva is also warning us against identity thinking and an obsession with control, as well as an infatuation with revealed truths that confirm these proclivities.

In Gillian Rose's last book, *Love's Work*, I glimpse a vision that Galina might well have developed had she lived. Rather than focus on *revealed religion*, Rose explores what she calls *unrevealed religion*, "which has hold of us without any evidences, natural or supernatural, without any credos or dogmas, liturgies or services." It is, she goes on to say, "the very religion that makes us protest, 'But I have no religion,' the very Protestantism against modernity that fuels our inner self-relation."[31] Rose claims that "this very protest founded modernity, an ethic without ethics, a religion without salvation," and that enlightenment rationality is "the dependant, the cousin-german" of this unrevealed religion, as is "reason's offspring, postmodern relativism."[32] I take these remarks as ironic commentaries on the impossibility of ever attaining a comprehensive and authoritative knowledge of the world, or of our ever being completely in control of it. In all experience—personal, social, scientific, or religious—there is a tension between two conceptions of control. The first implies management and mastery, in which the world bends to our will, and our knowledge promises to light up the darkness, offering us greater certainty in our relationships with objects and others. The second is dramatically different. In this more elusive vein, Rose writes "of a sense which, nevertheless, saves my life and which, once achieved, may induce the relinquishing of 'control' in the first sense—'control' means that when something untoward happens, some trauma or damage, whether inflicted by the commissions or omissions of others, or some cosmic force, one makes the initially unwelcome event one's own inner occupation. You work to adopt the most loveless, forlorn, aggressive child as your own, and do not leave her to develop into an even more vengeful monster, who constantly wishes you ill. *In ill-health as in unhappy love, this is the hardest work: it requires taking in before letting be.*"[33]

In Galina's last writings on the politics of religion, there is, curiously, no hint of this second notion of control as acceptance and yielding. Yet, even as she reprised Peter Berger's image of the sacred canopy, she was, as those closest to her knew, embracing a view of power born of the experience of powerlessness, a technique of the self that, as Foucault noted toward the end of his life, implied a shift away from the study of competing ideologies or identity politics to the study of how people can "effect a certain number of operations on their own bodies, on their souls, on their own thoughts," modifying themselves or acting "in a certain state of perfection, of happiness, of purity, of supernatural power."[34] Perhaps we can understand the gradual shift from the more reflexive tone of *Conjuring Hope* to the more conventionally academic style of Galina's final essays as a gesture toward a profession than demanded masks and jargons as the price of initiation. Perhaps it was a bid for greater presence at a time when her world was falling away, and even the project of understanding appeared irrelevant. This may also be the case for those who survive bereavement, for in the face of the overwhelming love that, paradoxically, wells up in us when we are thrown open to the ultimate, we pass beyond understanding, with our work of words, having reached the limit of what can be said, redeemed by our silence.

CHAPTER 10

I Am an Other

The double nature—confined and open—of the body-self, particularly in relation to listening and to speech, may be perturbed in two opposing ways: either the body may become too closed on itself, or it may merge with the other.

—René Devisch

Thornton Wilder's masterpiece, *The Bridge of San Luis Rey*, begins with a tragedy that seems to defy explanation. A rope bridge gives way as a group of travellers are crossing a deep canyon, and they are thrown to their deaths. A Franciscan priest who witnesses the accident is both stunned and mystified. "The bridge seemed to be among the things that last forever; it was unthinkable that it should break."[1] Brother Juniper doubts that a benevolent God would allow this fate to befall innocent people. There must surely be some reason for their deaths. "Why did this happen to those five?" Wilder's book recounts Brother Juniper's attempts to research the backgrounds of the victims and arrive at a theologically meaningful explanation of why they should have died at that time, and at that place. For those of us who repudiate the idea of divine omniscience and design, it is still not easy to accept that life may be devoid of ultimate meaning, and that accidents happen for no good reason. Though we may receive windfalls without much questioning, ill fortune tends to provoke great soul-searching. It seems outrageous, for example, that a young and beautiful woman should die of cancer, or that a brilliant writer, at the height of his powers, should perish in a car crash, while a corrupt tyrant enjoys health and happiness. Surely life is more than just a lottery. Surely the good do not deserve to suffer, or evil go unpunished. Surely there is some reason some of us should live in hell, while others inhabit paradise.

Faced with the unequal distribution of fortune and misfortune, human beings tend to embrace very different explanations. Some accept that inequalities are simply in the nature of things, or are divinely decreed. Others seek a person or persons who can be blamed for the unjust state of affairs. Still others refuse to accept inequality, repudiate "the blame game," and prefer to determine the *social* causes of human inequality. These different modes of *explaining* misfortune entail quite different courses of action. If one believes that some daemonic, extra-human agency is behind the differential distribution of fortune, one may be inclined to accept one's lot fatalistically. There is little one can do about it, except endure it stoically and perhaps pray that the powers-that-be that have deserted one today will visit one tomorrow, rewarding one's perseverance and faith. If one believes that one's misfortune has been caused by some malevolent other—a witch, a sorcerer, an enemy—one will, if one has the means to do so, seek to bring that malefactor to justice, or take one's revenge upon him or her. If one believes that social forces (class struggle, colonial history, racism or sexism, etc.) underlie the way things are, then one will seek to change the status quo through social action. In practice, however, these different modes of action and explanation are usually co-present and variously combined in any particular situation, which makes it impossible to justify the view that entire societies or particular individuals exemplify any one of these modes alone. Thus, while Brother Juniper presumes that God is benevolent, he cannot accept the tragic collapse of the bridge unless he finds clues in the biographies of the victims that explain why God allowed them to perish. This difficulty of working out the relative weight of different factors in explaining a particular event recalls the case of the Zande granary that collapses on and kills an unfortunate person who happens to be sleeping in its shade. It is readily acknowledged that the immediate cause is dry rot or termite damage, but the question as to why the granary collapsed *at that particular moment, killing that particular individual,* can only be answered by seeking, through divination, the "witch" that wished the victim dead. In Zande parlance, the "first spear" was the witch, while the "second spear" was the weakened structure of the granary.[2]

In modern states, arguments rage over whether the plight of the disadvantaged is a reflection of their personal failings or the historical and structural failings of society, and whether the individual or the state is responsible for redressing inequalities. Even if we accept Sartre's Marxian view that we both make our history and are made by it,[3] it is by no means clear in any particular situation what weighting we should assign free will and determinism.

The methodological difficulty of choosing between a "what" and a "who" is not unlike the problem anthropologists encounter with "structure" and "agency." To what extent do we explain a person's susceptibility to spirit possession in terms of their social marginality, their structural position? And if we introduce agency into the picture, what kind of agency can a person be said to possess when overwhelmed by a power over which he or she exercises so little control?[4]

Clearly, anthropological theorizing shares many of the same uncertainties that anthropologists find among the people they study.[5] While we historically prefer explanations of human behavior and thought that are focused on shared or collective factors—ethnic, cultural, social, class, caste, age, or gender—it is clear that no two individuals, born to the same roles and undergoing the same socialization, ever turn out to be identical. And every life course is in many ways unpredictable and unique, as George Devereux notes, invoking the Roman adage *Si bis faciunt idem, non est idem* (If two people do the same thing, it is not necessarily the same thing).[6]

This tension between different models for *explaining* any human situation—whether drawn from anthropology, philosophy, or so-called folk traditions—reflects the ambiguity of human *existence*, in which we are acted upon *by* the world to the same extent that we act *on* the world, wherein we are both determined and free, anonymous parts of an infinite whole, and autonomous members of finite and familial lifeworlds. Yet we persist, both in our lives and in our reflections on the human condition, in characterizing people as *either* closed in on themselves *or* merged with others when, for the most part, consciousness is continually wavering between these hypothetical extremes. Ironically, as René Devisch points out in his Yaka ethnography, a person who fully realized either of these extremes would be ill or insane.[7]

WILLING AND WAITING

One afternoon, in Freetown, I was walking down Spur Road in the direction of Lumley when a heavy lorry belching black smoke lumbered up the hill toward me. Printed in large letters above the windscreen were the words "Hard Work." No sooner had the lorry passed than a red poda poda appeared. Its logo, emblazoned on the cab, was "Blessings." This coincidence started me thinking about the interplay between stoic waiting and willful striving in everyday life and the different conceptions of a person's place in the social and cosmic scheme of things, for while patience implies accepting the status quo and not standing out from the crowd, striving may involve flouting custom and taking one's life into one's own hands.

According to a Kuranko adage, there is a lot of water in this world, but the water you drink is destined for you alone. If you are meant to live, the wherewithal of life will be there for you. If you are not meant to live, the wherewithal of life will be taken from you or given to someone else. In matters of life and death, divinities and ancestors have the last word. This is why people will sometimes put less effort into advancing a personal career than into divining the life course that has already been inscribed for them. In the West we are taught to assume responsibility for our own actions, to determine our own fates. If we work hard, apply ourselves, and do everything in our power to realize our ambitions and fulfill our dreams, then we will succeed. In West Africa one learns to be patient, to wait for doors to open and opportunities to arise. The powers-that-be, in their own good time and for reasons we cannot fathom, will give what they have to give and take what they have to take. If fortune smiles upon us, it is because we dutifully and stoically endured our time in the wilderness. If fortune passes us by, it is because we failed the test, ignored the advice of our elders, or fell foul of some sorcerer who stole what was meant for us.

This contrast between a fatalistic and a willful attitude to life may be overdrawn. In West Africa people are rarely so resigned to their fate that they do nothing to avert misfortune should a diviner see it coming, or ignore good fortune if it comes their way. No one is so bereft of any sense of oneself as an autonomous being that one is nothing more than an anonymous figure in a crowd. Even when people conform to certain protocols, doing their duty, going along with others without dissent, their reasons for doing so remain partly their own, and their experiences are seldom identical to the experiences of others.

In January 2002 I was staying with my old friend S. B. Marah in Freetown. As the president's brother-in-law, political ally, and right-hand man, S. B. had a large number of people at his beck and call—servants, security personnel, chauffeurs, and camp followers—and every day he received petitions from villagers and propositions from businessmen, entrepreneurs, and diplomats.

Among his most devoted assistants was a man in his forties called Fasili Marah, and in the run-up to the general election in 2002 S. B. had put pressure on the National Electoral Commission to hire his faithful underling. On the morning that the news reached us that Fasili's appointment had been confirmed, I congratulated Fasili on his good fortune. Though Fasili said that he owed everything to S. B., S. B. was quick to point out that "it was not for nothing," and that Fasili's good fortune was well deserved. "He has stuck with me through thick and thin, and it is only right that steadfastness and loyalty should be rewarded." There were several Kuranko elders at S. B.'s house that morning, and all concurred. One man added, however, that Fasili's success reflected the qualities of his mother, for, as the Kuranko see it, the blessings bestowed by one's paternal ancestors are contingent upon one's mother's behavior. If she is a hard-working, faithful, and dutiful wife to her husband, then her children will receive the blessings of their patrilineal forebears, and become *duwe dannu* (blessed children). If she fails in her duty by being lazy, unfaithful, or disobedient, then the path along which the patrilineal blessings flow will become blocked, and her children will be cursed. This is why the Kuranko say, "A man has many children; a woman bears them; a man's children are in her hands" (*Ke l dan sia; musu don den; ke l den wo bolo*) and observe that you are (i.e., your destiny is) in your mother's hands (*i i na le bolo*), or that the book your mother wrote is what you are reading now (*i na l kedi sebene, i wole karantine kedi*), which is to say that one's actions and disposition are direct reflections of one's mother's actions and disposition. In other words, though one's fate is ultimately determined by the ancestors and by God, all depends in practice on the dutiful work of women in serving their husbands and caring for their children. For many, such views encourage a fatalistic submission to life, a tendency to place one's hope in benefactors, mentors, or saviors—an attitude characteristic of many of those who now throng the new Pentecostal churches in the hope that good fortune will follow from giving up the little they do possess to the preachers and powers-that-be. For others, however, subjugating oneself in this way is seen to be both foolish and irresponsible. S. B., for example, took the view that "You are what you make of yourself." This was his constant refrain when upbraiding the young men who fetched his bathwater in the mornings, washed and ironed his clothes, helped him dress, carried his bags, and attended him. "If you don't work hard, you'll get nothing in this world. You must be honest and straightforward. Young people today want something for nothing. They are not serious. Even my own children, I often think about them all night long. I don't sleep for thinking of them." And S. B. told me how much he wanted his sons to "do well," to be men of substance, status, and influence. That they worked as waiters in London restaurants filled him with shame. "Would I want people to know my sons are servants?" he asked. "These useless jobs. Living underground because they do not have residence visas." When I pointed out to him that Abu and Chelmanseh were doing courses in hotel management in London and were not simply waiters, S. B. said he wanted to be proud of them, that he didn't want his sons to disappoint him. "These things weigh on my mind," he said. "After I am dead, what will happen?"

FOOLS RUSH IN WHERE ANGELS FEAR TO TREAD

That we in the West extol the virtues of hard work does not preclude fatalism from entering our thoughts, especially when our diligent labor and determined endeavors do not pay off. As the following story suggests, even the most ambitious and egotistical European will fall prey to fantasies of malevolent fate when his way is blocked and his efforts prove unavailing.

In 1868 a thirty-year-old Englishman called Winwood Reade arrived in Sierra Leone, determined, as he put it, "to open up a new region, and to have a red line of my own upon the map."[8]

Reade was the nephew of Charles Reade, whose adventure novel *The Cloister and the Hearth* had been published in 1861. For ten years, the lesser-known Reade had also sought to make his mark as a writer, publishing an account of a journey to Gabon in search of gorillas, a history of the Druids, and three novels. His novels were slated by critics for the banality of the dialogue and the shallowness of the characters. As for his tendentious travelogue, it fared little better, and he might well have taken the opening sentences of his uncle's best seller as a description of his own situation. "Not a day passes over the earth, but men and women of no note do great deeds, speak great words, and suffer noble sorrows. Of these obscure heroes, philosophers, and martyrs, the greater part will never be known till that hour, when many that are great shall be small, and the small great; but of others the world's knowledge may be said to sleep; their lives and characters lie hidden from nations in the annals that record them."

In Freetown, Reade rented a cottage in the hills. The rainy season was breathing its last. Ink-colored clouds slipped back from the bush. Indigo

lizards with bright-orange necks peered and skittered across mildewed concrete, and at dusk bats flitted upward from the direction of the sea, mewing
and squealing.

The city overwhelmed him—rutted streets sown with Bermuda grass, the
stench of open drains, the cryptic exuberance of the Krio market women
who plied their daily trade in thread, ribbons, fishhooks, nails, and madras
cottons and sat at night in the high windows of frame houses overlooking
the harbor. He cut his official visits to the minimum, preferring the humid
wilderness of the hills to the hubbub of the city. Every morning he wrote, and
in the afternoons he attempted to assign Latin names to the curious lacquered
shrubs—black, deep purple, and mottled lime—that filled his garden.

It was not until December that his vague ambitions metamorphosed into
a feasible plan. During a visit to the government interpreter, Reade chanced
upon a copy of Alexander Laing's *Travels in the Timanee, Kooranko and Soolima
Countries.* That night he read it through and resolved to travel to the source of
the Niger in the remote borderlands between anglophone Sierra Leone and
francophone Guinea. His years of inertia and mediocrity were over. He would
fulfill Laing's ambition and connect his own name forever with the Niger.
At the same time, he would study firsthand customs that might throw new
light on the history of religion.

He left Freetown in January 1869. Although the Royal Geographical Society had lent him a sextant and artificial horizon to make precise measurements at the Niger source, Reade regarded the instruments as encumbrances
and left them behind. As for finding his way north, he placed every confidence in Laing's 1822 map. But the map was far from accurate, and it took
Reade many months before he reached the town of Falaba in the far north,
where the Yalunka chief, who had never before seen a white man, offered the
stranger hospitality and protection.

Through his servant and interpreter, Abdulai, Reade learned that the
chief's domain did not extend as far as the Niger, and that Falaba was at war
with the Fula town of Dantilia. Mindful of Laing's tribulations in Falaba
forty-five years earlier, Reade decided not to risk angering his host by an-
nouncing his plans to travel through Fula lands.

Every day, caravans of gold, ivory, and hides passed through Falaba.
Laden donkeys and scores of bearers filed through the great palisades of cot-
ton trees, heading south toward the coast. Reade talked to the caravaners,
who told him that the Joliba, or great river, that Europeans called the Niger,

was but a three-day march to the east. The impatient Englishman heard the same fabulous stories of the source that Laing had heard in his time.

In his journal, Reade anticipated his goal. "I shall associate my name forever with its course, and earn a place in the history of Africa, for I shall strike it higher by at least a hundred miles than any other European. The Niger is only fifty miles off: let me reach it, and I have my reputation!"

Five weeks passed. Unable to endure further delays, Reade told the ruler of his plans.

He was immediately rebuffed—Fulas besiege us, enemies live in that direction, the country is unsafe. I cannot let you go!

The explorer lapsed into melancholia. Even the capture and execution of a Fula spy failed to arouse him. "All has been in vain. I have done nothing. I have merely reached a point where another traveller has been. I am close to the Niger, and yet I might as well be a thousand miles away. Am I never to succeed? For ten years I have been writing and writing, and fiasco has followed fiasco; that is my own fault; I have only to curse my own incapacity. But here I have done all that a man could do. I selected my route with prudence; I have followed it up with resolution; I have patiently submitted to tedious delays and vexatious degradations—yet all is in vain. It seems that this passion for glory by which I am tormented is an evil spirit devouring my life. Had I not been ambitious I might have been happy; but what am I now? A man who has mistaken his vocation. A man who has climbed in public and has fallen, and who must go through life with the stigma of failure upon him. Even if I write a good book, people will always be able to say, 'Yes he did that well enough; but he broke down in Africa, you know.' And then I shall have to answer such questions as these: 'Why did you not go to the Niger when you were so close? Well, I would not have given up. Don't you think that Baker or Livingstone would have managed to get on somehow or other?'"

His mental and moral exhaustion was now exacerbated by the effects of dysentery and fever. Unable to leave his sickbed, he succumbed to hallucinations. Preparing for death, he penned a rambling letter to an imaginary mistress, declaring his fidelity, assuring her of his tenacity of purpose.

Despite malaria and despair, Reade lived to learn that during his illness the Fula had attacked Falaba and been repulsed. The road to the south was now open; he was free to return whence he came.

During his convalescence in Freetown, the colonial secretary paid Reade a visit and formally forbade him from making further forays into the interior.

Reade protested. "Had Major Laing found everything easy, he would have left nothing in this country for me, his successor! My failure is eating into my soul. I would not care for captivity or sickness if I had only done something! I will go at it again. I will not leave Africa til I have written my name somewhere on the map!"

A month later Reade set off for Falaba, this time travelling light, determined, as he put it, to live off the land.

This time the Yalunka chief raised no objections to the white man travelling east. Reade took this to mean that his will had finally prevailed. But the open road simply meant that military campaigns had been called off with the onset of the rains and the demands of planting.

And so Reade reached Dantilia, and two days later he found his way to the banks of the Niger.

Elephant grass cut his hands as he thrust his way to the river's edge. As he watched the turbid water slipping by under a somber sky, an immense sadness took hold of him. By finding the river, he had escaped the opprobrium of complete failure, yet he felt no sense of success.

As three canoes crossed the river toward him, he asked his guide where they came from. Sankaran, his guide, answered. You will need their permission to go further.

Reade opened his journal. He wrote: "I feel all unstrung; it seems to me as if I am in a dream."

The Sankaran men drew their canoes onto the greasy riverbank. Abdulai asked how far they were from the source of the Joliba.

There are slave hunters there, he was told. All the towns are spoiled.

Reade patiently extracted more information. The river near the source was called the Tembiko. It was two days distant. The source belonged to a Kuranko clan, the Koroma, who killed a black cow there every year, casting the head into the river as a sacrifice to a djinn. If the offering was accepted, the djinn brought the cow back to life; its head would reappear downstream, with ears pricked up and eyes wide open.

Reade had heard these stories before. But new to him were the Sankaran men's reports of gold in the Bouré country far to the east. Even if the gold does not exist, Reade thought, I might reach Bamako, Mungo Park's highest point on the Niger, and so unite Laing's discoveries with Park's. This surely would win me a celebrated place in the history of African exploration.

Forgetting about the Niger source, he arranged to be ferried across the river, and hastened on through unmapped lands, intoxicated by every vista. "This is mine," he exclaimed. "Here no European has been; it is Reade's Land! That hill, that river, that lake. I can call them what I please!"

He reached Bamako in September. Though the gold proved illusory, he was convinced that he had done more than enough to secure his reputation.

Back in England he presented an account of his travels to the Royal Geographical Society, only to be taken to task for his lack of firsthand observations and precise measurements, and to be reminded of the great value that the society set upon the discovery of the *source* of the Niger and the calculation of its *height* above sea level. Mere descriptions, culled from African informants, were worthless.

Your lack of scientific data is regrettable, he was told. And your romantic inclination and impetuosity unsuited to the business of exploration. But there is much to discover, and you have made a courageous beginning.

Humiliated by this condescension, Winwood Reade withdrew from society, forgot about Africa, and wrote an encyclopedic denunciation of the established church. *The Martyrdom of Man* was published in 1872 to scathing reviews.

He began to imagine the friendship of a refined and intellectual woman, and to dream of the patient understanding, esteem, and pure pleasure that such a woman might give an unjustly maligned man. He composed letters to his imaginary mistress, addressing her as "Margaret" and assuring her that he desired only her devotion and regard. Gradually, these letters brought him back to Africa and led to the publication of *The African Sketch-Book* in 1873.

Beset by heart and liver ailments, and struggling to complete a novel called *The Outcast*, Reade died in 1875. Ironically, his fame would come to him posthumously through *The Martyrdom of Man* that, by 1940, had gone into its twenty-fourth edition.

I have always been struck by the coincidence that Winwood Reade was writing his self-pitying tracts about disappointed ambition at the same moment the sixteen-year-old Arthur Rimbaud was writing against the world in which he had been raised, and already envisaging a place like Africa, "far from everywhere," where he might lose himself and become another person entirely. Ironically, it is only in giving up the dream of making one's mark that one can fully become part of these worlds where great rivers arise and new understandings may be born.

The same year that Reade died, Rimbaud wrote his last poem.

CHAPTER 11

Yonder

Ian is a strange child. He likes to be away by himself and can never be found when he is wanted.

—Rose Fairweather, c. 1905

There is a compelling passage in Siri Hustvedt's essay "Yonder" that immediately brought to my mind the life and work of the painter Ian Fairweather. Hustvedt was born in America of Norwegian parents, and her childhood map of the world "consisted of two regions only: Minnesota and Norway, my here and my there."[1] This was the "yonder" her father described as a place "between here and there," a place that could not be occupied without it becoming "here" and thereby creating another elusive and indeterminate yonder, elsewhere. As writers, Hustvedt and her husband, Paul Auster, were fascinated by the similarity between this genealogical or geographical utopia and the writing of fiction. For though one writes in solitude, one imagines oneself inside the minds of characters located in myriad cities, disparate landscapes, and many roomed mansions elsewhere. What Hustvedt and Auster do not mention is that this dislocation of consciousness, this awayness, can be a trap, dropping the writer out of this world into an imaginary space that claims him or obsesses her with all the power of a mirage.

Such was the case with the painter Ian Fairweather. Born in Scotland in 1891, he spent a solitary childhood with various aunts after his parents returned to India when he was six months old. When he was ten, his father retired from the army and settled on Jersey in the English Channel. But it was too late for this lonely child to form the bonds he had been denied. Without a close relationship with his mother, he could not develop a sense of himself through her, or with an-other, and he was driven to fashion his identity alone. In the absence of mirroring, his self-image was negative. And because he probably did not like himself very much, he was loath to seek in friendships and social contacts the affirmation that might change this view. Unwilling to take a chance on the future, he fell back on the past, imagining he might slough off his own mundane skin and so retrieve the paradise found in a mother's love or a close-knit family. The Orient would become this imagined Eden from which he had been expelled.

At nineteen he was commissioned officer in the First Cheshire Regiment. Taken prisoner on his second day at the front, he spent World War I illustrating a POW magazine and doing ink drawings inspired by Japanese art. After the war he enrolled at the Slade, found it stultifying, and escaped to Canada and then China (in 1929).

I saw my first Fairweathers in the National Gallery of Australia, Canberra, in the early 1980s, and I was immediately drawn to them. The work refused categorization. Cubism, Chinese calligraphy, and even Aboriginal sand painting were all suggested, but the paintings—made of synthetic polymer paint and gouache brushed onto sheets of cheap cardboard and allowed to drip or run— had a presence and mystery that compelled me to return to them, over and over again. While *Turtle and Temple Gong* suggested an oriental origin for the abstract images, and *Monastery* and *Marriage at Cana* had Christian echoes, I could find no facts about the artist except that, before his death in 1974, he had lived a life of poverty and solitude on an island off the North Queensland coast.

For many years I kept postcards of two of Fairweather's paintings on my writing desk,[2] recognizing in this restive and reclusive individual an affinity I could not fully fathom.

Perhaps it had something to do with my own life at that time. I had recently lost my wife. I lived on the dole. Devoted to the welfare of my teenage daughter, I found it hard to make ends meet, though never rued my austere existence, writing every morning, taking long walks around a nearby mountain, shopping and preparing meals, being there when my daughter needed me. Did I somehow divine in Fairweather's distinctive paintings a similar marginality, an echo of my own hermetic life? Was his down-to-earth palette of dull blues and grays, rust red, smudged lilac, and yellow ochre evidence of some nameless loss, or his abstractions, his fascination with the East, a sign of disenchantment with the West? Could one even make such connections between art and reality when art conjured up places and forms bearing no resemblance to what we know as the real?

This was the burning question for me. For while I lived a fairly isolated life, often alone with my thoughts or unsure of myself in the company of others, I wanted art to do justice to the world not by mirroring it but by entering deeply into it, and I wondered whether this could be achieved through solitary meditation as much as through social engagement. As with art, so with the intellectual life—one had recourse to artifice, abstraction, and the arcane, to be sure, but this distancing from the empirical immediate could only be justified, in my view, if it led to an enhanced or a novel understanding of the world that lies around us, so familiar that we forget to look at it, so pedestrian that we dismiss it from our minds. And so, as I enlarged my knowledge of Fairweather's oeuvre, I grew even more admiring of the ordinariness of the subjects that had captured his attention—fish traps in a river, a house yard, a market, a birdcage, a gateway, a bridge over a canal—and the unstable materials on which he worked—plywood, butcher's paper, and cardboard. All this corresponded with my own fascination with the imponderabilia of everyday life, and the way that the most banal events or objects may illuminate the world.

As the Japanese moved south from Manchuria in the early 1930s, Fairweather began to search for a place of refuge. He stayed in Bali until his meager funds ran out, then came to Australia in February 1934. His first impressions of Melbourne presaged my own, thirty years later, walking the dismal and deserted weekend streets like a lost soul.

> I seem to have done nothing but pursue with burning feet (my sandshoes are wearing rather thin) a way through endless Finchleys and Golders Greens seeking a break—an open space—any let up in this colossal monotony. There is no break—it is a whole—a matriarchy—a million perfect homes . . . and the Sundays—oh the Sundays—the Salvation Army prowl the empty streets.[3]

Fairweather was lucky. He fell in with a small group of modernists who admired his seriousness and superior draftsmanship. But within a year he moved on—to the Philippines, Shanghai, Peking, Japan, all the while sending work back to London, where it was exhibited in the Redfern Gallery to critical praise. In 1938 he returned to Australia, but when war was declared, he travelled to Thailand, Malaya, Indochina, Singapore, and Calcutta in the hope that he might be of use, even at forty-eight, to the British army. Back in Australia in 1943, he did odd jobs, lived rough—often among other outcasts—in a makeshift shack, a derelict house[4]—until, in an old lifeboat he had bought for a song, he made landfall on Bribie Island, north of Brisbane, where he lived and worked, on and off, for the rest of his life.

Patricia Anderson has suggested that Fairweather's nomadism was born of a need to transmute direct experience into memory. It is not real places, people, or events he paints but his recollections of them. He moved in order that only the memory of his previous life remained, purged of the hardships he had endured, metamorphosed into abstract images.[5]

Here was a man who described himself as "selectively gregarious," whom others would call "pathologically reclusive," "profoundly melancholy," and "a strange, shy man with a cultured voice"[6] who painted at night in the penumbra of a hurricane lamp as though his Sisyphus-like task was to screen out the dross of his earthly existence in order to illuminate or protect an image of a world that could not be touched by the brutality of war, the cruelty of his fellow men, the drudgery of daily life, and the relentless passage of time. The more I read of Fairweather's ceaseless travels, his complete indifference to his personal appearance or home comforts, his penury and solitude, and his ability to paint under the most appallingly difficult conditions, the more I wondered whether this was a form of madness, though whether the blessed insanity of the maenad[7] and the bacchant[8] or the cursed insanity of the psychotic I could not say.[9]

Who in his right mind would have attempted to cross from Darwin to Timor on an improvised raft, as Fairweather did in April 1952?

Murray Bail calls it the act of a paranoid person. Hell, for this artist, was other people, who exhibited his work without his knowledge or consent, gloated and jeered at him, wished him ill. Like the hapless Hurtle Duffield in Patrick White's *The Vivisector*, Fairweather was the crook-necked white pullet that the other hens pecked at because it was different.[10] To leave the henhouse seemed the only solution. And so, after months of research in the Darwin Public Library, but with minimal navigation skills, he found materials in rubbish tips and scrap yards to build his raft. With three aluminum aircraft fuel tanks, a sail made from half-rotten hessian food parachutes, and ropes, wedges, fencing wire, and other bric-a-brac, he assembled his imitation Kon-Tiki, stashed his supplies of tinned food and water, and set sail. Sixteen days later, and already given up for dead, he made landfall on the island of Roti, west of Timor.

Perhaps, as Norman O. Brown suggests, madness is not the word for what we seek, but mystery. Whether we favor Dionysian excess or Apollonian discipline, we crave what the sedentary life of suburbia or academia cannot give—what Ezra Pound referred to as the mysteries that lie beyond the doors of "the outer courts of the same."[11] Yet, for we who spend so many hours writing, thinking, painting, sculpting, weaving, or practicing music in solitude, setting worldly concerns aside in order to conjure the voices, images, and forms that come unbidden only when we open our minds to them, do we not risk falling into fantasy and losing touch with the world in our haste to praise the ineffable, in our attachment to contemplation, in our search for the secret, the esoteric, and the occult? As Nance Lightfoot puts it, upbraiding Hurtle Duffield for being an "intellectual no-hope artist," indifferent to other people: "While you're all gummed up in the great art mystery, they're alive, and breakun their necks for love."[12]

Fairweather made no bones about his disenchantment with the Western world. In a letter to Lina Bryans in 1943, he wrote, "The painting I have done has always been an escape from our Western world—surrounded by it I seem to get sunk."[13] Like the islands on which he found temporary refuge or relief, Asia seemed to be a haven into which he could sail in his imagination, so that the quasi-calligraphic motifs on many of his works resemble screens or bars that give sanctuary to the vulnerable and indefinite figures within— mother and child, family groups, children, dancers, bathers, monks, and even the artist himself—all of whom possess the luminosity of stained glass.

HEADS IN THE CLOUDS

In Cambridge recently, a friend described her guitar teacher to me. He was a young man, so devoted to his music that he spent eight hours a day practicing, followed by hours reading poems by Lorca and Neruda that would help him refine his understanding of certain passages in pieces by Brazilian and Cuban composers. As my friend put it, "His head is in the clouds." I immediately thought of Ian Fairweather, and the metaphorical contrast that informs so much Western thought, at least since the Enlightenment, between the ethereal and the material. To have a strong sense of reality is to have one's feet firmly planted on the ground, to be down to earth. Reality is a matter of addressing the needs of income and livelihood; all else places one in jeopardy of becoming distracted, absentminded, even delusional. But surely what we need to know is when to let go and when to engage, when to submit and when to act. The imagination is as necessary to our health as the workaday imperatives with which it is contrasted. Just as sleep and dreaming are as vital to our health as food and water, so we sometimes need to distance ourselves from the world, the better to engage with it. *Reculer pour mieux sauter.* The difficulty is using art, religion, ritual, or fantasy to get some distance from the world that has become too much for us to bear or grasp without losing touch with that world. And again, I am struck by the recurring metaphors of storm and strife—of the world experienced as a minatory force, potentially overwhelming, engulfing, buffeting, drowning, swamping—and the countervailing images of calm, of water unruffled by wind, of stillness and silence—images of what we need if we are to hold our own, refresh our minds, and endure that buffeting.

I sometimes ask myself whether people living in tribal societies are better able to get the balance right.

But this broaches the question as to the status of thinkers, artists, and storytellers in such societies.

Early anthropologists regarded "preliterate" or "primitive" people as being so absorbed in the practicalities of everyday life that all of their ritual, art, and thought was subservient to the exigencies of survival. No one had either the leisure or the incentive for abstract thought, metaphysical speculation, rational inquiry, or systematic scientific experimentation. As Paul Radin wrote in 1927, it was widely assumed that there was "a dead level of intelligence among primitive peoples, that the individual is completely swamped by and submerged in the group, that thinkers and philosophers as such do not exist."[14] But in his determination to refute the views of Cassirer and Lévy-Bruhl, Radin promoted an equally spurious view of the primitive philosopher as skeptic, critic, ethicist, metaphysician, cosmologist, and sage. Instead of demystifying the Brahmanical conception of the philosopher as hero—a man of genius, capable of pondering the world from afar and grasping its inner workings—Radin and his successors looked for primitive philosophers who conformed to the Western stereotype.[15]

The metaphysical bias of Western philosophy has not only led European thinkers to measure or explain non-Western beliefs and practices solely in terms of their logical coherence or correspondence with objective reality; it has distracted us from exploring what Malinowski called "context of situation,"[16] namely, the ways in which speech and thought reflect personal, cultural, and practical interests that effectively delimit the range of what can be said or thought. Rather than eschew the view that language and thought can

transcend circumstance, many non-Western philosophers find their own traditions wanting when compared with the allegedly "systematic" and "speculative" thought of philosophers like Kant,[17] or focus on local sages and ritual
specialists who bear comparison with the hierophants of Western thought.
In this view, Africa appears to be interesting only insofar as it approximates
Western conceptions of civilization—monumental architecture, monothe-
istic religion, centralized states, advanced technologies—or possesses philosophers like Plato, sacred or learned texts, and deep cosmological knowledge
such as that falsely attributed to the Dogon sage Ogotemmêli by the French
ethnographer Marcel Griaule.[18] Even those philosophers who criticize this
kind of ethnocentrism, arguing that "the traditional and non-traditional
must be granted *de jure*, equal and reciprocal elucidatory value as theoretical
alternatives,"[19] turn to the "fathers of secrets" to elucidate the "high culture" or
"great tradition"[20] rather than explore the existential quandaries of ordinary
people which, in my view, is the milieu from which all thought springs.

It is to Michel Foucault that we owe our most trenchant critique of this
Aristotelian view of the intellectual as someone whose power of reason and
capacity for systematic understanding depend on his detachment from the
world rather than his participation in it. But we can go further than Foucault
and argue that thought is not merely an expression of a prevailing episteme
in which everyone participates to some extent; it is occasioned by existential
travails that cannot be reduced to any discursive regime or cultural ethos. In
other words, all thought is grounded in the situation of the thinker, and is an
attempt to come to terms with that situation, through stories and fantasies,
experimentation and speculation, reading and reflection, conversation and
consultation. As John Dewey observed, "thinking is not a case of spontaneous combustion; it does not occur just on 'general principles.' There is something specific which occasions and evokes it," namely, "some perplexity, confusion, or doubt."[21] Crisis provokes critique.

Where then, in any tradition, Melanesian, African, or European, does
thought reside?

It does not necessarily find expression in the work of great minds, isolated
in ivory towers, accessing libraries, using abstract language, scorning "low"
or "popular" culture, and proclaiming universal truths. Nor need it be located in myth, cosmology, proverbial wisdom, and beliefs (in witchcraft,
sorcery, ancestral influence, and ritual forms), as Wiredu and Hallen suggest.
Philosophy is neither a privileged vocation nor an activity that takes place in

a protected location. It is a mode of being-in-the-world, and as such it is inextricably a part of what we do, what we feel, and what we reckon with in the course of our everyday lives. This is the essence of Nietzsche's argument—that philosophical thinking is, like all conscious thinking, an "instinctive activity," and that every great philosophy is "a confession on the part of its author and a kind of involuntary and unconscious memoir."[22] It is a view that Foucault and Lévi-Strauss insisted on: that thought finds conscious expression in us, but is not necessarily generated by a self-conscious, thinking subject. For Heidegger, thought is similarly grounded—and may be compared with dwelling and building; it *is* a mode of constructive activity, a way of inhabiting the world.[23] For Heidegger's student Hannah Arendt, thought belongs to the vita activa—the social field of inter-est, interaction, and intersubjectivity. Here it makes its appearance as thoughtfulness, mindfulness, care, discernment, and judgment. For Kuranko, such social skills define what it is to be a moral person. Personhood (*morgoye*) consists in having regard for others (*gbiliye*) and showing them respect (*lembé*)—recognizing their status, paying them their due, contributing to their well-being. At the same time, personhood is consummated in self-restraint, bringing one's emotions under control, weighing one's words before speaking, thinking of the wider context in which one lives:

Morgo kume mir' la I konto I wo fo la (whatever word a person thinks of, that will he speak; i.e., think before you speak, lest you blurt out stupid ideas).

I mir' la koe mi ma, I wo l ke la (you thought of that, you do that; i.e., think before you act, lest your actions belie your intentions).

As my friend Sewa Koroma put it:

When people do things or say things, you have to think twice, think why, why they're doing this, is it because of this? I'm young. I've got to think that even if the [Diang] chief lived a long life or I die, I have kids coming up, and if I have access to the chieftaincy they might be interested, you know. People don't write history, they don't write things down. You have to remember everything. We say, *i tole kina i bimba ko* [your ear is as wise as your grandfather's words]. When my father was young he was listening to the elders talk about things that happened long before his time. Then he told me those stories, and I will tell them to my son. They're not written down, but if you listen you will know them. Those are the things you have to think about, that you have to know deep down. Ade [Sewa's wife] says, "You think too much," but I tell her there are things you have to think about, things beyond normal, so that you'll know.

Clearly, reflective thought involves getting beyond oneself—thinking of one's immediate situation from the standpoint of one's forebears' experience and understanding. This is not a quest for a transcendent view, but for identifying those factors and forces that lie in the penumbral regions beyond everyday, self-centered awareness. Reflective thought is not a matter of plumbing the psychic depths of other minds or achieving empathic understanding; rather, it is focused on one's relationships *with* others. The Kuranko refuse to speculate about other people's experience. "I am not inside them" (*n'de sa bu ro*), one is told, or "I do not know what is inside" (*n'de ma konto lon*). Empathic understanding is, moreover, not only thought to be impossible; it is regarded as largely irrelevant to behaving as a moral being possessing social intelligence or common sense (*hankilime*). The Kuranko emphasis is less on being of one mind than on moving with, working with, eating with, being with, and sitting with others (often in amicable silence). Accordingly, one of the greatest challenges to a Western anthropologist is how to acquire these techniques of practical mastery and mutuality in which a knowledge of the motives, mind-sets, and sentiments of others counts for far less than one's social skills in *interacting* convivially with them. As Paul Ricoeur phrased this in his last writing, our goal is not an identification with the other, which is, anyway, "neither possible nor desirable," but "an accompanying" that means that no one will have to live or die alone.[24]

A STORYTELLER'S STORY

I may seem to have strayed a long way from the life and work of Ian Fairweather. But I want to explore the thesis that art and philosophy carry the risk of estranging us from the world at the same time that they hold out the promise of helping us reengage more adroitly with it. It is perhaps this ambiguity that makes us suspicious of thinkers and artists, for they unsettle our certainties as well as show us new ways of understanding our existence. And so, in turning to the life and work of a Kuranko storyteller, I hope to bring into sharper relief the struggle that lies at the heart of all imaginative activity, both intellectual and artistic, to strike and sustain a balance between distancing oneself from the world and achieving a more vital involvement with it.

Flying over northern Sierra Leone, you see villages like islands in a sea of grassland and forest, interrupted by granite inselbergs and crisscrossed by

dirt paths and roads. This contrast between wilderness and settlement translates into a symbolic antinomy that is basic to local worldviews, narratives,
and rituals. The bush stands for awayness—an antinomian, extrasocial space
of untrammeled power and peril that is, paradoxically, the source of life-
giving energy, in the form of fertile farmland, game animals, herbal medicines, and bush spirits (djinn). While the town is a moral space, governed by
custom and law, it is only by venturing beyond the town that its vitality can
be sustained, and almost all Kuranko stories are allegories of the struggle to
reconcile the competing demands of being a part of a community and being
independent of it. This struggle also plays out in the mind of every storyteller, for in the questing hero the fabulist invokes a figure that stands apart
from the community yet whose discoveries in the wilderness may bring to
that community the vital powers, magical medicines, musical instruments,
and divinatory skills without which it could not exist. The stories may be set
in a remote and mythical place, a long time ago, but they are about the quandaries of life in the here and now. They may appear to be traditional, but they
are also the inventions of the living—imaginative means of coming to terms
with the complexities of existence.

Unlike most of my Kuranko informants, Keti Ferenke would never explain things away with the stock phrases "that is how it happened" (*maiya ta
ra nya na*), "that is how our ancestors let it happen" (*ma bimban' ya ta nya na*),
or "that is what we encountered" (*maiya min ta ra*); rather, he would address
every situation as a moral quandary demanding discussion and, hopefully,
resolution. The folktale (*tilei*) was the perfect vehicle for this pedagogy. Since
this narrative genre was ostensibly make-believe, a form of entertainment,
Keti Ferenke could cunningly conceal his serious and often provocative opinions in the stories he composed. Moreover, he could create his own stories
and pass them off as part of the canon. In Keti Ferenke I found a man with
an ironic and critical sense of his own culture, someone who respected conventional wisdom but saw that events in the real world constantly called that
wisdom into question.

Keti Ferenke's ability to observe his society from the margins stemmed,
undoubtedly, from the troubled circumstances of his early life. But though
he endured loss, he did not—like Ian Fairweather—suffer lovelessness, which
may explain why his view from the edge did not entail withdrawal from the
world but, rather, a deeply sympathetic engagement with others whose lives
had also been touched by tragedy.

The first set of events that would impact on him occurred before he was born.

For many years the chieftaincy of Diang had devolved within the Ferenke family. When Keti Ferenke's grandfather, Sewa Magba Koroma, died, the chief's son, Samaran Bala Koroma, succeeded him. But it was Bala's brother, Mamadu Sandi, who wielded the real power, a power that he abused by assaulting people, stealing other men's wives, and generally throwing his weight around. In this insufferable situation, a certain Alhaji Magba Kamara, whose mother hailed from Diang, decided to intervene. Having had a few years of schooling, Magba wrote a letter to the British district commissioner that purported to be from an exasperated and weary chief Bala, asking that he be allowed to resign the chieftaincy. Magba took the letter to Bala and explained that it was from the government and thus required his signature before development work in Diang could be approved. The illiterate Bala thus signed away his chieftaincy, and the staff of office was taken from him.

Elections for a new chief were now called, and candidates presented themselves from the two ruling lineages of the Koroma clan—the "Magbas" and the "Ferenkes."

At this time rumors had spread that the new paramount chief would be a Muslim. But since none of the candidates were Muslims, people were mystified. Fearing the worst, Mamadu Sandi and his followers drove the Muslim Mandingos from Kondembaia, the main town in Diang. But some of the old men knew of whom the diviners had been speaking, and they travelled to Kono in search of Sheku Magba, a young man who had been apprenticed to a Muslim teacher at an early age and in whom many of the Magba family placed their hopes.

Sheku returned home to find himself at the center of arguments among the Magbas, some of whom felt he was too young to be chief, as well as attacked by the Ferenkes, who did not want their power to devolve to the junior line, or to a Muslim.

However, the elections were won by the Magbas, Sheku Magba became paramount chief, and the Ferenkes became politically marginalized.

Not only political strife cast its shadows over Keti Ferenke's early life. His sister and brother both died when they were young, and in his tenth or eleventh year, tragedy struck again.

When his maternal grandmother died in Kamadugu Sukurela (a ten-mile walk from Kondembaia), Keti Ferenke's mother asked him to go at once to Tongoma in Kono to inform his classificatory sister of the death and bring her back to Kondembaia for the funeral. But his mother was suffering from a severe headache and Keti Ferenke was reluctant to leave her.

Only when she insisted did he leave. It was the twenty-ninth of the month before Ramadan. Two days later he reached Tongoma and informed his sister that their grandmother had died. But it was now Ramadan, and Keti Ferenke's brother-in-law would not allow his wife to travel until the fast month had ended.

While he was away in Tongoma, Keti Ferenke's mother died. People were wailing, "Ferenke has not come yet, Ferenke has not come yet, Ferenke has not come yet." Although the tragic news had reached towns throughout the chiefdom, people kept the news from Keti Ferenke, and he only learned of what had happened in his absence when he returned to Kondembaia and found himself in the middle of the funeral rites. It was now the middle of the month of Ramadan.

On the last day of the month Keti Ferenke's father went to the mosque. It was a Friday. But as Kona Sumban joined the others to pray, he began trembling and could not stand without support. People urged him to go home and rest, but he insisted he would be all right. As prayers ended, it was clear to everyone that Kona Sumban was seriously ill. They helped him to his house, but he died later that day. "It was a terrible thing," Keti Ferenke remembered. "From Friday, through Saturday, until Sunday, no one could bury him because his death had been so sudden and so strange."

In explaining these distant events to me, Keti Ferenke spoke fatalistically. "What Allah had destined had happened." But he also spoke of how he was received into his father's elder brother's household and cared for as a son. "My father had gone, but chief Bala was still alive. So I was not heartbroken. I found no fault with my elder father, who provided bridewealth for me to marry and cared for me as a father. Indeed, I feel that my own father never died. So my heart is at peace."

What I could not ask, and did not know how to ask, was whether his skill in composing thought-provoking stories had helped him make a virtue of his marginality.

In Keti Ferenke's comments on the value of intelligence, one glimpses an answer to this question.

Consider the following exposition on the power of social nous or intelligence (hankili):

To start with, my great-great-grandfather was a chief. Down to my grandfather, they were all chiefs. Until my father, they were chiefs. Now, when you are born into a ruling house you will be told many things. If you are a fool you'll be none the wiser, but if you are clever you will inspect everything carefully. And when you lie down, you will think over certain things. If you do this, it is good. That is how I think of things.

We say *kina wo* and *kina wo* [near homophones]. They are not one [the first means "beehive." the second means "elder"]. If you hear *kina* [elder], he knows almost everything. But if you hear *kina* [beehive], it does not know anything. The elder could be found in the younger, and the younger could be found in the elder.

Even if a person is a child but behaves like an elder, then he is an elder. If he thinks like an elder, then he is an elder. Even if a person is old and senior, if he behaves like a child, then he is a child. Therefore, this matter of seniority comes not only from the fact that one is born first, or from the fact that one is big and strong; it also concerns the manner in which one behaves and does things. For example, you will see some old men who have nothing; they are not called "big men" [*morgo ba*, "elders"]. But some young men have wealth; because of that, they are called *morgo ba*. Therefore, whatever Allah has put in your head, that is what will make you what you are. I am speaking now, but some of these words of wisdom [*kuma kore*] that I am explaining to you are not known by everyone. You may ask a man and he may know them. But I have explained them to you. Therefore, am I not the elder? Therefore, if you hear the word *kina* you should know that it is intelligence [*hankili*] that really defines it.

Where Keti Ferenke and I differed was in the way we explained intellectual giftedness. Where he saw it as innate—a divine gift—I saw it as partly genetic, but mostly acquired. Yet our *experience* of creative apperception was identical, for creative ideas and "divine" inspiration were seen to arise on the thresholds between sleep and wakefulness, night and day, confusion and clarity.

"It is Allah who endows a person with the ability to think and tell stories," Keti Ferenke told me. "It was my destiny to tell stories. When my father went to a diviner before I was born, the diviner told him that his next-born child would be very clever." These remarks are consonant with the Kuranko idea that a storyteller simply "sets down" or "lays out" something that has been given to him or put into his mind; he is, therefore, a *til'sale*, "one who sets down *tileinu* (stories)." In this sense a storyteller is like a diviner. The diviner is "one who lays out pebbles," though it is God or a bush spirit who implants the idea of how to interpret the patterns in the diviner's mind.

"When you are told something," Keti Ferenke said, "it is good if it stays in your mind. Ideas come into my head, just like that. I am not asleep. I am not in a dream. But when I think of them, I put them together as a story. I could never stop thinking of stories, though I could stop myself telling them." And he went on to describe how, as he worked on his farm or lounged in his hammock at home, he would try to develop a narrative that did justice to the idea that had been seeded in his mind, bringing it to life in an entertaining and edifying way.

Not only did ideas come to him when he was relaxed and susceptible to "divine" (we might say "unconscious") inspiration; it soon became clear to me that his stories themselves were plotted, like folktales throughout the world, as a series of critical episodes or encounters, usually three in number, interrupting the narrative flow and creating moments of impasse and heightened suspense that are preludes to a breakthrough, a surprising intervention, a novel perspective. In Kuranko stories, these moments of hiatus and tension usually occur at a socio-spatial threshold—a river's edge, a ford, a crossroads, a bridge, the perimeter of a village, or chiefdom—or at the temporal borderland between the rainy and dry seasons, or night and day. Spatial and seasonal boundaries thus provide the Kuranko with concrete images of existential limits in the same way that images of the no-man's-land between *ius humanum* and *ius divinum,* or of a censoring ego that regulates traffic across the threshold between the unconscious and conscious, provide the European social imaginary with its metaphors of border situations. But in both lifeworlds, it is quasi-human figures—djinn and fetishes,[25] scapegoats and homo sacer[26]—that demarcate and embody the ambiguous zone where we cease to be recognizable to ourselves yet may see ourselves more completely than at any other time.

In Kuranko stories, these moments of maximum suspense are not only signified spatially by images of borders; they are viscerally experienced as a shift from narrative to song. At such moments of narrative hiatus, the storyteller's voice is joined with a chorus of voices, adults and children alike all chiming in. Signaling a transition from one critical episode to another, songs not only increase the intensity of audience participation; they enable everyone to actively share in the telling of the tale rather than remain spellbound as passive listeners. Not only does the song mediate an individual listener's close identification with the protagonist, who is stuck in a quandary and sings in sorrow or for supernatural help; the song helps break the impasse or spell, allowing the story to proceed toward its denouement.

Structurally, therefore, every Kuranko story encapsulates the interrupted rhythm of life itself—its periods of unreflective routine, its unpredicted moments of adversity and bewilderment, its ritualized return to normalcy. Kuranko stories play out, as it were, the existential aporias of everyday life— the descent of order into chaos, the desolating losses that follow death or migration, the estrangement of kin, the brutality of power, the falling out of friends. Like other forms of play (*tolon*), Kuranko stories safely enact, in ways that admit of artificial resolution, the dilemmas of life. But the operative word is "artificial," for everyone knows that life can never be cajoled into conforming to the scenarios one wishes upon it, and it is not for nothing that stories are told in the twilight zone between day and night, between waking and sleeping, when one can for a moment accept the illusion that what one can imagine or think is also a measure of what one can actually do.

CHAPTER 12

Reading *Siddhartha* to Freya at Forest Lake

Then one is no longer disturbed by the play of opposites.

—Patañjali

It was the summer before our daughter, Freya, began high school, and my wife and I had rented a cabin at Forest Lake. Freya brought Hermann Hesse's *Siddhartha* along. She was obliged to read the book before her first week of classes but was finding it hard going. The prose was tautologous and inelegant, the philosophy obtuse, and it was only a matter of time before she asked if I could read it to her and explain what it was about. And so we sat on the porch together in the evening, as a ruby-throated hummingbird flickered at the nectar-filled bird feeder and a fisherman in an aluminum dinghy drifted slowly around the edge of the lake, casting his fly upon the water. I tried to explain the Eastern view of enlightenment: how one seeks to distance oneself from the distractions of this world—the craving for wealth or fame, possessions, home comforts, luxury goods—in order to be more attuned to the mysteries of existence. But to Freya, at fourteen, it was inexplicable that one should deny oneself the pleasures of life and go wandering in a forest, neglecting one's appearance, depriving oneself of basic comforts, and exposing oneself to the elements.

"But there are elemental pleasures," I said, "that are different from the pleasures of everyday life. When you go swimming in the lake, and go out far, don't you sometimes feel as if your body and the water flowed together, that the swimming was so natural and effortless that it just happens, and you are in your element, like a fish?"

Freya understood.

"That is close to what Siddhartha sought," I said. "That oneness with the world."

"But I like clothes," Freya said. "I like looking good. I like good food. Is that wrong?"

"No," I said. "But we can bring a lot of unhappiness upon ourselves by thinking that we absolutely must have these things if we are to have a life. One doesn't have to live without these things, but it may be useful to know that the greatest fulfillment in life does not come from them. That is why people sometimes give things up, at least for a while, depriving themselves of sleep, food, shelter, speech, and sex. It helps them get their lives into perspective, to see what is real and what is illusory."

"Then why did Siddhartha have an affair with Kamala, and become a merchant, and live the life of the world? Why didn't he stay in the forest, or go with the Buddha?"

"Because the road of excess can also lead to the palace of wisdom. Because overindulging in the things of this world can have the same effect as depriving yourself of them. These are all experiments with yourself, as you search for the right balance between being a part of the world and remaining apart from it. Sometimes we need to take a break from the world, like coming here to Forest Lake. But if we lived here all year round, we might get bored with it. Same with books. They can help us understand the world, but sometimes it is good to get away from books and simply experience things as they are, like this lake and the pines around it. That was why Siddhartha could not follow the Buddha, as Govinda did. The *teachings* of the Buddha would have got in the way of Siddhartha understanding the meaning of those teachings in his own way, in his time."

"I know that," Freya said. "Sometimes I don't listen to my teachers or my books, but if I am interested in a subject I read about it in my own way and learn about it for myself."

I sit on the jetty as the sun goes down, inhaling the dry odor of pines, the scent of resin. A late breeze disturbs the surface of the lake. I also feel it on my face. On the yonder shore—a splash of sunlight on a mown lawn, a red barn. Nearer at hand—trampled pinecones, fallen branches, moss-covered stones, saplings, and a bough lifted and badgered by a sudden gust of wind. Below me, the shallows are amber in the sunlight. A shoal of small fish passes through them as through a glass of ale. The wind flips the page of my notebook against the back of my hand, and I stop writing.

In my amateurish attempts to explain Buddhism to my daughter, I had become aware of the foolishness of trying to characterize any human life in terms of a worldview, religious or secular.[1] To explain the life of an individual Buddhist in terms of Buddhist scripture would be as absurd as looking for the Sermon on the Mount in the life of a Christian. "The whole is the false,"[2] Adorno wrote, turning Hegel on his head. What one discovers in any biography is never an entire culture or ethos, but only fragments. A life is an improvisation in which those fragments represent our fitful, opportunistic inventions of a language that speaks to our changing circumstances.

I began to think of my own life, then, and of its many metamorphoses, its unceasing movement between solitude and sociality.

The role of outsider came easily to me; it enabled me to make a virtue out of my social ineptitude. Roaming the hills around my hometown, walking alone in the bush, or tracing the course of a local stream, I was at peace. Among my peers, I felt lost. Yet I was determined to redress this imbalance, to overcome my shyness, to write my way into the world.

That willpower was so necessary to achieving this indicates how habituated I had become to solitude. And in times of great adversity, when my will failed me, I would yield to my older impulse and retreat from the world as a hurt animal might retreat to a mountain lair to lick its wounds. Alone I might be, but never lonely.

When I took up yoga, I found a new pretext for distancing myself from the world, just as Hesse may have found in Buddhist notions of nonattachment a rationale for abandoning his wife and children, for whom he felt deep ambivalence. So absorbed did I become in yogic practices for disciplining body, breath, and mind that I was scarcely aware of how remote and disinterested I now seemed to my friends. All balance between self-absorption and worldly involvement was lost. I could sit in a full lotus, or stand equally still, on my head or my feet, but I moved among my friends carelessly or indifferently. I achieved physical strength and poise, calmness and concentration of mind, but at the expense of my ability to respond fully and sympathetically to others. Indeed, it took me several years to realize that yoga, as the word itself implies, is a way of integrating or harmonizing self and world, and not a justification for world renunciation. This view was underscored by B. K. S. Iyengar, who established the tradition in which I trained.

There is a . . . balance to be achieved between the philosophical life and the practical life.[3]

Religious life is not to withdraw from the everyday world . . . I am within and I am without. That is known as balance. If we can live like that, it is religion.[4]

People sometimes ask me whether it is possible to practise yoga and lead a normal family life. Is my own example not enough to give you the answer? In my early days, many people tried to tempt me to become a sannyasin. I said, "No, I will marry. I will see the struggles and the upheavals of the world, and I will practise." So I am an old soldier. I have six children and I still practise yoga. I have not abandoned my responsibilities towards other people. I can live in life as a witness without being part and parcel of the action. I may be here, I may speak, I may help other people, but I can become completely detached in a split second. That is what yoga has given me.[5]

It is impossible to speak of the practice of yoga without addressing the question of belief—of the worldview in which the practices are embedded. Although yoga has been understood very differently in different Indian traditions, and by different Indian practitioners and preceptors,[6] there would appear to be greater discontinuities between Indian and Western conceptions of yoga than there are within India itself. Iyengar's autobiographical essays and yoga commentaries, for example, are so replete with allusions to Hindu religious and social values, prophetic dreams and visions, ayurvedic medical philosophy and Patañjali's *Yoga Sūtras*, that one could easily conclude that yoga was intrinsically Indian and only partially within the reach of Westerners.[7] Two arguments can be made against this assumption. First, the ethical restraints (yama) and disciplines (nyama), named by Patañjali as the first two branches of yoga, are not unique to yoga. It is only with the third and fourth branches—techniques of the body and breath—that yoga proper begins.[8] As Iyengar notes, mastery and enlightenment can be attained through diligence in one or two of the branches and do not require mastery of them all. "Mahatma Gandhi did not practice all the aspects of yoga. He only followed two of its principles—non-violence and truth. . . . If a part of yama could make Mahatma Gandhi so great, so pure, so honest and so divine, should it not be possible to take another limb of yoga—asana—and through it reach the highest level of spiritual development?"[9] Second, yoga is universal. Citing Patañjali's description of yoga as sarvabhauma (bhauma = world; sarva = all), Iyengar asks: "Two thousand five hundred years ago Patañjali did not divide East from West. Why should we do so today?"[10] However, Iyengar's stronger argument for the universality of yoga derives not from Patañjali, whose knowledge of the "West" was probably limited and indirect, but from his own experience as a well-travelled teacher and therapist who has seen that many of the physical ailments and existential quandaries that human beings come up against are similar throughout the world. "So do not get carried away by the words which are used in different countries," he concludes. "The essence is the same. Look into the essence and do not be misled by the names."[11]

This was borne out by my own practice of Iyengar yoga over a period of thirty-seven years. The eight "limbs" of yoga, as enunciated by Patañjali— yama (ethical constraints), niyama (purifying disciplines), asanas (techniques of the body), pranayama (techniques of the breath), pratyahara (inwardness), dharana (inward focus), dhyana (trained contemplation), samadhi (the peace that passeth all understanding)—are neither exotic nor uniquely Indian. Indeed, yoga practice does not, of itself, require or entail any particular ethos or worldview. One may become a vegetarian, as I did, but there is no *necessary* relationship between doing yoga and embracing an ethic of ahimsa (nonviolence), truthfulness (satya), or nonpossessiveness (aparigraha). Nor does it follow that assuming postures named after various animal and plant species implies a totemic or shamanistic disposition.[12] As for yogic training, this is a matter of practice, not precept. As Iyengar put it, "To a beginner, do not explain; just put him in the correct pose (to give him the feeling, the understanding). One can know all theory, yet in practice know nothing."[13]

Not everyone would share this nondoctrinaire point of view. For many people, practice and credo are mutually entailed. To merely go through the motions of meditating or praying without experiencing the religious rationale for the practice is bad faith. Belief is seen as a script or blueprint that guides our actions, and our actions should, it is implied, bear out our belief.

My own view is very different. That one may experience, through yoga practice, an exhilarating consonance of body and mind, and even, at times, experience an undistracted, euphoric state of being in which the boundaries between oneself and the world disappear cannot be taken as evidence that one has attained a superior state, let alone a divine one, or that one is now warranted to capitalize on one's experience as a guru or sage. Experience, in itself, proves nothing. It gives no good grounds for making epistemological or eschatological claims. It is to Kant that we owe this argument against what he termed "the parlogisms of pure reason," in particular, the mistake of moving from a necessary feature of our *representations* of the world to a conclusion about the world's actual *nature*. We may have a strong sense of being substantial selves that remain consistent over time, or we may have had an overwhelming experience of satori (disappearance of the ego, union with the One), but in neither case can we draw ontological conclusions about the nature of the experiencing subject or the objective nature of the cosmos. Accordingly, to momentarily enjoy a sense of union between body and mind does not mean that Descartes's separation of body (res extensa) from mind (res cogitans) is untenable, any more than the ability to still one's discursive consciousness is a sign of enlightenment. As Agehananda Bharati puts it, "If there is some ulterior Truth somehow linked to [mystical] experience, we cannot know it."[14] Moreover, the zero-experiences that Christians call grace and Hindus call samadhi may never come to those whose entire lives have been devoted to attaining these states, yet come unbidden to many who have never gone in quest of them.[15]

Our tendency to ontologize and exoticize experience is understandable. Without a strong personal experience of God's presence and power, it would be difficult to sustain a belief in His existence. But enlightenment may also be understood as not finding God, of being able to resist jumping to the conclusion that certain experiences confirm the existence of one of the extrahuman or extrasensory entities with which every social imaginary is replete, of seeing these entities as props or means of coping with and finding satisfaction in a world that defies our best attempts to know and control it. Divinities—like subtle bodies, biofields, astral forces, and auras—are heuristic, not ontological, categories. To place them in brackets, suspending the question as to whether they really exist, does not necessarily lead us to dismiss them as illusions, for they are *necessary* illusions that can have real consequences for our well-being.

Agehananda Bharati has labored these same points in his own attempts to demystify religious experience. "Mystical experience does not confer the status of objective existence on what has been experienced," he writes. Nor does the existence or nonexistence of the Godhead make "the slightest difference to my meditation or my ritual."[16] In short, Bharati's embrace of Indian mythology, theology, and ritualism bypasses belief. Moreover, it entails the view that the bonds of belief are inimical to emancipation.[17] Iyengar's approach to yoga is remarkably similar. Yoga practice is not grounded in belief, he observes, but faith. "When I was suffering from tuberculosis and got healthy through yoga, I did not believe that yoga was going to cure me. It cured me. That gave me faith. Faith is not belief. It is more than belief. You may believe something and not act on it, but faith is something you experience. You cannot ignore it. If you ignore it, it is not faith. Belief is objective—you may take it or leave it. But faith is subjective—you cannot throw it out."[18]

There are echoes here of Karl Jaspers's view that faith is neither a possession nor a form of knowledge.[19] Rather, it belongs to the perennially uncertain space between all that lies within our grasp and all that eludes it.

The impulse to retreat from the world may thus be understood as a strategy for recovering a sense of security and stability in the face of circumstances that overwhelm us, a way of standing still or reorienting ourselves when worldly involvements bewilder or break us. Faith is a recognition that it is possible to come to terms with such experience, to periodically die to this world and reenter it anew.

In a BBC interview with Wole Soyinka, the seventy-two-year-old Nigerian writer is sitting on a stone wall. Behind him is a dirt road and some mango trees. The man who spent two years and four months in prison during the Nigerian civil war—a year and ten months of it in solitary confinement—speaks of the difference between involuntary and voluntary withdrawal from the world. Incarceration and solitary confinement are forms of torture, he says. Ways of "breaking the mind." "But to retreat to my childhood home and spend my days in seclusion here, I cannot get enough of it. I am a glutton for tranquility. My selfish search is always for a place like this." Elsewhere, he observes, "I cannot wait to repossess the bush, or maybe it is the other way around, let the bush repossess me. The bush and its furtive breath. Refuge and solace."[20] Yet despite the dangers of political engagement, Soyinka suggests that the writer who needs peace and quiet in order to work also needs the turmoil of the world if he is to have something to write about. This paradox is embodied in the combative-creative figure of Ogun that Soyinka has made his tutelary deity. "He could be such a peaceful person, yet he could go to war at a pinch." In the same vein, Soyinka speaks of activism and art as Siamese twins that cannot be operated upon without one or both of them dying.[21]

Imperturbability can be a virtue. To "keep your head when all about you are losing theirs and blaming it on you,"[22] to remain calm in the midst of chaos, is a kind of transcendence. But it is not a transcendent *state* that is achieved, but an acceptance of the "incompleteness of the world, the imperfectability of man [and] the impossibility of a permanently valid world order."[23] In short, the stone is always situated within the stream, buffeted and abraded by it.

By contrast, there are those who seek stone as a symbol of solidity and constancy—a place outside the turbulence of life's seas and streams.

In the fall of 2009 I travelled to Denmark for a conference of anthropologists and philosophers, all of whom were doing research on questions of ontological trust and uncertainty.

During my flight from Boston to Rejkyavik, I left my seat to stretch my legs and fell into conversation with a man around my age who, with his wife, was on his way to join a cruise that would take them on a circumnavigation of the North Atlantic. He was wearing a baseball cap with the insignia of a parachute regiment, and a fisherman's shirt whose pockets were crammed with pens, reading glasses, and gadgets. No sooner had Paul Herrick introduced himself and told me his destination than he asked whether there was anything I had wanted to do in my life but hadn't, whether there was anything I now regretted having not done or left unexplored. It occurred to me that he had been watching the Rob Reiner movie *The Bucket List*, about two terminally ill men who escape a cancer ward and head off on a road trip with a wish list of things to do before they die—driving a Formula One car, skydiving, climbing the pyramids, going on a lion safari in Africa, and so on.

"No, I don't think there is," I said.

"Then you're a fortunate man," Paul said.

"What about you?" I asked.

Paul, it turned out, was one of those people who ask all the questions. So he responded to my question with another of his own.

"What's the difference between man and the animals?"

I hazarded a few guesses, already trying to figure out how to extricate myself politely from this situation. "Language? Intra-specific violence? Conceptual thought?"

"Man seeks perfection," Paul announced, answering his own question and ignoring my own. And he explained how this and other profound insights into the human condition were contained in *The Urantia Book*.

First published in Chicago by the Urantia Foundation in 1955, *The Urantia Book* claims to have been given by celestial beings as a revelation to our planet, Urantia. Paul first read it when he came out of the army in 1962. It took him a year and a half to get through its more than two thousand pages.

"I was fascinated," Paul said, but I thought it was bullshit. Then I read it again. Halfway through, I realized it was the truth. It all made perfect sense. Let me tell you, that moment was the biggest thrill of my life. I was a young daredevil. I'd scuba dived in the Arctic, skydived, done stunt flying. I was one of the guys who formed The Golden Knights.[24] Been a thrill seeker all my life,[25] but, like I say, *The Urantia Book*, when I realized what it was, that was the biggest thrill I'd ever experienced."

Our conversation ended with sudden turbulence; the "fasten seatbelts" sign came on, and Paul and I were asked to return to our seats. Half an hour later, when we had regained stable air, Paul sought me out again. I left my seat and we worked our way back to the toilet area where there was space to stand. Paul was apologetic at first for boring me with his talk of Urantia. "You probably think I'm crazy. You probably want to hide somewhere so you don't have to hear me go on about Urantia."

I assured him that this was not the case. His story intrigued me. I was particularly interested in something he had said about faith: "You must pursue and keep faith with what is real for you, even if it has little reality for anyone else. Like me wanting to hold the world record for the most aircraft types jumped from. So far I've jumped from one hundred and sixteen different types of aircraft, and I'm looking for more."

Paul paused. "I think I know what you're driving at. You want to know what brought me to *The Urantia Book*."

In 1960, two years before he read *The Urantia Book*, Paul had made a routine parachute jump. His main chute failed to open. It was a streamer. He tried to deploy the reserve chute. Nothing happened. He realized he was going to die. In a desperate effort to deploy the reserve chute, he grabbed it ("They had no 'pilots' in those days") and hurled it toward the horizon. "It almost tore me in two, the force of it. But I survived." Paul went on to say that he had been raised in the Methodist Church. "But something about it was implausible. I couldn't accept it, and I didn't like organized religion. I had to come to the answers in my own way. My son is an aeronautical engineer, like me. A brilliant one. I talk to him, he listens, but he doesn't see what I see. My sisters are the same, except they won't even listen. They're fundamentalists. One burned a *Urantia Book*, page by page. The work of the devil, she called it. You can talk to a person until you're blue in the face. It's not going to happen. For some, it comes gradually; for others, it comes as a shock. Like a sledgehammer. It knocks you sideways. It opens you up to what's really going on out there. You can't prove a thing, you can't touch it or see it, but when you know it's there you know it more surely than you know I'm standing here talking to you."

I told Paul I was an anthropologist. I wanted to tell him that I had also been frustrated getting my message across—trying through my writing to reach a broad audience and disabuse people of their mistaken notions of non-Western peoples. But Paul presumed I dug up bones and ancient civilizations, and was keen to know what I would make of the chronology revealed in *The Urantia Book* and the "four epochal events."

"You know much more about anthropology than I do," Paul said, "but I'll bet you'll have many aha moments when you read *The Urantia Book*. It will tie together and fill in the gaps in your knowledge of anthropology. You will suddenly know what to look for, and where to look, that your colleagues don't. You will be able to explain the heretofore unexplainable."

I set little store by revealed knowledge, so I could not follow Paul to where he wanted to take me. And when, in due course, Paul sent me excerpts from *The Urantia Book* that advocated eugenic solutions to the "problem" of racially or intellectually "degenerate" and "socially unfit" forms of humanity, I called an end to our correspondence.

Nevertheless, for months thereafter, I wondered how someone who sought risks in life should be attracted to a book of bogus revelations, a work of the fascist imagination in which devotion to a single absolute authority figure goes hand in hand with obedience to some absolute law.

We all have to find answers that work for us, and we arrive at them in our own way. But what attitude does an intellectual adopt in the face of the multifarious worldviews to which people become attached, and the universal claims that are made for them? Can we achieve Jaspers's "philosophical faith" that accepts the finite limits of what we may know, and *not* fall into nihilism, relativism, or despair?[26]

About the time I wrote these lines and posed this question, I happened to read Kendra Goodson's final essay for my 2009 course "The Shock of the New." In her essay, Kendra describes one of her first nights on call as a hospital chaplain, when a seventeen-year-old man was brought to the emergency room with a gunshot wound to the head. The wound was self-inflicted, and the young man died soon after admission. "As a chaplain," Kendra writes, "I was supposed to be offering words of hope and comfort," and so she led the grieving family in prayer. But as the father began to weep into his hands,

Kendra said something "that I regretted as soon as it had slipped out—'It doesn't make sense.'" She then placed her hand on the father's back. Soon after, his sobbing began to subside, and "as he wiped tears from his face, he looked at me and said, 'You're right, it doesn't make sense.' I was astonished," Kendra writes, "to see relief in his eyes as he said these words," as if facing up to the arbitrariness and precariousness of existence were not paralyzing but healing.

Reviewing the conversations, encounters, and stories that I have juxtaposed in this book, I see far less evidence of union, reconciliation, or balance than of struggle and of aporias, suggesting an inescapable sense that no one life ever encompasses or comprehends Life itself, that no one is identical to the class to which he or she ostensibly belongs, and that we are just as bound to project our own self-understandings onto the world at large as we are fated to be shaped by events and influences that remain beyond our practical and conceptual grasp. In Nietzsche's exhortations that philosophy be more experimental, in the radical empiricism of William James, with its emphasis on the intransitive as well as the transitive aspects of our experience, in Karl Jaspers's notions of the encompassing and the limit, in Theodor Adorno's negative dialectics and Jacques Derrida's deconstructionism, one glimpses a lineage of ideas that disavow the possibility of closing the gap between the way we represent the world to ourselves and the way the world is actually constituted. Rather than seek, through science or rational analysis, new ways of creating certain knowledge, these thinkers urge us to describe all that gets excluded in such quests for certainty. By opening our minds to the unsettling strangeness that lies on the margins of what we think we know and can name, our world maps may lose their value but we enter other worlds thereby, not with dread but exhilaration, realizing the truth of Sextus Empiricus's argument[27] that skepticism may be embraced as a way of life (*agoge*) or disposition (*dunamis*) as well as an aporetic method of thought, and that the suspension of judgment (*epoché*) may help us achieve inner tranquility and peace of mind (*ataraxia*).

CHAPTER 13

On the Work and Writing of Ethnography

What would be the value of the passion for knowledge if it resulted only in a certain amount of knowledgeableness and not, in one way or another and to the extent possible, in the knower's straying afield of himself . . . to think differently, instead of legitimating what is already known?

—Michel Foucault

Having explored several variations on the theme of human existence as a continual interplay between the hypothetical poles of being-in-oneself and being-with-others, it is only appropriate that I should consider in this closing chapter the methodological ramifications of this theme in the work and writing of ethnography.

My focus is the ethical question of how it is possible, in our ethnographic fieldwork and writing, to reconcile our intellectual preoccupations with the often radically different preoccupations of our interlocutors. How, in brief, can we strike a balance between doing justice to the people who accept us into their communities, sharing their life experiences and scarce resources, *and* satisfy the demands of the profession to which we belong and from which we make our living?

This dilemma also finds expression in our existential struggle in the field to maintain a balance between preserving and losing our sense of personal identity.

Montaigne provides a telling example of this dilemma in his essay on the imagination. In the house of a wealthy and elderly man "who suffered with his lungs," Montaigne meets the attending physician who, when asked by the patient how he might be cured, answers that one way would be for him to infect Monsieur Montaigne, who is in good health, with a liking for his company. "If he were to fix his gaze on the freshness of my complexion," Montaigne writes, "and his thoughts on the youthful gaiety and vigour with which I overflowed, and if he were to feast his senses on my flourishing state of health, his own condition might well improve." In the same ironic vein, Montaigne then points out that what the physician forgot to mention was that Montaigne's health "might at the same time deteriorate."[1]

Are we then justified in speaking of a "healthy" or "safe" distance that should be kept between oneself and others, whether they are well or ill?

FIELDWORK

It is customary among the Kuranko that having received a stranger into one's home and given him or her hospitality and protection, one is expected to accompany the guest halfway on his or her journey home. This custom of "escorting" (*blessala*) or "going along with" (*kata ma so*) makes a good metaphor for fieldwork, for while one's hosts are obliged to look after their "stranger,"[2] the stranger is expected to reciprocate by respecting local protocols, being attentive to the rules of the household in which he or she is lodged, and mindful of what is expected of him or her in return for what is given. That one's very humanity is contingent on being accepted into this other lifeworld, albeit as a dependent and a potential risk, is shown by the excessive gratitude with which the novice ethnographer often attempts to ritually repay his or her hosts. Weston La Barre once observed that "out of professional pride, anthropologists seldom admit the quite characteristic depression and paranoia of 'culture shock' they have all experienced during the first few weeks or months of fieldwork."[3] But it is not only the alien and the unknown that disorient one in the field, for one is often already marginal in the culture in which one has grown up, and desperate for validation. That one "comes out of the field experience with a mildly fanatic love" for one's particular people, espousing a commitment to their interests and with "deeply gratifying personal friendships that over-ride great cultural and age differences" is, La Barre argues, not because one's real character was acknowledged and appreciated but because the other "rescued one's humanity" at a time when one was vulnerable and struggling to find one's feet. One's indebtedness to the other finds expression in an overcompensatory gesture of praising the other as a friend or kinsman or kinswoman. I think there is more than a grain of truth in La Barre's remarks, and it rings true of my earliest relationships with Kuranko collaborators.

Initially, the people with whom one associates are often marginal in their own lifeworld—outliers, so to speak, who are halfway to being rank outsiders like oneself. But one's relationships with people met in the course of fieldwork change over time, and the deepening of personal ties transforms the kind of conversations and interactions one has, as well as the kind of understandings one acquires, and these transformations may compromise the nomothetic project of anthropology itself—which, in its insistence on explaining human thought and behavior in terms of culture, history, or global processes, finds it difficult to accommodate the idiosyncratic and affective dimensions of social life. Fieldwork that begins with an overwhelming sense of alienation from one's host community may therefore lead to an equally overwhelming sense of identification with it.

But in "going along" with those on whom one's personal well-being and professional research depend, one is not obliged to "go all the way," uncritically accommodating all that is asked of one or accepting all that one's hosts do or say. The crucial ethical demand is that one not foreclose conversations because one presumes to know the origins, motives, or meaning of the other's thoughts or emotions, and that one not judge the views of the other solely from the standpoint of one's own worldview. Just as any conversation requires that one is attentive to what others have to say, without being obliged to embrace their point of view, so being a good guest implies a willingness to meet one's hosts halfway—less a question of an empathic identification with the other which is, as Paul Ricoeur points out, "neither possible nor desirable," or of cultivated disinterest, but of a "favorable attitude" toward the other, manifest in the act of "accompanying."[4] One seeks to strike a balance, as it were, between having it all one's own way and becoming so submerged in the lifeworld of the other that one's own sense of self is utterly eclipsed. The indeterminate character of ethnographic research reflects this tension between a disposition to cling to habitual ways of thinking and acting (because they are second nature and provide a sense of personal stability in an unstable world) and a desire to open oneself up to the possibility of seeing and doing things in radically different ways, even though these might initially seem "unnatural."

When I first lived in a Kuranko village I preferred to light my own fire to boil water for drinking or bathing. I regarded this mundane task as having little bearing on my research work, and, inevitably, my method of building a fire was careless and wasteful of wood. Though villagers possibly joked about my fire lighting, they did not criticize or censure me, which was remarkable considering the scarcity of firewood and the time consumed in gathering it. One day, for no apparent reason, I observed how Kuranko women kindled and tended a fire, and I sought to imitate their technique, which involved careful placement of the firestones, never using more than three lengths of split wood at one time, laying each piece carefully between the firestones, and gently pushing them into the fire as the ends burned away. When I took pains to make a fire in this way, I became aware of the intelligence of the technique, which maximized the scarce firewood (which women have to split and tote from up to a mile and a half away), produced exactly the amount of heat required for cooking, and enabled instant control of the flame. This practical mimesis afforded me insight into how people maximized both fuel and human energy; it made me see the close kinship between economy of effort and grace of movement; it helped me realize the common sense that informs even the most elementary tasks in a Kuranko village.

Many of my insights into Kuranko social life followed from a comparable cultivation of practical skills: hoeing on a farm, dancing (as one body), trimming the wick of a kerosene lantern, eating with the fingers of my right hand, weaving a mat, entertaining a guest.

During my first few months of fieldwork, I would seek out a quiet and unoccupied room to write up my field notes. Constantly interrupted by my concerned hosts, who were uncertain as to whether I needed companionship or preferred my own company, I moved to the verandah of the house, where I could do my work without giving offense. However, whenever someone came by to chat or sit with me, I felt obliged to offer a cup of tea and engage in small talk. As with my fire lighting, so with my socializing—it took me a long time before I noticed how others performed these tasks, and even longer before I began emulating local usages. This meant breaking my characteristically Western middle-class habit of making conversation with a guest and of filling silences with trivial observations. Among the Kuranko, neighborliness (*siginyorgoye*, lit. "sitting partnership") is expressed through customary greetings and the sharing of food and drink. But mutual recognition does not require constant conversation and is best consummated in amicable silence—the art of simply being-with-another, an art of copresence. By learning to rely on observation and imitation rather than interrogation, I went a long way toward a participatory understanding of local praxis, literally putting myself in the place of the other, inhabiting his or her world.

George Devereux has shown that one's personality inevitably colors the character of one's observations and that the "royal road to an authentic, rather than fictitious, objectivity" is perforce the way of *informed* subjectivity.[5] But subjectivity is social and somatic in character, and not necessary a synonym for solipsism or self-centeredness. To participate bodily in the everyday practical life of another society may be a creative technique that helps one grasp the sense of an activity by using one's body as others do, just as eating as locals eat, working at the pace that locals work, and going along with local priorities may carry one into an understanding that could not be attained through questioning, interviewing, or conceptual guesswork alone. In other words, ethnographic practice is always more than a matter of observing. Understanding cannot be attained simply by *seeing* (either through inspection or introspection); it implicates all the senses to varying degrees and involves a bodily relationship with the objects and others around us.[6] This means that ethnographic practice subsumes the allegedly disinterested understanding of *epistêmê* in *technê*, where even theory building is construed as a technique, on a par with word processors, plows, and defense mechanisms, whereby human beings seek to make their relations with the world and with others more practically and socially viable.

There are resonances here of Heidegger's discussion of equipment and equipmentality. Heidegger's argument is that we never encounter things as having a self-evident identity. Things, like other people, reveal themselves in relation to us, just as we disclose ourselves in the ways we relate to them. Thus, simply by looking at a hammer we can deduce little about its function. The hammer only reveals its "being" when it is picked up and put to use. In Heidegger's words, "The kind of Being which equipment possesses—in which it manifests itself in its own right—we call 'readiness-to-hand' (*Zuhandenheit*)."[7] Heidegger then goes on to say that "theoretical behavior is just looking, without circumspection." And he argues that understanding depends on our ability to grasp the "readiness-to-hand" of everything from a forest to a fire or an acre of farmland. The meaning of these things resides in their physical implementation.

Can we extend this argument to intersubjectivity and claim that our knowledge of others and of their lifeworlds is contingent on the ways we engage and interact with them? Such a claim implies that it is more fruitful to understand oneself and the other in relation to the situation in which we find ourselves, and that dispositions, identities, roles, and cultural schemata are potentialities, "ready-to-hand," that come into play strategically, opportunistically, and variously as our interests shift and our situation alters. Bernard Stiegler refers to this ongoing process of becoming as *individuation*, though he is careful not to conflate this term with *individualization*, since any interaction entails I *and* We identifications,[8] and both are constantly under revision as circumstances change.

To focus on human situations involves calling into question the view that people speak and act in certain ways because they are culturally, historically, or biogenetically predisposed to do so. But while explanations based on disposition are alluringly parsimonious and seemingly coherent, explanations based on situations offer far less intellectual satisfaction, partly because situations are usually too complex and involve too many points of view to allow much analytical certainty. A way out of this impasse is to learn how to draw a line between what can and cannot be expressed in explanatory language.

In his *Tractatus Logico-Philosophicus*, Ludwig Wittgenstein remarks that "even when all possible scientific questions have been answered, the problems of life remain completely untouched," and he goes on to say that "there are, indeed, things that cannot be put into words. They make themselves manifest. They are what is mystical."[9] Gabriel Marcel made a similar distinction between a "problem" that admits of a solution and a "mystery" that can never be entirely solved.

> A problem is something met with which bars my passage. It is before me in its entirety. A mystery, on the other hand, is something in which I find myself caught up, and whose essence is therefore not to be before me in its entirety. It is as though in this province the distinction between in me and before me loses its meaning.[10]

If our essays in understanding can only go partway toward explaining "all that is the case,"[11] does our task then become one of judging when to tell and when to show?

Much ethnographic writing is so replete with explanatory language and so bereft of sustained descriptions of life as lived that one might easily conclude that the ethnographer is seeking to mask with discursive prose a complexity that he or she cannot psychologically tolerate. What passes for theory is thus a defense against the anxiety of the inexplicable, the ineffable, the contradictory, the ambiguous.[12]

Herein lies the case for existential-phenomenological anthropology. Many of the topics on which phenomenologists and existentialists have focused lie at the boundaries of what traditional empiricism, philosophy, religious studies, and social science have defined as their respective preserves. Rather than the analysis or interpretation of texts, we also look to the contexts in which texts are produced, used, abused, or invoked. Rather than the life of the mind, we also consider the life of the body, the senses, the emotions, the imagination, and the material objects we fashion, deploy, and value in our everyday lives. Rather than assuming that our experience of the world may be directly inferred from the ways in which we represent the world to ourselves and to others, we focus on the lack of fit, the slippage between our immediate experience and the conceptual forms whereby that experience is mediated. Rather than isolate the human subject as an arbiter of meaning, a bounded self, a singular existent, we switch our attention to what transpires *between* subjects and the ways in which our sense of self is contingent on the behaviors, responses, and dispositions of others and the situations in which we find ourselves. Rather than speak of stable and identifiable entities—whether these be personalities, innate dispositions, cultures, religions, or historical periods—we prefer to deconstruct such categories, exploring the mutable and multifarious character of our actual being-in-the-world, and suspending all assumptions as to the epistemological truth of the descriptive labels we deploy in creating the illusion that the world can be subject to our knowledge and control. Our focus is the human struggle for being—the ongoing, resourceful, and various ways in which we work, alone and together, to affirm life in the face of death, salvage life in face of adversity, and make life fulfilling rather than empty of meaning. But life is always lived *within* limits, no matter how much we fantasize that life may be made limitless—and these limits include the limits of our ability to comprehend and control life, the limits of our ability to endure hardship, the limits of our ability to articulate what it is we think we know, and the limits of our ability to reverse time as if it were like a passage of music that we could replay endlessly until we got it right.

WRITING

Perhaps no philosopher wrestled more with this question of the limits of meaning, of logic, and of thought than Ludwig Wittgenstein, whose *Tractatus* concludes with the famous remark, "What we cannot speak about we must pass over in silence." But Wittgenstein also argues that even when the philosopher has nothing to say, he may have something to show—obliquely, analogically, descriptively. There are inadvertent echoes here of Husserl's and Heidegger's conception of phenomenology as descriptive showing—a method of bringing something into the light of day, of revealing what it looks like, what it appears to be.[13] For an ethnographer, therefore, two vital questions arise: first, when do we allow our interlocutors to speak, fully acknowledging their voices, their points of view, and not occlude their voices and views with our own?; second, when do we presume to *say* what is the case, when do we *show* what cannot be said, and when do we keep *silent*?

The trick is of what I have elsewhere called "writing intersubjectivity,"[14] developing a paratactic style that interleaves story and essay, strikes a balance between the voice of the author and the voices of his or her interlocutors, and leaves space for the reader to rethink whatever is being said or shown. One's writing preserves the oscillations in lived experience between moments of complete engagement and moments of detached reflection, while echoing the continual switching in everyday life between moments of self-absorption and moments of absorption in others. Ideally, one's writing shows how understandings emerge from the space between people—a space of conversation, negotiation, and encounter that switches unpredictably between accord and discord, attunement and disharmony. Indeed, the wealth of vernacular images derived from music and applied to both writing and sociality attests to the profound similarities between our relations with others and our sense of sound. Fieldwork is a way of sounding the other out—giving him or her a hearing, getting a sense of the world from his or her point of view. By extension, sound writing echoes the events, encounters, and conversations that make up our everyday life in another society, bringing them back to life on the printed page while at the same time offering our reflections on them.

We may have reached a moment of neorealism in the history of the academy when in-depth, detailed, direct recountings of experience will be considered as illuminating, edifying, and thoughtful as the experience-distant jargon extolled by the rationalists of the Enlightenment. David Shields calls this "reality hunger," an increased interest in and appetite for "seemingly unprocessed, unfiltered, uncensored, and unprofessional" material, and a blurring of distinctions between fiction and nonfiction, description and analysis, and anthropology and autobiography.[15] Arousing emotion, moving a reader, describing the living context in which one's thoughts unfold, and using artistic devices—narrative, imagery, idiomatic speech, montage—are valid ways of communicating a point of view, making an argument, or revealing a truth. It is becoming acceptable to stir or disturb one's audience in the same way that music or movies do. Rather than distrusting prose that evokes a slice of life, a lived event, or a personal experience, we are learning to distrust forms of discourse in which the assertion of authority requires an autocratic manner. We crave sincerity as much as scholarship, direct testimony as much as indirect speech. The world of thought is being brought back to life. The test of the soundness of philosophy—and, by extension, the writing of philosophy—is whether, in the words of John Dewey, it ends "in conclusions which, when they are referred back to ordinary life-experiences and their predicaments, render them more significant, more luminous to us, and make out dealings with them more fruitful . . . does it yield the enrichment and increase of power of ordinary things."[16] And so we ask, how may anthropology or philosophy become what Ivan Illich called "a tool for conviviality"?[17]

In addressing this question, my concern is with techniques of writing that enable us to resonate with and remain in touch with the events, persons, and things being written about, writing that does justice to life, that makes sense, that rings true. This is not a call for reverting to old ideas of writing as mimesis or representation—mirroring the nature of the world or creating naturalistic images. Sound writing may capture or convey the spirit of lived experience by radical departures from naturalistic conventions, in the same way that literary dialogue can sound real without resembling actual conversation.

SOUND PROPERTIES OF THE WRITTEN WORD

Writing carries traces of sound and speech, in the same way that our moments of solitude carry traces of our social lives. This is why the question of whether speech is more authentic than writing is as absurd as the question of whether individuality is a more authentic mode of being than participation in collective life. As with the Gestalt image of figure and ground, these different modalities are mutually entailed and mutually arising. There is, to cite Jacques Derrida, a "metaphysical exchange" and "circular complicity of the metaphors of the eye and the ear."[18]

Consider Ngugi Wa Thiong'o's childhood memoir *Dreams in a Time of War*, in which the Gikuyu and Kenyan writer describes his first experiences of school at age nine and the Gikuyu primer with which he learned to read.

At first he is attracted to the pictures that accompany the text, and only gradually does he learn to tackle long passages that lack any illustrations. One passage he reads over and over again until suddenly, one day, he begins to hear music in the words:

> God has given the Agĩkũyũ a beautiful country
> Abundant in water, food and luscious bush
> The Agĩkũyũ should praise the Lord all the time
> For he has ever been generous to them.

"Even when not reading it," Ngugi writes, "I can hear the music." He continues, "The choice and arrangements of the words, the cadences. I can't pick any one thing that makes it so beautiful and long-lived in my memory. I realize that even written words can carry the music I loved in stories, particularly the choric melody. And yet this is not a story; it is a descriptive statement. It does not carry an illustration. It is a picture in itself and yet more than a picture and a description. It is music. Written words can also sing."[19]

There is a long tradition in scholarship of seeing oral and literate technologies of communication as entailing radically different sensibilities and essentially different ontologies. It is argued that the transition from orality to literacy entails a dramatic transformation in consciousness in which words cease to sing,[20] intellectuality becomes divorced from feeling, the arts of memory atrophy, vision is privileged over all other senses, thought becomes independent of conventional wisdom, and the reader is alienated from his or her community.[21] These arguments are often informed by a romantic view that oral cultures enshrine a more ecologically balanced and socially attuned mode of existence in which the life of the community takes precedence over the life of the mind—as in Walter Benjamin's lament that modernity prefers information processing to storytelling, data to wisdom,[22] echoing Socrates's conviction that writing is a phantom, undermining memory, poisoning/drugging the mind, and leading us astray.[23]

I want to contest the assumption that orality and literacy are mutually antithetical and that writing necessarily entails a loss of authentic values, eclipsing oral modes of expression and undermining social bonds. I also want to argue against the view that we can characterize and contrast entire societies in terms of their dominant technology of communication—or, for that matter, their dominant modes of government, economic life, or social organization. As George Devereux pointed out many years ago, a complete understanding of any social formation demands that we explore the ambiva-lence that arises from the copresence of manifest and latent patterns,[24] and hence the tension that exists between that which is publicly emphasized and that which is publicly suppressed, between dominant and subdominant leit-motifs, alternative ethical values, and different modes of consciousness. No society exists or has ever existed that comprises individuals whose conscious-ness is wholly self-absorbed or entirely diffused into the collective, even though these polar positions may find expression in dominant ideologies. Just as persons exist both in their own right and in relation to others, so writing and orality imply both divergent and overlapping modes of commu-nication. This undoubtedly explains the apparent contradictions in Walter Ong's celebrated work, where he claims a "vast difference" between literacy and orality only to speak of this relationship as "complementary" and assert that "writing can never dispense with orality."[25] In this vein, he writes that "in all the wonderful worlds that writing opens, the spoken word still resides and lives. Written texts all have to be related somehow, directly or indirectly, to the world of sound, the natural habitat of language, to yield their mean-ings."[26] Jacques Derrida takes this argument even further, arguing that writ-ing is haunted by a sense of all that lies beyond its margins in the same way that philosophy is inevitably written in the shadows of the nonphilosophical. Derrida uses the image of the tympanum to capture this sense of sound, al-beit muffled, that counters the apparent silence of a text, or the reader of a text, and is vital to the intelligibility of the written word.[27]

I have a tin ear and cannot hold the simplest tune or learn a foreign lan-guage by listening alone. Much as I admire John Blacking's *How Musical Is Man?*, his thesis that everyone has a capacity for music[28] does not apply to me. If deafness is a disability, so, arguably, is tone deafness—the inability to discern, recall, or mimic sound. But it is said that people deficient in one area of the sensorium will compensate by developing skills and sensitivities in another, and Oliver Sacks describes how a person with expressive aphasia (speechlessness) may still be able to sing "very tunefully and with great feel-ing, but only getting two or three words of [a] song."[29] My eidetic memory is excellent. And since childhood I have depended on the written word to make good my aural-oral ineptitude. Yet writing has never been, for me, a substi-tute for speech, any more than scholarly pursuits have been inimical to soci-ality. One mode of being or communicating does not necessarily preclude another. And so when I ask whether the oral is entirely absent when I read or write, I can confidently say no, since in composing this very sentence I am murmuring the words as I write them down, trying to get a feel for how they will resound in the sequence I am testing on my tongue, seeking a structural balance that will be easy on the ear. Fiction writers often confess a similar sense of hearing voices, of writing down dialogue they have heard, and of assessing its verisimilitude less against the standard of recorded speech than against an inner standard of what rings true. The idea is very old that thinking is a form of talking to oneself, which is why people who undergo surgery on their vocal chords are told not to read until the lesions heal. In brief, the distinctions we like to make between speech and writing, or speech and thought, are largely artificial, and there are greater phenomenological continuities between these conventionally contrasted activities than we are ordinarily aware of.

Consider, for example, the opening lines of Seamus Heaney's poem *Oysters*:

Our shells clacked on their plates.
My tongue was a filling estuary,
My palate hung with starlight:
As I tasted the salty Pleiades
Orion dipped his foot into the water.

Alive and violated
They lay on their beds of ice:
Bivalves: the split bulb
And philandering sigh of ocean.
Millions of them ripped and shucked and scattered.[30]

Is it not true that as one reads these lines, one also hears them—and, furthermore, that one sees and tastes the brine-slicked bivalves lying in their flaking, ice-caked shells on a pewter plate? Surely the written word not only conjures sound and sense; it is haunted by sound textures; it possesses metrical properties. And is this not true of both self-consciously rhythmic and tonal poetry *and* the less carefully composed, atonal prose of a novel, an essay, or a tract?

The inextinguishable presence of a voice in a written text may be a result of synesthesia[31]—a faculty that all human beings share to some degree, making it inevitable that one area of the sensorium will evoke others, including touch—which may explain why we speak of a piece of writing as a text—a term that derives, like texture, from the action of weaving. Whether written or spoken, language is always interwoven with threads of experience that are, strictly speaking, beyond words. Writing puts a spin on the ineffable, making it seem to be sayable, or subtly indicates what is outside its ability to signify.[32] We might therefore say that the *look* of a particular writer's prose, or our sense of his or her style, will evoke a memory of his or her voice—or, if we have never heard the writer speak, summon "a" voice that goes with the text, that makes it audible.

Despite these claims that literacy never entirely divorces itself from orality, the view is still held, particularly in the academy, that a logical, analytically coherent, and thoughtful disquisition on any subject requires the suppression of what Derrida, following Husserl, called "the sensory face of language."[33] Making experience intelligible requires the subjugation of its sensible properties, including sound.

I now turn to exploring in more detail the analogy I have drawn between the *technical* relationship of experience to writing and the *social* relationship of private to public life. I begin by spelling out some of the principles that have guided my own experiments in sound writing, and I go on to provide an example of these principles in practice.

Just as sound ethnographic writing is careful not to mute the voice of the ethnographer *or* his or her interlocutors, it does not exclude the reader. Rather, it invites the reader to enter into the text, to feel free to get his or her own sense of the scene or events unfolding, and to arrive at his or her interpretation of what the text conveys. This is what Eugenio Montale meant by "the second life of art."[34] While the author owns the process of authoring a text, painting a picture, performing a role, he or she cannot lay claim to the work once it has been put into circulation in the public sphere. For the work is now not only available to readers or audiences; it belongs to them; it is theirs to interpret according to their own persuasions and predilections.

Second, sound writing reflects sound research. And the key to sound research is openness and inclusivity. This implies an observational alertness to what is happening in the field. But, more important, perhaps, is one's *social* sensitivity to the people who have accepted one into their households and everyday lives. Sound research is, therefore, not simply a matter of suspending preconceptions and going with the flow; it is predicated on an awareness that the quality of what one may know is determined by the quality of one's relationships with those one comes to know in the course of fieldwork.

Third, it is imperative that one allows one's empirical material to determine any interpretative response. This means paying meticulous attention to vernacular expressions, local figures of speech, and ontological metaphors. These, rather than any theory one has acquired, provide the windows through which one may glimpse the inner workings of another lifeworld. In his field-work with ex-combatants in Guinea-Bissau, Henrik Vigh became familiar with the vernacular term *dubria*. Young men would use the word in describing their struggle for work, to make ends meet, or to find sources of enjoyment in an impoverished social environment. One informant conveyed the meaning of *dubria* to Henrik by moving his upper body in a disjointed yet rhythmical sway, looking somewhat as if he were shadowboxing: arms along his side, weaving and bobbing his torso back and forth as though dodging invisible pulls and pushes. "*Dubria!*" Pedro exclaimed. "You *dubria* ... so that you can see your life." Henrik realized that *dubriagem* connoted the "use of shrewdness and craftiness to navigate dangerous or difficult terrain," and his concept of navigation as "motion within motion"—action in an unstable environment when you are yourself destabilized—was born of listening hard to what his informants were telling him.[35]

Fourth, one must entertain the possibility that every situation calls for a different response. Just as joking and avoidance are universal strategies for dealing with socially ambiguous or non-negotiable relationships, so the ethnographer sometimes turns to contemplation, sometimes to writing, sometimes to speech, or sometimes to direct action in seeking the most appropriate way of responding to what others say or do, or demand. But even when one writes, there is always the question of what kind of writing is called for.

A WRITING SAMPLE

In early 2002 I returned to Sierra Leone after many years away. I took with me a book I had hastily bought at Gatwick Airport, and I would read and reread this book during the following weeks, finding in its elegiac tone echoes of the devastated social landscape and tragic stories to which I would bear witness. When I came to write of that time, W. G. Sebald's *Austerlitz* haunted every phrase, every sentence, imparting to my narrative something of the strange interplay of resignation and resilience that I encountered in Sierra Leone. In the following pages I describe an episode in my journey north, in the company of my old friend, S. B. Marah, a few weeks before peace was officially declared. This was S. B.'s first visit to his political constituency in a long time, and a way of mending the political fabric torn apart by years of pillaging, violence, neglect, and scarcity. I hope this text will exemplify what I have been saying about sound writing, as well as provide a variation on the theme that has run like a red thread throughout this book, namely, that it is extraordinarily difficult, in a society of scarcity, to strike a balance between acquiring what one deems vital for one's own well-being and providing others with what is vital to theirs. How can there be social justice when the basic requirements of existence—food, shelter, and water—are insufficient to go around, so that one person's feast is always another's famine, one person's gain is inevitably another person's loss? The beef has, therefore, dual meanings: connoting an argument or a point of ethical contention, as well as denoting a cattle beast, a source of life energy and power.

THE BEEF

For two days, a young steer had been tethered by a short rope to a mango tree at the edge of the compound. It was a gift to S. B., meant to be taken to Freetown, along with several goats. Constrained by the rope, the steer was unable to stretch its neck to the ground; all it could do was occasionally nose or lick dew from the long grass that was within its reach. When it defecated, it held its tail horizontal, its spine as straight as a spirit-level, and the tuft of hair by its penis twitched when it finished urinating. So forlorn did this animal seem that I became convinced that it knew its imminent fate.

On the morning that we packed the vehicles, preparing to leave Kabala, it became obvious that there was not enough room in the back of the pickup for the steer. As the Big Men discussed their quandary, I sat some distance away, listening to an elderly man recount the history of Mande to a young newspaper reporter—passing from a description of Sundiata, who ruled the empire in the mid-fourteenth century, to an account of the first clans, the origins of the xylophone, and the birth of praise singing. Old Musa's spectacle frames were tied upside down to his cap, because this was the only way the one remaining lens could cover his one good eye. Earlier in the day he had asked if I could send him some new glasses from Freetown—just as Leba had asked for a camera and the musicians had begged me to help them buy new guitars and amplifiers.

When I noticed that the Big Men and soldiers were gathering by the mango tree, I went down into the courtyard to talk with Leba, who said he had come to say good-bye. "They are killing the beef," he observed. And as we watched from a distance, saying nothing, the steer was forced to the ground and its throat cut. The carcass was then cut into portions, and the head, neck, forequarters, rump, underbelly, entrails, hide, heart, and liver were set out in separate piles on some banana leaves. Nearby, ten vultures stood their ground, occasionally flapping their ungainly wings and craning their necks toward the kill.

Suddenly a young man standing next to Leba muttered something about how short life was. When I asked him what he meant, he said: "The way they slaughter these cows for these ministers. If we the young men wanted some of that beef, those Big Men would fight us, juju-way. They'd say, 'If any young man looks at the meat, let him beware.' So they make you afraid to go there. That is why we young people should not open our eyes too much on the meat. The big men could make us impotent. Or they could shoot us with their fetish guns."

I knew that many older men were similarly possessive of their young wives, but this was the first time I'd heard of possessiveness toward meat—though one heard rumors of so-called Leopard Societies that, in days gone by, committed ritual murders so that Big Men might augment their power by eating the vital organs of children. The logic ran as follows: children, women, and cattle were wealth. A man's capacity to father children, marry many times, and acquire cattle was a sign of power. And status and stature were intimately linked. It was not for nothing that one of S. B.'s praise names in the north was simba, elephant—an allusion to his physical bulk as much as his commanding presence, his social standing, and his political power. Still, it amused me that so many Big Men were immobilized by their own obesity—sluggish, unwell, and impotent. Was this why they were so preoccupied with the virility and appetite of young men? If so, the young men, denied meat and obliged to do the Big Men's bidding, seemed to find little consolation in the fact that what they lacked in status they made up for in strength and vitality.

When we drove off, I noticed that the vultures were clumsily quarreling around the spot where the steer had been butchered and picking at the blood-blackened earth.

The sun was hot. The summit of Albitaiya was lost in the haze of the harmattan. In the backseat of the 4Runner I felt cramped and uncomfortable. Underfoot were several bags of meat, including the steer's severed head. Copies of the Noble Qur'an in English, which Fasili had mysteriously acquired in Kabala, kept falling on my head. And our police escort again filled the landscape with its wailing sirens as we drove over the rice and clothing that villagers had spread on the roadside to dry or through smoke from burning elephant grass.

At Fadugu the police Land Rover left us, and as if released from an obligation to behave itself, the 4Runner began to lose compression and suffer from brake failure. Yet even as we labored up the last hill toward Makeni, S. B. was pressing his nephew to overtake slower-moving poda podas, and urging us on. "Le' we go, le' we go," he said, as if his impatience and willpower would be instantly transmitted to the vehicle and it would obey. By the time we crawled the last few yards into a roadside repair shop, I realized it had taken us five hours to travel seventy miles. The hood of the 4Runner was quickly opened and propped up, and the engine exposed to the scrutiny of a dozen or so grease monkeys, while the Big Men issued advice, diagnoses, and orders from the makeshift seats that had been brought out for them. "This car na too slow," S. B. observed. "It don vex us too much," added his acolyte Fasili. Watching the Big Men as they sat unmoving and unmoved in front of a rusty, wheel-less vehicle that had been chocked up with driveshafts and a wooden mortar, I had a flashback to Gatwick Airport, when I had found myself with several hours to kill before my flight. The departure lounge had been almost deserted, though not far from where I was sitting a young businessman was talking on his mobile phone. As I listened to his conversation with diminishing interest, a woman started vacuuming the walkway between us. As she drew near, I lifted my feet so she could reach under the seat. But when she moved on to where the man in the suit was talking on his mobile phone, he ignored her completely. It wasn't as if he could not see her; he simply did not want to acknowledge her. Nor, it appeared, did she expect anything of him. When he showed no sign of moving either his feet or his bag, the woman left the space around him as it was—littered with candy wrappers and used telephone cards. Trivial in itself, this incident left me troubled. Not only did I want to know why certain people, as a matter of principle, will make absolutely no concession to those they consider their inferiors; it made me ask myself why I felt so acutely uncomfortable with status distinctions, and sought, wherever possible, to avoid or nullify them. Recollecting this incident at Gatwick also reminded me of how awkward I sometimes felt at the hotel in Freetown where I had lodged before travelling up-country. Where most people would readily accept being waited on—for, after all, this is what waiters are paid to do—I felt embarrassed by the deferential or obsequious rigmarole and could not abide having someone pour water into my glass, place a napkin over my lap, or call me sir. No one could be less suited for high office than myself. Indeed, so assiduous was my need to avoid the trappings of authority and privilege that I instinctively sought the margins and the shadows—the world of the underdog or the young.

I wandered away across the tamped, grease-and-oil-stained earth, past the decaying mud-brick building that served as an office, the lean-tos under which old car seats, cylinder blocks, radiators, differentials, mufflers, and cannibalized engine parts had been stacked, to where I could sit alone, collect my thoughts, and scribble some notes. Then I strolled up the road to buy a bread roll and a tin of sardines from which to make a sandwich.

When I returned to the vehicle, S. B.'s nephew, who was known as small S. B., explained that the brake fluid line to the rear wheels had been burned through by the broken muffler and had to be replaced. The air filter also required cleaning. As one of the grease monkeys was dispatched into town to find a spare brake fluid line, food was brought for the Big Men—for the third time that day. But eating did not interrupt their critical commentary on the mechanics' efforts. "Why you no fix em before now?" the Alhaji asked testily. "Come on bo, le we go now," S. B. added, with a weariness that appeared to preclude any response. Dr. K. said nothing. He was too busy ordering one of the mechanic's boys to uncap two bottles of Heineken beer for him as he tugged rubbery strands of meat from a boiled goat's head. "Kam eat," he said to me. When I explained I did not eat meat, he was incredulous. "Where do you get your protein?" he asked. "Where do you get your strength?"

"We Africans have tough stomachs," Fasili observed.

"It's not stomach," I said. "It's heart. I don't eat meat for health reasons."

When he had finished eating, Dr. K. removed his gray safari shirt and summoned a small boy to scratch his back. He was like a hippo, as dour as he was massive. And while he picked his teeth with a sliver of wood, the boy started to massage his enormous shoulders.

S. B. was being ear-bashed by two local men who had lost their local businesses in the war.

Makeni, I knew, had been a Revolutionary United Front (RUF) stronghold. Even now there were billboards at the roundabouts in the center of the town with photos of Foday Sankoh and RUF political slogans.

Perhaps this was why S. B. showed so little sympathy for their plight. "No one went into exile here," he asserted. "You have only yourselves to blame for what happened here."

"We had nowhere to go," one of the Makeni men replied.

And then, as if to elicit my understanding, the second man described how well the RUF was organized. "They would send small boys to spy on prominent people," he said. "The kids would disguise themselves as cigarette sellers or petty traders. They would carry messages. We never knew who they were. They would get information about a place before they attacked it."

"You know," S. B. said wryly, "one time the RUF entered a mosque and asked, 'Anyone here believe in God?' No, we don't, everyone said. Even the Imam. No, no, he said, I do not believe!"

The Makeni men both laughed.

"But seriously," S. B. said, "the SLPP [Sierra Leone People's Party] expects people to work for the country. Government is composed of people. You should not fear to speak the truth to your government. The government does not want to hurt you. As long as you are on the right side, you have nothing to fear."

As S. B. was talking, a truck had pulled in at the roadside. Intrigued by the slogan emblazoned on its side—*Fear Not the World but the People*—I walked over to the truck to see what it carried and was dismayed to find that twenty-five steers were crammed together on the back, their horns roped to wooden beams that were in turn lashed to a metal frame covering the vehicle's tray. The animals were unable to move. The flank of one had been so badly lacerated by the jolting of the truck over degraded roads that its hip bone was exposed. They had been packed top to tail, in rows of five, to maximize space. Their muzzles were dry, foam flecked their mouths, their eyes were closed with pain and exhaustion, and their heads had been forced up over the rumps of the animals in front. From time to time an unbearable moan was released from the herd, and I was reminded instantly of the bobby calves I used to hear baying mournfully in the night when I was child, as they waited out the hours of darkness in a cramped railway wagon on a siding in my hometown before going on to the slaughterhouse the next day.

The driver and his mate tilted the cab of the truck forward and began inspecting the engine, while a couple of other young men clambered up onto the back of the truck and walked over the steers, checking the lashings.

"You should have brought your camera, Mr. Mike." It was small S. B., who had sidled up to me unseen.

"I was thinking," I said, "that this is how Africans were once packed in the slave ships, head to foot, to save space."

But where I saw slaves, or imagined myself, small S. B. saw only cows. And I did not feel inclined to share with him my ruminations on when, and under what circumstances, we might extend human rights to animals or, for that matter, deny these rights to our fellow human beings, treating them as if they were mere chattels or beasts. Yet it was suddenly very clear to me that my own notion of rights reflected the egalitarian ethos of the country in which I was raised. In tribal societies such as Kuranko, one's worth was ostensibly relative to one's patrimony, rank, and title, which is why, I guess, the Big Men always wore their status on their sleeves—Honorable, Doctor, Paramount Chief. In such a society, one's due was generally reckoned in terms of birth, not worth. A chief was due a retinue, and tithes, not to mention praise and honor. A father was owed his children's respect. And a wife was duty bound to honor her husband, and to obey him without question. For the Kuranko, this calculus of social distinction was both categorical and unambiguous. People were superior to animals, first-born were superior to second-born, men were superior to women, adults were superior to children, the patriline was superior to the matriline, rulers were superior to commoners, and commoners were superior to praise singers, blacksmiths, and leather workers. At the bottom of the social scale, finabas—the bards and custodians of chiefly traditions—were superior to no one, except perhaps slaves. In practice, however, the worth of a person was far less fixed than this schema would suggest. When Keti Ferenke explained this to me many years ago, he began by punning on the word *kina*, which, depending on a subtle difference in pronunciation, could mean either beehive or elder. His argument was that someone who is nominally elder could lose the right to be considered superior if he behaved unjustly or idiotically. A person could be an elder, a status superior, he said, but if he acted like a child, he *was* a child. Superiority, he noted, derived not only from being born first, or from being big and powerful; it also stemmed from the way one behaved. For Keti Ferenke, whose pride in his own intellectual adroitness was, at least in my company, undisguised, a person's true worth was defined by his or her social gumption, or nous, though other innate traits, such as temperament, bearing, and moral courage, might also elevate a person beyond his or her given social position. Consider the myth of Saramba, for instance, a warrior chief of great renown, whose jealous half brothers decided to waylay and murder him. When Saramba's humble finaba, Musa Kule, got wind of the plot, he devised a plan to save his master's life. After persuading the ruler to exchange clothes with him, Musa Kule rode the chief's horse ahead along the road where the ambush had been laid. As a result, Musa Kule was killed instead of the chief. In recognition of his sacrifice, Saramba declared that from that day hence their descendants should be considered equals, because the moral qualities of the lowborn fina had effectively eclipsed the status superiority of his master.

Subtle reciprocities are disclosed here. The relationship between respect paid and recognition returned, for example, or the implicit understanding that a chief will give his protection to those who submit to his authority and place themselves in his hands. But what if a chief or political leader turns into a tyrant—seizing people's property, taking advantage of his subjects, repaying tribute with obloquy? What if a husband abuses his dutiful and obedient wife? And should the young have regard for the ancestral order of things when it is evoked only to bolster the powers and prerogatives of an elite that is indifferent to their needs, contemptuous of their aspirations, and blind to their talents? For many young people in Sierra Leone, their patience with autocracy, traditional or modern, has worn thin. For them, their due was determined by need, and this is not delimited by their inferior station in life but by what they imagine might be theirs as citizens of the world. These questions, born of my Kuranko research, were, I realized, not unrelated to the RUF rebellion, but at that moment, as if to derail my train of thought, small S. B. said that the 4Runner had been repaired and we could be on our way.

As I walked back to the 4Runner, I found the boss mechanic negotiating with S. B. for a little extra money. The mechanic's son was at his father's side. He was about the same age as my own son. As the father spoke to S. B., he cradled his son's head in his hand. Then he ran his hand over the boy's shoulders and back, pressing him to his side. And all the while, the boy was beaming with happiness. One and one another. The two of them mirroring my relationship with my own son. Myself a part of *and* apart from their life-world, at once close and distant.

Spinoza was right, I think, in persuading us not to speak of ontologically different *types or entities* but of different *aspects or modes* of the one inexhaustible reality.[36] Anthropology can only become a truly dialectical science when it finds ways of doing justice to the interplay of particular and universal perspectives, singular and shared modes of human being, in fieldwork, analysis, and writing alike.

ACKNOWLEDGMENTS

My greatest debt is to friends who allowed me to publish their stories, experiences, and opinions in this book—Keith Egan, Brijen Gupta, Sewa Magba Koroma, Fiona Murphy, Neni Panourgiá, Jørgen Pedersen, McGinty Salt, and Sofka Zinovieff. I am also grateful to other friends for comments on drafts of this work—Davíd Carrasco, Charles Hallisey, Robert Desjarlais, Adam Lyons, Don Seeman, and Tyler Zoanni. Acknowledgment is also due to friends who have passed on, yet figure in the pages of this book, as in my life, as spiritual interlocutors—Peter Fisher, Peter Herbst, Pauline Jackson, Keti Ferenke Koroma, Galina Lindquist, and Richard Rorty. Lulie El-Ashry provided timely research assistance. And my sincere thanks are due to Reed Malcolm for his generous support of my work. Finally, I thank the following copyright holders for material reprinted here with their permission: Berghahn Books, Inc., for "After Understanding: A Memoir of Galina Lindquist," in *Religion, Politics and Globalization: Anthropological Approaches*, ed. Dan Handelman and Galina Lindquist (New York: Berghahn, 2011), pages xv–xix; Duke University Press, for excerpts from *The Palm at the End of the Mind: Relatedness, Religiosity and the Real* (Duke University Press, 2009), pages 162–67, and from *In Sierra Leone* (Duke University Press, 2004, 2005), pages 41–48.

NOTES

I. PREAMBLE

Chapter epigraph: Jean-Paul Sartre, "The Itinerary of a Thought," in *Between Existentialism and Marxism*, trans. John Matthews (London: Verso, 1983), 42.

1. Gregory Bateson and Margaret Mead, *Balinese Character: A Photographic Analysis*, vol. 2 (New York: Special Publications of the New York Academy of Sciences, 1942), 3. Also relevant here is Émile Durkheim's argument in *The Elementary Forms of the Religious Life*, that episodes of emotional intensity, delirium, "collective effervescence," and transgression are essential to social viability. *The Elementary Forms of the Religious Life*, trans. Joseph Ward Swain (New York: The Free Press, 1965), 258–59. The critical point is that such forms of uninhibited union allow "people to transcend the limits of their own personality and *become part of a larger and more powerful whole*." Sébastien Tutenges, "Louder! Wilder! Danish Youth at an International Nightlife Resort" (PhD thesis, University of Copenhagen, 2010), 28–29, emphasis added. These observations also bring to mind Elias Canetti's comments on the potential of a crowd to transcend difference. "Only together can men free themselves from their burdens of distance; and this, precisely, is what happens in a crowd. During the discharge distinctions are thrown off and all feel *equal*." *Crowds and Power*, trans. Carol Stewart (New York: Farrar, Straus and Giroux, 1984), 18, emphasis in original.

2. Bateson and Mead, *Balinese Character*, 3.

3. Ibid., 68.

4. *Moby Dick; or, The Whale* (Harmondsworth: Penguin, 1986), 497.

5. Daniel Stern, *The Interpersonal World of the Infant: A View from Psychoanalysis and Developmental Psychology* (New York: Basic Books, 1985), 74–75. Ed Tronick's more recent summary of ongoing research on primary intersubjectivity emphasizes the *collaboration* of infant and parent in regulating interaction and laying down the

neuro-behavioral foundations of a "dyadic consciousness"—incorporating complex information, experience, and mutual mappings into a relatively coherent whole that functions as a self-regulating system, effectively expanding the consciousness of one person into the consciousness of another. Dyadic consciousness begins in the stage of primary intersubjectivity, and, should an infant be "deprived of the experience of expanding his or her states of consciousness in collaboration with the other . . . this limits the infant's experience and forces the infant into self-regulatory patterns that eventually compromise the child's development." Ed Tronick, *The Neurobehavioral and Social-Emotional Development of Infants and Children* (New York: W. W. Norton, 2007), 292. See also Allan N. Schore, *Affect Regulation and the Repair of the Self* (New York: W. W. Norton, 2003), 37–41.

6. Karl Jaspers's axiom is crucial: "To analyze existence is to analyze consciousness." *Philosophy*, vol. 1, trans. E. B. Ashton (Chicago: University of Chicago Press, 1969), 49.

7. Laing's account of this dynamic and anxious relationship between being separate from and being connected to others echoes Otto Rank's conception of human existence as a perpetual oscillation between a highly individuated consciousness of oneself and a generalized consciousness of one's connectedness to others. These modes of awareness reflect the will to separate and the will to unite. Otto Rank, *Will Therapy: An Analysis of the Therapeutic Process in Terms of Relationship* (New York: Knopf, 1936), 31. Deeply influenced by Rank's thinking, Ernest Becker summarized the human dilemma as follows: "Man wants the impossible: He wants to lose his isolation and keep it at the same time. He can't stand the sense of separateness, and yet he can't allow the complete suffocation of his vitality. He wants to expand by merging with the powerful beyond that transcends him, yet he wants while merging with it to remain individual and aloof." *The Denial of Death* (New York: The Free Press, 1973), 155.

8. R. D. Laing, *The Divided Self* (Harmondsworth: Penguin, 1965), 26, emphasis in original. One of the most compelling ethnographic explorations of this tension between autonomy and interdependence is Robert Desjarlais's study of the Yolmo of Nepal. Desjarlais speaks of "two contradictory cultural values: those of independence and interdependence. Yolmo wa, though deeply communal beings, also profess a strong notion of individuality, with this dialectic fostering a conflict between the desire for autonomy and the need for independence." This sociocultural dynamic, he adds, is "common to Tibeto-Burman peoples of the Himalayan region." *Body and Emotion: The Aesthetics of Illness and Healing in the Nepal Himalayas* (Philadelphia: University of Pennsylvania Press, 1992), 47.

9. As Maurice Natanson puts it, "the paradox of the individual within the social [is] a 'metaphysical constant' of mundane existence." *Anonymity: A Study in the Philosophy of Alfred Schutz* (Bloomington: Indiana University Press, 1986), 143–44.

10. Garrett Hardin, "The Tragedy of the Commons," *Science* 162 (December 1968): 1243–48.

11. John Donne, "Meditation XVII," Devotions upon Emergent Occasions, in *The Complete Poetry and Selected Prose of John Donne*, ed. Charles M. Coffin (New York: Modern Library, 1952), 440–41.

12. In *The Varieties of Religious Experience* (New York: New American Library, 1958), William James cites Alphonse Daudet's recollections of his brother's death in support of the hypothesis that our tendency to apprehend the world in diametrically opposite ways drives us to seek experiences of unification. "The first time I perceived that I was two was at the death of my brother, Henri, when my father cried out so dramatically, 'He is dead, he is dead!' While my first self wept, my second self thought, 'How truly given was that cry, how fine it would be at the theatre.' I was fourteen at the time" (141). I cannot agree with either Daudet or James that such different attitudes imply psychological disharmony, discord, or "duplexity" since they are both modes of consciousness common to everyone and should not be ontologized as alternative personality types.

13. Philip M. Bromberg, *Standing in the Spaces: Essays on Clinical Process, Trauma, and Dissociation* (New York: Psychology Press, 2001), 57.

14. Henry James, *Roderick Hudson* (New York: Penguin Books, 1969), 27.

15. John Dewey, *Experience and Nature* (New York: Dover, 1958), 7. More recently Pierre Hadot has made a similar case for philosophy as a way of life, "a preparatory exercise for wisdom," involving "spiritual exercises" that might include dietary or discursive regimes, meditations or conversations, or practical action or intellectual reflection. *Philosophy as a Way of Life: Spiritual Exercises from Socrates to Foucault*, trans. Michael Chase (Oxford: Blackwell, 1995).

16. This ethnographic method was, however, employed earlier by the American anthropologists Frank Hamilton Cushing and Franz Boas.

17. Hortense Powdermaker, *Stranger and Friend* (New York: W. W. Norton, 1966).

18. Paul Ricoeur regards the dialectic between different modes of thought—detachment and involvement—as grounded in the *ontological* contrast between having a unique identity (ipse) and being identical with all other human beings (idem). Hence, the "dialectical tie between selfhood and otherness [is] more fundamental than the articulation between reflection and analysis." Ricoeur, *Oneself as Another*, trans. Kathleen Blamey (Chicago: University of Chicago Press, 1992), 317.

19. Ibid., 3.

20. Theodor Adorno observes: "Only at a remove from life can the mental life exist, and truly engage the empirical." But, he adds, "Distance is not a safety-zone but a field of tension" since thought can never attain the complete detachment that it longs for, and its vitality will always depend on its faithfulness to the complexity of the life it cannot contain in concepts or grasp in its entirety. *Minima Moralia: Reflections from Damaged Life*, trans. E. F. N. Jephcott (London: Verso, 1978), 128.

21. See Basil Bernstein's work on "primary socialization" in *Class, Codes and Control* (London: Routledge and Kegan Paul, 1975).

22. John Dewey, *How We Think* (Buffalo, NY: Prometheus Books, 1991), 138.

23. Claude Lévi-Strauss, *The Savage Mind* (*La Pensée Sauvage*) (London: Weidenfeld and Nicolson, 1966), 13.

24. Ibid., 3.

25. Claude Lévi-Strauss, *Totemism*, trans. Rodney Needham (Harmondsworth: Penguin, 1969), 158–59. My own fieldwork among the Kuku Yalanji of southeast Cape York, Australia, provides a second example. Two intermarrying moieties, Dabu and Walla, are named after two kinds of bees—one yellow-bodied and the other black-bodied—thus establishing their simultaneous identity *and* difference. Michael Jackson, *Minima Ethnographica: Intersubjectivity and the Anthropological Project* (Chicago: University of Chicago Press, 1999), 180.

26. That philological and unconscious connections may be traced among words such as "knee," "know," "narrate," "generate," "generation," and "can" suggests that an ability to go out into the world, independently, "on one's own two feet," is basic to knowing how to exist socially and to reproduce one's kind. H. A. Bunker and B. D. Lewis, "A Psychoanalytic Notation on the Root GN, KN, CN," in *Psychoanalysis and Culture*, ed. G. B. Wilbur and W. Muensterberger (New York: International Universities Press, 1965), 363–67.

27. Dewey, *How We Think*, 12.

28. Tronick, *Neurobehavioral and Social-Emotional Development*, 289.

29. Aldous Huxley, *Eyeless in Gaza* (London: Flamingo, 1994), 3.

30. *Letters of Aldous Huxley*, ed. Grover Smith (London: Chatto and Windus, 1969), 400.

31. The phrase is from the title of F. Mathias Alexander's *Constructive Conscious Control of the Individual* (London: Methuen, 1924).

32. Huxley, *Eyeless in Gaza*, 235.

33. John Dewey, *Human Nature and Conduct: An Introduction to Social Psychology* (New York: Holt, 1922), 30.

34. Ibid., 35–37.

35. Derek Freeman, "Totem and Taboo: A Reappraisal," in *Man and His Culture: Psychoanalytic Anthropology after "Totem and Taboo,"* ed. W. Muensterberger (New York: Taplinger, 1969), 53–78.

36. Sigmund Freud, *Totem and Taboo: Some Points of Agreement between the Mental Lives of Savages and Neurotics*, trans. James Strachey (London: Routledge and Kegan Paul, 1960), 141–42.

37. Ibid., 143.

38. Freeman, "Totem and Taboo," 66–78.

39. Sigmund Freud, *Moses and Monotheism: Three Essays* (New York: Alfred Knopf, 1939), 131. Cited by Derek Freeman, 74.

40. Henry Miller, *The Books in My Life* (New York: New Directions, 1969), 75, emphasis in original.

41. Michel Foucault, *The Order of Things: An Archaeology of the Human Sciences* (London: Tavistock, 1970), 387.

42. James Miller, *The Passion of Michel Foucault* (New York: Simon and Schuster, 1993), 379.

43. Ibid., 355.

44. Ibid., 366–70. Foucault's discovery of the fascist in himself recalls Adorno's recollections of five school yard bullies "who set upon a single schoolfellow, thrashed him and, when he complained to the teacher, defamed him a traitor to the class." These were, Adorno writes, "the warning signs of the German awakening [and] I recognized them all in the features of Hitler's dictatorship." Adorno, *Minima Moralia*, 192–93.

45. Lionel Trilling, "Introduction" to *Homage to Catalonia*, by George Orwell (New York: Harcourt Brace Jovanovich, 1952), xi–x; quotation from p. x.

46. Ibid., xvi.

47. Paul Ricoeur, *Freud and Philosophy: An Essay in Interpretation*, trans. Denis Savage (New Haven, CT: Yale University Press, 1970), 32–36.

48. Henry Ellenberger, *The Discovery of the Unconscious* (New York: Basic Books, 1970), 537.

49. Claude Lévi-Strauss, *Tristes Tropiques* (London: Jonathan Cape, 1973), 57–58. Cf. Heidegger's adaptation of the Greek notion of aletheia ("unconcealment") as philosophical method. Unlike Lévi-Strauss, Heidegger is careful *not* to claim that what one discloses is necessarily the truth. "The End of Philosophy and the Task of Thinking," in *Martin Heidegger: Basic Writings*, ed. David Farrell Krell (New York: Harper & Row, 1977), 386–92.

50. Carla Stang, *A Walk to the River in Amazonia: Ordinary Reality for the Mehinaku Indians* (New York: Berghahn, 2009), 48–52.

51. The English word "mask" derives from the Arabic maskhara, which also gives us, via the Italian, the word "mascara" and, via the French, the word "masque" (a theatrical or musical entertainment), with its connotations of dissimulation, assumed appearance, disguise, pretense, and false-seeming.

52. Foucault, *Order of Things*, 326.

53. Plato, *The Republic*, 2d ed., trans. Desmond Lee (Harmondsworth: Penguin, 1974), 264.

54. Ibid., 370–71.

55. Hannah Arendt, *The Human Condition* (Chicago: University of Chicago Press, 1958), 50, 51–52.

56. Hanna Fenichel Pitkin, *The Attack of the Blob: Hannah Arendt's Concept of the Social* (Chicago: University of Chicago Press, 1998).

57. *Das Man* signifies people in the abstract: "the they," "the others," the undifferentiated crowd.

58. Cited by Walter Benjamin, *The Writer of Modern Life: Essays on Charles Baudelaire* (Cambridge, MA: The Belknap Press of Harvard University Press, 2006), 209–10.

59. This image echoes the final scene of Marcel Carné's great film *Les Enfants du Paradis* (1945).

60. Natsume Soseki, *Kusamakura*, trans. Meredith McKinney (Harmondsworth: Penguin, 2008), 143–44.

61. Otto Rank, *Will Therapy: An Analysis of the Therapeutic Process in Terms of Relationship* (New York: Knopf, 1936), 31.

62. Ernest Becker, *The Denial of Death* (New York: The Free Press, 1973), 155.

2. THE PHILOSOPHER WHO WOULD NOT BE KING

Chapter epigraph: Richard Rorty, *Philosophy and Social Hope* (London: Penguin, 1999), 11.

1. Not so, in the view of Stanley Cavell, who has long acknowledged the ways in which his philosophizing "tends perpetually to intersect the autobiographical," observing that Wittgenstein, more than any other philosopher of the twentieth century, has shown "how it happens that a certain strain of philosophy inescapably takes on autobiography, or . . . an abstraction of autobiography." Stanley Cavell, *Little Did I Know: Excerpts from Memory* (Stanford, CA: Stanford University Press, 2010), 2, 6.

2. *Philosophy and the Mirror of Nature* (Princeton, NJ: Princeton University Press, 1979).

3. *Philosophy and Social Hope* (London: Penguin, 1999), 6.

4. Ibid., 7–8.

5. Richard Rorty, "Trotsky and the Wild Orchids," in *Wild Orchids and Trotsky*, ed. Mark Edmundson (Harmondsworth: Penguin, 1993), 29–50; quotation from pp. 34–35.

6. *Philosophy and Social Hope*, 266.

7. Published in the November 2007 issue of *Poetry* magazine.

8. Bruce Kapferer, *The Feast of the Sorcerer: Practices of Consciousness and Power* (Chicago: University of Chicago Press, 1997), 1.

9. Kapferer, *Feast of the Sorcerer*, 48–50.

10. Richard Rorty, *Contingency, Irony, and Solidarity* (Cambridge: Cambridge University Press, 1989), xv.

11. Ibid., xvi.

12. *Philosophy and Social Hope*, 227.

13. Ibid.

3. HERMIT IN THE WATER OF LIFE

The chapter title is taken from the fifth volume of Thomas Merton's journals, *Dancing in the Water of Life: Seeking Peace in the Hermitage*, ed. Robert E. Daggy (San Francisco: HarperCollins, 1997), 243.

The chapter epigraph is from an untitled, unpublished poem by Brijen K. Gupta.

1. Brijen K. Gupta was born on September 17, 1929.

2. For many years I thought the poem was Brijen's, but it was written by Winifred Rawlins, a Quaker friend. *The Fire Within* (New York: Golden Quill Press, 1959), 36.

3. Albert J. Raboteau, *A Fire in the Bones: Reflections on African-American Religious History* (Boston: Beacon Press, 1995).

4. Thomas Merton, *Conjectures of a Guilty Bystander* (Garden City, NY: Doubleday, 1966), 140–41.

5. Arthur Koestler, *The Yogi and the Commissar and Other Essays* (London: Jonathan Cape, 1985), 10–11.

6. In 1964, though not yet a U.S. citizen, Brijen was arrested for civil disobedience in Tougaloo, Mississippi, an incident that led, ironically, "to a lifelong friendship with the deputy sheriff," who Brijen described as "a rabid racist."

7. Ashis Nandy, *The Intimate Enemy: Loss and Recovery of Self under Colonialism* (Oxford: Oxford University Press, 1988), 90.

8. Agehananda Bharati, *The Ochre Robe* (Seattle: University of Washington Press, 1962), 244. See also *The Tantric Tradition* (London: Rider, 1965).

9. See William A. Gerhard and Brijen K. Gupta, "Literature: The Phenomenological Art," *Man and World* 3, no. 2 (1970): 102–15.

10. Dr. Ram Manohar Lohia (1910–1967) was an Indian freedom fighter and a Socialist political leader who helped establish the Congress Socialist Party in 1934 and wrote numerous articles on the feasibility of a Socialist India.

11. Dr. Sarvepalli Radhakrishnan (1888–1975) was an Indian philosopher and statesman. One of India's most acclaimed scholars of comparative religion and philosophy, he tried to build a bridge between East and West by showing that their philosophical systems were mutually intelligible. He was the first vice president of India (1952–1962) and the second president of India (1962–1967).

12. R. L. Nigam joined the DAV English faculty while Brijen was at Benares Hindu University. They became lifelong friends.

13. Cārvāka (also known as Lokāyata) is a materialist, skeptical Indian philosophy that eschews religious foundations. It is named after its founder, Cārvāka, author of the Bārhaspatya-sūtras.

14. Maharishi Ramana (1879–1950) inspired Paul Brunton's *In Search of Secret India* (London: Rider & Co.,1934).

15. J. A. Chadwick (1899–1939) was educated at Cambridge and became a Fellow of Trinity College.

16. Gertrude Emerson Sen (1892–1982) was also a geographer and explorer and the author of *Voiceless India* (London: George Allen & Unwin, 1931).

17. Born in 1898, Nixon joined the Royal Flying Corps and served in a fighting squadron during the First World War. "His direct experiences with the death and destruction of warfare filled him with a sense of futility and meaninglessness.... After the war Nixon enrolled in King's College at Cambridge University to study English literature. There he discovered Buddhism, being particularly attracted to the life story of the Buddha. Like many others interested in Buddhism at that time,

Nixon became involved with the Theosophical Society." David Haberman, "A Cross-Cultural Adventure: The Transformation of Ronald Nixon," *Religion* 23 (1993): 217–27.

18. As George Orwell observes, Gandhi's struggle was not against sexuality per se but against intimate and preferential attachments that, by their passionate and exclusive nature, prove inimical to the service of God and humanity. "Reflections on Gandhi," *Partisan Review* 6, no. 1 (1949): 85–92.

19. Horace G. Alexander (1889–1989) was a teacher and writer who headed the British Quaker relief effort in India. A champion of Indian independence from Britain, he was a friend of Gandhi and was Gandhi's host on a visit to England when negotiations for independence began in the mid-1940s.

20. Anandamayi Ma (1896–1981) was a visionary, renowned for her spiritual powers (siddhis) and intense religious emotionality. She described herself as bereft or empty of any sense of personal identity, completely at one with the great void (mahasunya) to which she ascribed her actions, emotions, and yogic abilities.

21. Brijen cannot recall how he came to know Gwen Catchpool. "She and her husband Corder (who was to fall to his death mountain climbing in 1952) had been Quaker representatives in Nazi Germany. They now lived at 49 Parliament Hill, Hampstead, which was for years to come my second home. At some point she wrote to Horace Alexander asking him if I was real, and Alexander, surprised that I was in correspondence with her, suggested that I seek her advice in getting to England/ Europe."

22. T. R. V. Murti's (1902–1986) great work is *The Central Philosophy of Buddhism: A Study of Madhyamika System* (London: G. Allen and Unwin, 1955).

23. After graduating from Benares Hindu University, Beena Banerjee went to Calcutta, where she and her husband, the distinguished journalist Hamdi Bey, enriched the city's intellectual life.

24. Abraham Johannes Muste (1885–1967) was a Christian Socialist, active in the pacifist movement, the labor movement, and the U.S. civil rights movement. Author of *Non-Violence in an Aggressive World* (New York: Harper & Bros., 1940), Muste was also a minister of the Religious Society of Friends and general secretary of the Amalgamated Textile Workers of America from 1920 to 1921. As executive director of the Fellowship of Reconciliation, he became an advisor to Martin Luther King Jr.

25. The Catholic Worker was both the name of a newspaper and a movement aimed at realizing in the individual and in society the teachings of Christ. "The principles of the movement called for the rejection of capitalism as far as that is possible and the establishment of a 'distributist' economy" in which workers owned the means of production and distribution. William O. Paulsell, *Tough Minds, Tender Hearts: Six Prophets of Social Justice* (New York: Paulist Press, 1990), 92.

26. Thomas Merton, *Turning toward the World: The Pivotal Years*, ed. Victor A. Kramer (San Francisco: HarperSanFrancisco, 1996), 291.

27. Thomas Merton, *Dancing in the Water of Life: Seeking Peace in the Hermitage*, ed. Robert E. Daggy (San Francisco: HarperSanFrancisco, 1997), 259.

28. Bernard McGinn, "Withdrawal and Return: Reflections on Monastic Retreat from the World," *Spiritus* 6, no. 2 (2006): 149–72.

29. Pendle Hill was established in Wallingford, Pennsylvania, in 1930 as a Quaker study center designed to prepare its adult students for service both in the Religious Society of Friends and in the world. The founders envisioned a new Quaker School of Social and Religious Education that would be "a vital center of spiritual culture" and "a place for training leaders" [Rufus Jones, Preliminary Announcement, 1929].

30. Perhaps the most renowned historian of his time, Toynbee's focus was the rise and fall of civilizations. Unlike Spengler, who regarded decline as inevitable, Toynbee argued that a society's longevity and vitality depended on how creatively it responded to physical and social challenges. That civilizations so often sink into a slough of nationalism, militarism, and despotism led him to argue that "Civilizations die from suicide, not by murder."

31. The line is from Merton's *Dancing in the Water of Life*, 243.

32. Scott Milross Buchanan (1895–1968) was an American educator, philosopher, and foundation consultant, renowned as the founder of the Great Books program at St. John's College, Annapolis, Maryland. Brijen first met Buchanan in 1954 and was introduced to the Toynbee seminar by him. Brijen regarded Buchanan as one of his greatest mentors.

33. Milton Mayer, "The Christer," *Fellowship* 18, no. 1 (1952): 1–10.

34. With other members of the Socialist Workers Party, Brijen distanced himself from Schachtman in 1959, when he became a neoconservative, cold war warrior.

35. The date of Brijen wife's, Ginny's, nervous breakdown.

36. *Sirajuddaullah and the East India Company, 1756–1757: Background to the Foundation of British Rule in India* (Leiden: E. J. Brill, 1962, rev. ed., 1966).

37. Val was my brother-in-law, and it was through him that I was introduced to Brijen.

38. McGinn, "Withdrawal and Return," 153.

39. *Ochre Robe*, 10.

40. In anthropological parlance, a kindred is a group of individuals related to one another not through descent alone but through a person's *chosen* affiliations to a pivotal figure. Derek Freeman, "On the Concept of the Kindred," *Journal of the Royal Anthropological Institute* 91 (1961): 192–220.

4. WRITING WORKSHOP

Chapter epigraph: David Mamet, *On Directing Film* (London: Faber and Faber, 1991), 6.

1. Glenn Kurtz, *Practicing: A Musician's Return to Music* (New York: Alfred A. Knopf, 2007), 209.

2. Ibid., 204.

3. Ibid., 211.

4. Ibid., 179–80.

5. Keith Egan, "Walking Back to Happiness? Modern Pilgrimage and the Expression of Suffering on Spain's Camino de Santiago," *The International Journal of Travel and Travel; Writing* 11, no. 1 (2010): 107–32; quotation from p. 115.

6. W. B. Yeats, *Collected Poems* (London: Macmillan, 1958), 268.

7. Donald Schell, cited in Egan, "Walking Back," 113.

8. "Stream and Sun at Glendalough," in Yeats, *Collected Poems*, 288–89.

9. Seamus Heaney, "St. Kevin and the Blackbird," in *The Spirit Level* (London: Faber, 1996), 24.

10. Henry David Thoreau, *Walden* (Boston: Beacon Press, 1997), 76.

11. Nancy Scheper-Hughes, Preface to the 1982 paperback edition of *Saints, Scholars, and Schizophrenics: Mental Illness in Rural Ireland* (Berkeley: University of California Press, 2001), xviii.

12. Cited by Michael Viney, "The Yank in the Corner," *The Irish Times*, August 6, 1983.

13. Joan Didion, *Slouching toward Bethlehem* (New York: Farrar, Straus & Giroux, 1968), xvi.

14. Nancy Scheper-Hughes, "Ire in Ireland," *Ethnography* 1, no. 1 (2000): 117–40; quotations from pp. 120, 127.

15. Scheper-Hughes, *Saints, Scholars, and Schizophrenics*, 311.

16. Immanuel Kant, *Groundwork of the Metaphysic of Morals*, trans. H. J. Patton (New York: Harper & Row, 1964), 98 and passim.

5. HOW MUCH HOME DOES A PERSON NEED?

The title is from Jean Améry, *At the Mind's Limits*, trans. Sidney Rosenfeld and Stella P. Rosenfeld (London: Granta Books, 1999), 41.

Chapter epigraph: John Berger, *And Our Faces, My Heart, Brief as Photos* (London: Writers and Readers, 1984), 67.

1. The terms are Arthur Kleinman and Joan Kleinman's. "Suffering and Its Professional Transformation: Toward an Ethnography of Interpersonal Experience," *Culture, Medicine and Psychiatry* 15, no. 3 (1991): 275–301.

2. *Anthropology through the Looking-Glass: Critical Ethnography on the Margins of Europe* (Cambridge: Cambridge University Press, 1987).

3. Identity connotes both equality *and* distinction; while *idem* suggests that one is the same as others, *ipse* suggests that one is unique in contrast to others. Hannah Arendt, *The Human Condition* (Chicago: University of Chicago Press, 1958), 175. See also Paul Ricoeur, *Oneself as Another*, trans. Kathleen Blamey (Chicago: University of Chicago Press, 1992), 2–3, 116.

4. Michael Jackson, *The Politics of Storytelling: Violence, Transgression and Intersubjectivity* (Copenhagen: Museum Tusculanum Press, 2002).

5. Maxine Gordon, "Dexter Gordon in Europe," liner notes from *Dexter Gordon Live in '63 & '64* (DVD Jazz Icons, cat. no. 19002: Naxos), 4–5.

6. Though intellectuals and musicians were open to the African American expatriates, other Danes were not. When Louis Armstrong first came to Denmark in 1933, he was referred to in the local press as "the ape from the jungle" and "nothing to do with music." Jørgen Pedersen, personal communication, May 15, 2009.

7. Justin B. Richland, "On Neoliberalism and Other Social Diseases: The 2008 Sociocultural Anthropology Year in Review," *American Anthropologist* 111, no. 2 (June 2009): 170–76.

8. Jeroen de Valk, *Ben Webster: His Life and Music* (Berkeley: Berkeley Hills Books, 2001), 139. Also see Frank Büchmann Møller, *Someone to Watch Over Me: The Life and Music of Ben Webster* (Ann Arbor: University of Michigan Press, 2006), 273.

9. Vincent Crapanzano writes eloquently of how a Moroccan friend compared the "in-between" (*barzakh* and *barzakh*) to the "silence between words and to dreams." *Imaginative Horizons: An Essay in Literary-Philosophical Anthropology* (Chicago: University of Chicago Press, 2003), 57. See also Paul Stoller's comments on the "between" in medieval Sufism, as well as in his own research experiences with Songhay spirit possession. *The Power of the Between: An Anthropological Odyssey* (Chicago: University of Chicago Press, 2009), 1–11.

10. George Orwell, "Reflections on Gandhi," *Partisan Review* 16 (January 1949), 85–92.

11. Søren Kierkegaard, *Fear and Trembling*, trans. Howard V. Hong and Edna H. Hong (Princeton, NJ: Princeton University Press, 1983), 47.

12. Albert Camus, *American Journals*, trans. Hugh Levick (New York: Paragon House, 1987), 60.

13. Camus, *American Journals*, 69.

14. Cited in Oliver Todd, *Albert Camus: A Life* (New York: Vintage, 1998), 194.

15. Ibid., 404.

16. Nella Larsen, *Quicksand*, ed. Thadious M. Davis (New York: Penguin, 2002), 64.

17. George Hutchinson, *In Search of Nella Larsen: A Biography of the Color Line* (Cambridge, MA: Belknap Press of Harvard University Press, 2006), 25.

18. David Leeming, *James Baldwin: A Biography* (New York: Henry Holt, 1994), 240.

19. Cited in Lena Ahlin, *The "New Negro" in the Old World: Culture and Performance in James Weldon Johnson, Jessie Fauset, and Nella Larsen* (Lund: Department of English, Lund University, 2006), 103.

20. Henry Louis Gates Jr., "White Like Me," *New Yorker*, June 17, 1996, 66–81.

21. Zora Neale Hurston, "How It Feels to Be Colored Me," in *I Love Myself When I Am Laughing: A Zora Neale Hurston Reader*, ed. Alice Walker (Old Westbury, NY: The Feminist Press, 1979), 153.

22. Published in *Ms.*, March 3, 1975, 74–79, 84–89.

23. Hurston, "How It Feels," 154–55, emphasis in original. In arguing that her interest lay "in what makes a man or a woman do such and such-and-so, regardless of his color," Zora Hurston was at pains to avoid self-defensiveness and self-pity. But by celebrating her own belligerent individualism at the expense of describing racial

discrimination, she risks bracketing out experiences that were central to the everyday reality of life for other African Americans living under the regime of Jim Crow. Robert E. Hemenway, *Zora Neale Hurston: A Literary Biography* (Urbana: University of Illinois Press, 1977), 281.

24. "I was born in the nightmare of the white man's mind." Kalamu ya Salaam and James Baldwin, "James Baldwin: Looking towards the Eighties," in *Conversations with James Baldwin*, ed. Fred Standley and Louis H. Pratt (Jackson, MS: University Press of Mississippi, 1989), 177–85, especially p. 181.

25. James Baldwin, *Nobody Knows My Name: More Notes of a Native Son* (New York: Dell, 1961), 17; emphasis in original.

6. CLEARINGS IN THE BUSH

Chapter epigraph: From T. S. Eliot, *Little Gidding*.

1. Arthur Schopenhauer, *The Essays*, trans. T. Bailey Saunders (New York: Wiley, 1926), 26, emphasis in original.

2. Arthur Schopenhauer, "Aphorisms on the Wisdom of Life," in *Parerga and Paralipomena: Short Philosophical Essays*, vol. 1, trans. E. F. J. Payne (Oxford: Clarendon Press, 1974), 321.

3. Arthur Schopenhauer, "Similes, Parables and Fables," in *Parerga and Paralipomena*, 651–52.

4. Sigmund Freud, *Group Psychology and the Analysis of the Ego*, trans. James Strachey (New York: Norton, 1959), 33.

5. Dominque Zahan, *The Bambara* (Leiden: E. J. Brill, 1974), 5.

6. *Parerga and Paralipomena*, vols. 2, 3.

7. Primo Levi, *Other People's Trades*, trans. Raymond Rosenthal (London: Michael Joseph, 1989), vii.

8. Given the evidence of police abuse of Aboriginal detainees, it may be irrelevant to distinguish between real or imaginary voices. What is significant is the grave danger, dissociation, and disorientation that come from being isolated from one's own kith and kin, at the mercy of strangers with a reputation for racist brutality, and subject to the terrors of the dark.

9. A "reformed Aboriginal alcoholic" quoted in Ernest M. Hunter, "Aboriginal Suicides in Custody: A View from the Kimberley," *Australian and New Zealand Journal of Psychiatry* 22 (1988): 273–82; quotation from p. 279.

10. Peter's parents survived the Nazi years by migrating to South America.

11. As "enemy aliens," the German refugees were not allowed to handle weapons.

12. Patricia Dobrez and Peter Herbst, *The Art of the Boyds: Generations of Artistic Achievement* (Sydney: Bay Books, 1990), 198.

13. Ibid.

14. Peter writes that, in the 1940s and 1950s, artists and academics enjoyed "an easy fellowship" with professional people, trade unionists, writers, radicals, and public servants in the pubs. "Such unconstrained and pleasurable interchange of

ideas in the vernacular is now only a memory. Neither the art scene nor the desperately defensive modern university favours such openness. The philosophers have become so technical, so 'professional,' that few people outside the seminar-room have much hope of understanding them." *Art of the Boyds*, 201.

15. Ibid., 206.

16. Ibid., 108.

17. Ibid., 112.

18. Ibid., 115.

19. Ibid., 162.

7. THE GULF OF CORINTH

Chapter epigraph: Lawrence Durrell, "The Tree of Idleness," in *Collected Poems* (London: Faber and Faber, 1960), 51.

1. Perhaps the most powerful and eloquent of these critiques is Christopher Lasch's *The Culture of Narcissism: American Life in an Age of Diminishing Expectations* (New York: Norton, 1978).

2. Ibid., 5.

3. Erich Fromm, *Man for Himself: An Enquiry into the Psychology of Ethics* (London: Routledge and Kegan Paul, 1949), 237.

4. Ibid., 96, emphasis added.

5. Ibid., 129, emphasis in original.

6. William Faulkner, *Requiem for a Nun*, act 1, scene 3.

7. I had been living in Menton since late August 1982 with my first wife Pauline and my daughter Heidi. Heidi, my firstborn daughter, was thirteen at this time.

8. Billy Moss, an officer in the Coldstream Guards, was Leigh Fermor's collaborator in the kidnapping.

9. Deborah Devonshire, "Patrick Leigh Fermor," in *In Tearing Haste: Letters between Deborah Devonshire and Patrick Leigh Fermor*, ed. Charlotte Mosley (London: John Murray, 2008), xv–xvi. There are two minor errors in this account: the guerillas reached Mt. Ida *three* days after the kidnapping, and Leigh Fermor read *five* stanzas of Horace's *Ad Thaliarchum* 1. ix.

10. Patrick Leigh Fermor, *A Time of Gifts* (New York: New York Review of Books, 2005), 86.

11. Maurice Cardiff, *Friend Abroad: Memories of Lawrence Durrell, Freya Stark, Patrick Leigh-Fermor, Peggy Guggenheim and Others* (London: The Radcliffe Press, 1997), 19.

12. Patrick Leigh Fermor, *A Time to Keep Silence* (New York: New York Review of Books, 1982), xvii. Even in his youth, Leigh Fermor had experienced the attraction of monastic life, describing in *A Time of Gifts* his visit to the Benedictine Abbey at Göttweig, where an Irish monk "of immense age and great charm" showed the young wayfarer around. "I envied his airy and comfortable cell, his desk laden with books, and his view over the mountains and the river" (*A Time of Gifts*, 187).

13. These details are culled from Sofka's *Eurydice Street: A Place in Athens* (London: Granta Books, 2004), 13.

14. Virginia Woolf, *Jacob's Room* (New York: Harcourt Brace Jovanovich, 1960), 151.

15. Neni Panourgiá, *Dangerous Citizens: The Greek Left and the Terror of the State* (New York: Fordham University Press, 2009), 56.

16. Ibid., 57.

17. Ibid., 19.

18. Ibid., 92–93.

19. "Exiles on the Greek islands where concentration camps were established for the Leftists in 1947, as Civil War was raging, saw Oedipus from a different light, so to speak. Beaten, tortured, and pressured to sign declarations that they were not what they maintained to be (Leftists) but something that they were not (Christian nationalists), they found themselves somatically in the place of Oedipus: with swollen feet from bastinado, gouged eyes from strikes on the head, being asked to answer the unanswerable question, are you (with us) or are you not? —all the while being told the same thing, you will become human (*ánthropoi*) or you will die" (111). See Neni Panourgiá, "Fragments of Oedipus: Anthropology at the Edges of History," in *Ethnographica Moralia: Experiments in Interpretive Anthropology*, ed. Neni Panourgiá and George Marcus (New York: Fordham University Press, 2008), 97–112.

20. The term is J. M. Coetzee's. See "All Autobiography Is 'Autre-biography': J. M. Coetzee Interviewed by David Atwell," in *Selves in Question: Interviews on Southern African Auto/Biography*, ed. J. L. Coullie et al. (Honolulu, 2006).

21. As Neni remarks often in her book, storytelling is dangerous. Even close family would tell her to be careful what she wrote, what was necessary to remember, and what was wisest to suppress. "You know better than I do," an uncle told her, "*scripta manet* and there are still a lot of people alive from that time" (*Dangerous Citizens*, 20).

22. Simon Critchley, "Have a Happy Afterlife," *International Herald Tribune*, June 25, 2009.

23. Robert Graves, *The Greek Myths*, vol. 1 (Harmondsworth: Penguin, 1955), 41.

24. Octavio Paz, *The Labyrinth of Solitude* (New York: Grove Press, 1985), 209.

25. Michael Jackson, "The Gulf of Corinth," in *Being of Two Minds* (Wellington: Steele Roberts Publishers, 2011), 15–16.

26. Sofka, *Eurydice Street*, 27.

27. Henry Miller, *The Colossus of Maroussi* (London: Heinemann, 1960), 79.

28. George Orwell, "Inside the Whale," in *Selected Essays* (Harmondsworth: Penguin, 1957), 9–50.

29. Miller, *Colossus*, 82.

8. IT'S OTHER PEOPLE WHO ARE MY OLD AGE

Chapter epigraph: Maurice Merleau-Ponty, *The Phenomenology of Perception*, trans. Colin Smith (London: Routledge, 1989), 347.

1. Jean-Paul Sartre and Benny Levy, *Hope Now: The 1980 Interviews*, trans. Adrian Van Den Houten (Chicago: University of Chicago Press, 2007), 72.

2. Lawrence Durrell, *Balthazar* (London: Faber and Faber, 1958), 14–15.

3. Jean-Paul Sartre, *Search for a Method*, trans. H. Barnes (New York: Vintage, 1968), 91.

4. Jean-Paul Sartre, "Itinerary of a Thought," *New Left Review* 58 (1969): 43–66; quotation from p. 45.

5. "The mixed Maori population of Pukekohe have given themselves a name—Nga Hau E Wha (The Four Winds)—which expresses their varied backgrounds. The Four Winds of Maoridom appear to have been caught in the stronger current of change, and it is worthwhile considering the direction in which they are blowing." B. Kernot, "Which Way Are the Winds Blowing," *Te Ao Hou* 42 (March 1963): 20.

6. By contrast, Joan Metge, who studied under Piddington several years earlier, recalls him as a "gifted teacher [whose] carefully crafted lectures were made memorable by a fund of jokes." *Dictionary of New Zealand Biography*, vol. 5 (Wellington, N.Z.: Allen & Unwin; Dept. of Internal Affairs, 1990–2000), 411.

7. Ralph Piddington, *An Introduction to Social Anthropology*, vol. 1 (London: Oliver and Boyd, 1952), 14.

8. Piddington, *An Introduction to Social Anthropology*, vol. 2 (London: Oliver and Boyd, 1952), 543.

9. Ibid., 546.

10. Ibid., 549.

11. Ibid., 781.

12. D. J. Mulvaney, "Australian Anthropology: Foundations and Funding," *Aboriginal History* 17, no. 2 (1993): 105–28. See also Geoffrey Gray, "'Piddington's Indiscretion': Ralph Piddington, the Australian National Research Council and Academic Freedom." *Oceania* 64, no. 3 (1994): 217–45.

13. Ralph Piddington, "Aborigines on Cattle Stations Are in Slavery: Anthropologist Piddington Backs World's Probe Demand." *The World*, January 14, 1932, 1.

14. Ralph Piddington, "Treatment of Aborigines: World's Plea for Better Conditions Receives Attention Abroad." *The World*, July 7, 1932, 6–7.

15. A. O. Neville, the chief protector at this time, may be familiar to some readers from his portrayal in the 2002 film *Rabbit Proof Fence*. A diehard paternalist, Neville believed that biological absorption was the key to "uplifting the Native race." In defense of policies of forced settlement, removing children from parents, surveillance, discipline, and punishment, Neville argued that Aboriginals had to be protected from themselves whether they liked it or not. "They cannot remain as they are. The sore spot requires the application of the surgeon's knife for the good of the patient, and probably against the patient's will." Cited in Stephen Kinnane, *Shadow Lines* (Fremantle, Western Australia: Fremantle Arts Centre Press, 2003), 253.

16. Geoffrey G. Gray, *A Cautious Silence: The Politics of Australian Anthropology* (Canberra: Aboriginal Studies Press, 2007), 113.

17. Mulvaney, "Australian Anthropology," 122–23.

9. OBJECTS IN MIRROR ARE CLOSER THAN THEY APPEAR

Chapter title is taken from words stenciled on the rearview mirrors of most modern cars.

Chapter epigraph: Galina Lindquist, *Conjuring Hope: Healing and Magic in Contemporary Russia* (New York: Berghahn, 2006), 192.

1. Galina Lindquist, *Conjuring Hope: Healing and Magic in Contemporary Russia* (New York: Berghahn, 2006), xiv.

2. Galina Lindquist, "In Search of the Magical Flow: Magic and Market in Contemporary Russia," *Urban Anthropology* 29, no. 4 (2000): 315–57.

3. Lindquist, *Conjuring Hope*, 199.

4. Ibid., 80.

5. Ibid., 229.

6. Maurice Merleau-Ponty, "From Mauss to Lévi-Strauss," in *Signs*, trans. R. C. McLeary (Evanston, IL: Northwestern University Press, 1964), 119.

7. During Galina's last field trip in Tuva, she was brutally informed by a local woman healer that she had cancer. Feigning great distress, the healer offered not only to cure Galina's cancer but to collaborate in writing a book with her. In a posthumously published paper, Galina describes the overwhelming dread this diagnosis caused her and how—when she had recovered her equilibrium—she came to value the insights this traumatic episode had given her into how healers work by intimidating their clients, asserting their authority, and inspiring belief in their powers. But as for accepting the healer's offer, Galina speaks of this moment as a baptism of fire: "I must admit that I was not prepared to go that far: the face of the Other as the face of death was too much for me." Galina Lindquist, personal communication, 2007.

8. Gillian Rose, *Love's Work: A Reckoning with Life* (New York: Schocken Books, 1995).

9. *The Cloude of Unknowyng* is an anonymous fourteenth century work of Christian mysticism that emphasizes spiritual union with God through contemplative prayer and love rather than thought and knowledge.

10. D. W. Winnicott, *Playing and Reality* (Harmondsworth: Penguin, 1974), 126–27.

11. Maurice Merleau-Ponty, *Phenomenology of Perception*, trans. Colin Smith (London: Routledge, 1962), 353.

12. Ibid., 359.

13. Ibid., 354.

14. Martin Heidegger, *Being and Time*, trans. John Macquarie and Edward Robinson (New York: Harper and Row, 1962), 226–27.

15. Michael Oakeshott, *Rationalism in Politics and Other Essays* (London: Methuen, 1962), 119.

16. Galina Lindquist, "'Being a Hostage to the Other': Levinas's Ethical Epistemology and Dysphoric Fieldwork Experiences." In *Anthropological Fieldwork: A*

Relational Process, ed. Dimitrina Spencers and James Davies (Newcastle upon Tyne: Cambridge Scholars Publishing, 2010), 195–203.

17. In his magisterial comparative study of doctrines of rebirth in Buddhist, Greek, and Amerindian traditions, Gananath Obeyesekere shows that despite "vast differences" these doctrines have "important structural similarities and variations based on a shared belief in reincarnation." *Imagining Karma: Ethical Transformations in Amerindian, Buddhist, and Greek Rebirth* (Berkeley: University of California Press 2002), xiv. Obeyesekere's preoccupation with deductive models and "elementary structures" unfortunately precludes explorations of the experiential bases of such eschatologies.

18. Norbert Elias, *Involvement and Detachment*, trans. Edmund Jephcott (Oxford: Basil Blackwell, 1987), xviii.

19. Meyer Fortes, *Oedipus and Job in West African Religion* (Cambridge: Cambridge University Press, 1983), 15.

20. Ibid., 23.

21. Robin Horton even suggests that West African cosmologies "probably represent attempts by other people to conceptualize motivational conflicts in an essentially Freudian way," as if Freud's analysis is analytically more sophisticated and therapeutically more useful than these primitive precursors. Robin Horton, "Destiny and the Unconscious in West Africa," *Africa* 31, no. 2 (1961): 115.

22. Alma Gottlieb, *The Afterlife Is Where We Come From: The Culture of Infancy in West Africa* (Chicago: University of Chicago Press, 2004), 79.

23. Ibid., 80.

24. Ibid., 79.

25. "The appallingly high mortality rate for infants and young children . . . looms large in the consciousness of every Beng mother," writes Alma Gottlieb (*Afterlife*, 93).

26. Ibid., 88.

27. Ibid., 98.

28. Ibid., 273–76.

29. Merleau-Ponty, *Phenomenology of Perception*, 358.

30. Nicolas Wood, "Strains of a Balkan Ballad," *International Herald Tribune*, November 14, 2004.

31. Rose, *Love's Work*, 135–36.

32. Ibid., 139.

33. Ibid., 98, emphasis added.

34. Michael Foucault, "First Howison Lecture on 'Truth and Subjectivity,'" October 20, 1980. Cited by James Miller, *The Passion of Michel Foucault* (New York: Simon and Schuster, 1993), 321–22.

10. I AM AN OTHER

"Je est un autre" is Arthur Rimbaud's famous declaration of his determination to become other than the person he has been raised to be. In "Letter to Paul Demeny," Charlesville, May 15, 1871.

Chapter epigraph: René Devisch, "The Human Body as a Vehicle for Emotions among the Yaka of Zaire," in *Personhood and Agency: The Experience of Self and Other in African Cultures*, ed. Michael Jackson and Ivan Karp (Stockholm: Almqvist & Wiksell, 1990), 115–33; quotation from p. 127.

1. Thornton Wilder, *The Bridge of San Luis Rey* (New York: HarperCollins, 1998), 5.

2. E. E. Evans-Pritchard, "Zande Therapeutics," in *Essays Presented to C. G. Seligman*, ed. E. E. Evans-Pritchard, Raymond Firth, and Bronislaw Malinowski (London: Kegan Paul, Trench, Trubner & Co., 1934), 49–61, especially p. 59.

3. Jean-Paul Sartre, *Search for a Method*, trans. Hazel Barnes (New York: Vintage, 1968), 85–90.

4. On the "mixing of voluntary and involuntary elements" in possession cults, see Ivan Karp, "Power and Capacity in Iteso Rituals of Possession," in *Personhood and Agency: The Experience of Self and Other in African Cultures*, ed. Michael Jackson and Ivan Karp (Stockholm: Almqvist & Wiksell, 1990), 79–93, quotation from p. 84.

5. That the *appearance* of the world is a product of the *means* whereby we observe is, of course, a central tenet of quantum mechanics, as spelled out in Heisenberg's uncertainty principle.

6. George Devereux, *Ethnopsychoanalysis: Psychoanalysis and Anthropology as Complementary Frames of Reference* (Berkeley: University of California Press, 1978), 125.

7. A person who is too self-enclosed is compared to "fermenting cassava paste that is indissolubly bound in a bushel," while someone who is overly effusive and spontaneous is censured as socially dead to the world. Among the Kuranko, a self-absorbed individual is compared to a fat grub called "sonson," which is so oily that it can be fried without additional oil being added to the pan, "stewing in its own juice," while one who cannot contain one's emotions, control one's mouth, or curb one's appetite is similarly "deaf" to the protocols of social life and said to be equally "crazy."

8. For details of Reade's travels in Sierra Leone I have drawn on the following sources: W. Winwood Reade, *Savage Africa*, 2 vols. (London: Smith, Elder & Co., 1864); W. Winwood Reade, *The African Sketch-Book*, vol. 2 (London: Smith, Elder & Co., 1873); and F. Legge, introduction to W. Winwood Reade, *The Martyrdom of Man* (London: Smith, Elder & Co., 1872).

11. YONDER

Chapter epigraph: Ian Fairweather's sister, Nourma Abbot-Smith, in *Ian Fairweather: Profile of a Painter* (St. Lucia: University of Queensland Press, 1978), 1. Cited in Murray Bail, *Fairweather* (Sydney: Murdoch Books, 1981), 11.

1. Siri Hustvedt, "Yonder," in *A Plea for Eros* (New York: Picador, 2006), 2.

2. I discovered, years later, that Patrick White acquired Fairweather's *Gethsemane* in 1958, the year it was painted. It hung over White's writing desk on Martin Road, in Centennial Park, for many years, until he gave it to the Art Gallery of New South Wales in 1974. White visited Fairweather on Bribie Island in 1961, and his

fictionalized version of Fairweather (Hurtle Duffield) is the central figure in his 1970 novel *The Vivisector*.

3. Cited in Murray Bail, *Fairweather* (Sydney: Murdoch Books, 1981), 29.

4. Later, in Darwin, he lived in a concrete mixer and then in an abandoned, rat-infested railway wagon, showing, as Murray Bail puts it, "a peculiar preference for discomfort, difficulty" (ibid., 94).

5. Patricia Anderson, "Ian Fairweather: A Web of Memory and Feeling," *Art & Australia* (Summer 2006): 252–56.

6. "Ian Fairweather: A Reclusive Australian Painter," *The Economist* (April 16, 2009).

7. In Roman mythology, maenads were the female followers of Dionysus. Their name literally translates as "raving ones," for Dionysus inspired the maenads to ecstasy through dancing and drunken intoxication. As they lost self-control, they would shout excitedly, engage in uncontrolled sexual behavior, and ritualistically hunt and tear animals to pieces, devouring the raw flesh.

8. "Blessed is he who has the good fortune to know the mysteries of the gods, who sanctifies his life and initiates his soul, a bacchant on the mountains, in holy purifications." See Norman O. Brown, "Apocalypse: The Place of Mystery in the Life of the Mind," *Harper's Magazine* (May 1961): 47.

9. The same questions inform Patrick White's account of Hurtle Duffield, for whom his paintings are more real than the people he paints. White prefaces *The Vivisector* with quotations from Rimbaud, Blake, Saint Augustine, and Ben Nicholson to suggest the intimate links between art and the *mysterium tremendum* of religious experience.

10. Patrick White, *The Vivisector* (Harmondsworth: Penguin, 1970), 9.

11. Ezra Pound, *Guide to Kulchur* (New York: New Directions, 1970), 144–45.

12. White, *Vivisector*, 197.

13. Cited in Bail, *Fairweather*, 68.

14. Paul Radin, *Primitive Man as Philosopher* (New York: Dover, 1957), xii.

15. See, for example, Robert Redfield, "Thinker and Intellectual in Primitive Society," in *Primitive Views of the World*, ed. Stanley Diamond (New York: Columbia University Press, 1964), 33–48.

16. On Malinowski's pragmatic and ethnographic theory of language, see "The Problem of Meaning in Primitive Languages," Supplement I, in *The Meaning of Meaning: A Study of the Influence of Language upon Thought and of the Science of Symbolism*, ed. C. K. Ogden and I. A. Richards (New York: Harcourt Brace, 1953), 296–336.

17. Kwasi Wiredu, *Cultural Universals and Particulars: An African Perspective* (Bloomington: Indiana University Press, 1996), 114.

18. Walter van Beek, "Dogon Restudied: A Field Evaluation of the Work of Marcel Griaule," *Current Anthropolo1ogy* 32, no. 2 (1991): 139–67.

19. Barry Hallen, "A Philosopher's Approach to Traditional Culture," *Theoria to Theory* 9 (1975): 259–72, 261.

20. Ibid., 264. See also Barry Hallen and J. O. Sodipo, *Knowledge, Belief and Witchcraft: Analytic Experiments in African Philosophy* (London: Ethnographica, 1986), 8–9.

21. John Dewey, *How We Think* (Buffalo, NY: Prometheus Books, 1991), 12.

22. Friedrich Nietzsche, *Beyond Good and Evil: Prelude to a Philosophy of the Future*, trans. R. J. Hollingdale (Harmondsworth: Penguin, 1973), 17, 19.

23. Martin Heidegger, *Poetry, Language, Thought*, trans. Albert Hofstadter (New York: Harper & Row, 1971), 146–51.

24. Paul Ricoeur, *Living Up to Death*, trans. David Pellauer (Chicago: University of Chicago Press, 2009), 17.

25. These foregoing points are fully explored and amply illustrated in my study of Kuranko storytelling. Michael Jackson, *Allegories of the Wilderness: Ethics and Ambiguity in Kuranko Narratives* (Bloomington: Indiana University Press, 1982).

26. Giorgio Agamben, *Homo Sacer: Sovereign Power and Bare Life*, trans. Daniel Heller-Roazen (Stanford, CA: Stanford University Press, 1998).

12. READING *SIDDHARTHA* TO FREYA AT FOREST LAKE

Chapter epigraph: *The Yoga-Sūtra of Patañjali*, trans. Chip Hartranft (Boston: Shambhala, 2003), 37.

1. I would later share these reflections with my colleague Charlie Hallisey. In Charlie's view, Hesse's narrative was both Eurocentric and simplistic. It echoed Victorian narratives of a questing hero, as well as the perennial adolescent search for a path or true vocation. Hesse's Siddhartha is like Goldilocks, Charlie said. Someone venturing out into the world, testing and tasting other people's food and furniture, looking for what works for her, what feels "just right." And he mentioned the Danish writer Karl Gjellerup who, like Hermann Hesse, fell under the spell of Buddhism, and published *Pilgrimen Kamanita* ("The Pilgrim Kamanita") in 1906, a fictional journey of an Indian merchant's son from a youthful life of prosperity and carnal pleasure to death, rebirth, and nirvana.

2. Theodor Adorno, *Minima Moralia: Reflections from Damaged Life*, trans. E. F. N. Jephcott (London: Verso, 1978), 50.

3. B. K. S. Iyengar, *The Tree of Yoga* (Boston: Shambhala, 1989), 10.

4. Ibid., 11.

5. Ibid., 27.

6. Mircea Eliade, *Yoga: Immortality and Freedom*, trans. Willard R. Trask (Princeton, NJ: Princeton University Press, 1970), 7–9.

7. B. K. S. Iyengar, *Body the Shrine, Yoga Thy Light* (Bombay: B. I. Taraporewala, 1978), 15–16, 29, 61. Also see Iyengar, *Tree of Yoga*, 89–92.

8. Eliade, *Yoga*, 53.

9. Iyengar, *Tree of Yoga*, 46.

10. Ibid., 14.

11. Ibid., 16.

12. This probably reflects the origin of yoga in the ancient non-Vedic Natha cult, linked with the worship of Siva as Lord of all the animals (Pasupati Siva). The culture of the body among the Nath Siddhas was also associated with the dynamic interplay of sun and moon. The word "hatha yoga" signified the unification (yoking) of ha (sun) and tha (moon), which itself connoted a ritualistic bringing together of the two primordial elements of which all being, including human being, is composed—variously expressed as the creative and the destructive, Siva and Shakti, male and female. Shashi Bhushan Dasgupta, *Obscure Religious Cults* (Calcutta: Firma K. L. Mukhopadhyay, 1962), 229–46.

13. B. K. S. Iyengar, unpublished notes from Yoga Darsana, London, July 1970.

14. Agehananda Bharati, *The Light at the Center: Context and Pretext of Modern Mysticism* (Santa Barbara, CA: Ross Erikson, 1976), 78.

15. Ibid., 66.

16. Agehananda Bharati, *The Ochre Robe* (Seattle: University of Washington Press, 1962), 84.

17. Ibid., 83.

18. Iyengar, *Tree of Yoga*, 37.

19. Karl Jaspers, *Way to Wisdom*, trans. Ralph Manheim (New Haven, CT: Yale University Press, 1954), 51.

20. Wole Soyinka, *You Must Set Forth at Dawn: A Memoir* (New York: Random House, 2006), 7.

21. Wole Soyinka, "Running to Stand Still," http://www.pwf.cz/en/archives/interviews/1177.html.

22. The opening lines of Rudyard Kipling's "If."

23. Karl Jaspers, "On My Philosophy," in *Existentialism from Dostoyevsky to Sartre*, ed. and trans. Walter Kaufmann (New York: Meridian Books, 1956), 153.

24. In 1959 thirteen men collaborated in forming the Strategic Army Corps Sport Parachute Team to compete in what was, at the time, a Communist-dominated sport. The skydiving team performed so well that on June 1, 1961, the army officially recognized, designated, and activated the team as the U.S. Army Parachute Team.

25. A few weeks after our encounter on the Icelandair flight, Paul sent me pictures from the eighteen-day cruise that he and his wife had taken. Here he was on a 70-mph, rigid-hull inflatable boat ride in Norway, on an aerial assault course 100 feet above the ground in Scotland, rolling down a hill in a ball (zorbing) in Northern Ireland, snorkeling in a dry suit in 35-degree water in Iceland, and kayaking in Greenland. "We also had 80-mph and 21-foot waves part of the trip," he added. "Some fun."

26. Karl Jaspers, *The Perennial Scope of Philosophy*, trans. Ralph Manheim (New York: Philosophical Library, 1949), 1–46.

27. Sextus Empiricus, *The Skeptic Way: Sextus Empiricus's "Outlines of Pyrrhonism,"* trans. Benson Mates (New York: Oxford University Press, 1996), 89.

13. ON THE WORK AND WRITING OF ETHNOGRAPHY

Chapter epigraph: Michel Foucault, *The Use of Pleasure*, vol. 2, *The History of Sexuality*, trans. R. Hurley (New York: Vintage, 1990), 8–9.

1. Michel de Montaigne, *Essays*, trans. J. M. Cohen (Harmondsworth: Penguin, 1958), 37.

2. The Kuranko term *sundan* connotes "guest" or "stranger" and resonates with comparable terms in other West African languages.

3. Weston La Barre, *The Ghost Dance: Origins of Religion* (New York: Dell, 1972), 52.

4. Paul Ricoeur, *Living Up to Death*, trans. David Pellauer (Chicago: University of Chicago Press, 2009), 17.

5. George Devereux, *From Anxiety to Method in the Behavioral Sciences* (The Hague: Mouton, 1967), xvi–xvii.

6. This is the central thesis of Maurice Merleau-Ponty's *Phenomenology of Perception*, trans. Colin Smith (London: Routledge, 1962). Also see Don Ihde, "Scientific Visualism," in *Readings in the Philosophy of Technology*, ed. David M. Kaplan (Lanham, MD: Rowman and Littlefield, 2004), 469–86.

7. Martin Heidegger, *Being and Time*, trans. John Macquarrie and Edward Robinson (New York: HarperCollins, 1962), 98, emphasis in original.

8. Bernard Stiegler, *Acting Out*, trans. David Barison, Daniel Ross, and Patrick Crogan (Stanford, CA: Stanford University Press, 2009), 4.

9. Ludwig Wittgenstein, *Tractatus Logico-Philosophicus*, trans. D. F. Pears and B. F. McGuiness (Atlantic Highlands, NJ: Humanities Press, 1974), 73.

10. Gabriel Marcel, *Being and Having*, trans. Katharine Farrer (Boston: Beacon Press, 1951), 100.

11. Wittgenstein, *Tractatus*, 5.

12. See Devereux, *Anxiety to Method*, xvi–xx.

13. Martin Heidegger, *Being and Time*, trans. John Macquarrie and Edward Robinson (New York: HarperCollins, 1962), 51–55.

14. Michael Jackson, *Minima Ethnographica: Intersubjectivity and the Anthropological Project* (Chicago: University of Chicago Press, 1998), 32–36.

15. David Shields, *Reality Hunger: A Manifesto* (New York: Alfred A. Knopf, 2010), 5.

16. John Dewey, *Experience and Nature* (New York: Dover, 1958), 7. More recently, Pierre Hadot has made a similar case for "philosophy as a way of life"—less a theoretical discourse than a "practice, an *askesis*, and a transformation of the self." See *What Is Ancient Philosophy*, trans. Michael Chase (Cambridge, MA: Belknap Press of Harvard University Press, 2002), 275.

17. Ivan Illich, *Tools for Conviviality* (New York: Harper and Row, 1973).

18. Jacques Derrida, "Tympan," in *Margins of Philosophy*, trans. Alan Bass (Chicago: University of Chicago Press, 1984), xiii.

19. Ngugi Wa Thiong'o, *Dreams in a Time of War: A Childhood Memoir* (New York: Pantheon, 2010), 65.

20. David Howes speaks of this as "a crisis of intonation" and describes the "dwindling power" of traditional songs in the Trobriand Islands, where older people lament the passing of a "golden age of orality," when the measure of human greatness was the resounding quality of one's vocal presence. See *Sensual Relations: Engaging the Senses in Culture and Social Theory* (Ann Arbor: University of Michigan Press, 2003), 64–67.

21. J. C. Carothers, "Culture, Psychiatry and the Written Word," *Psychiatry* 22 (1959): 307–20. Also see Jack Goody, ed., *Literacy in Traditional Societies* (Cambridge: Cambridge University Press, 1968); Marshall McLuhan, *The Gutenberg Galaxy* (London: Routledge and Kegan Paul, 1962); Walter J. Ong, *Orality and Literacy: The Technologizing of the Word* (London: Methuen, 1982); David Riesman, "The Oral and Written Traditions," in *Explorations in Communications*, ed. Edmund Carpenter and Marshall McLuhan (Boston: Beacon Press, 1960), 109–16.

22. Walter Benjamin, "The Storyteller," in *Illuminations*, trans. Harry Zohn (New York: Schocken Books, 1968), 83–109.

23. Plato, *Phaedrus*, trans. Christopher Rowe (Harmondsworth: Penguin, 2005), 61–64. See also Jacques Derrida, "Plato's Pharmacy," in *Dissemination*, trans. Barbara Johnson (London: Athlone, 1981), 66–94.

24. "Each culture contains the negation of its manifest pattern and nuclear values, through a tacit affirmation of contrary latent patterns and marginal values. The complete real pattern of a culture is a product of a functional interplay between officially affirmed and officially negated patterns possessing mass." Devereux, *Anxiety to Method*, 212.

25. Walter J. Ong, *Orality and Literacy* (New York: Routledge, 2002), 13, 5, 8.

26. Ibid., 8. This argument has also been made, eloquently and empirically, by William A. Graham in his study of the vocal and sensual character of scriptural texts, and he cites examples of how scripture is not only written but "recited, read aloud, chanted, sung, quoted in debate, memorized in childhood, meditated upon in murmur and full voice," its sacrality realized in the life of a vocal community. *Beyond the Written Word: Oral Aspects of Scripture in the History of Religion* (Cambridge: Cambridge University Press, 1987), ix, 7–8.

27. Derrida, *Margins of Philosophy*, x–xii.

28. John Blacking argues that "the essential differences between music in one society and another may be social and not musical. If English music may seem to be more complex than Venda music and practiced by a smaller number of people, it is because of the consequences of the division of labor in society, and not because the English are less musical or their music is cognitively more complex." *How Musical Is Man?* (Seattle: University of Washington Press, 1973), 102.

29. Oliver Sacks, *Musicophilia: Tales of Music and the Brain* (New York: Vintage, 2007), 232.

30. Seamus Heaney, *Field Work* (London: Faber and Faber, 1979), 11.

31. Oliver Sacks provides wonderful examples of musical synesthesia in which musical keys and chords are strongly associated with colors and tastes. See "The Key of Clear Green: Synesthesia and Music," in Sacks, *Musicophilia*, chap. 14.

32. Cf. Jacques Derrida's comments on the textual metaphor of language in *Margins of Philosophy*, 160–61.

33. Ibid., 161.

34. Eugenio Montale, *The Second Life of Art: Selected Essays*, trans. Jonathan Galassi (New York: Ecco Press, 1982).

35. The term is no longer current in Portuguese, though it is cognate with the French *se debrouiller*, meaning to fend for oneself, to get by in a murky situation in which one cannot see far ahead (*brouillard* = fog). Henrik Vigh, *Navigating Terrains of War: Youth and Soldiering in Guinea-Bissau* (New York: Berghahn, 2006), 128–30.

36. Benedict de Spinoza, *Ethics*, trans. Edwin Curley (Harmondsworth: Penguin, 1996), part 1, 16, 23. I deliberately mistranslate "God" as "Reality."

INDEX

Aboriginal people: avoidance strategies of, 87; and drinking, 88; on ghosts, 85–87; treatment of, 80–81, 83, 113–14. *See also* Kuku Yalanji people; Warlpiri people
absence. *See* detachment
Adorno, Theodor, 158, 166, 193n20
Aesop, 192
African Sketch-Book, The (W. Reade), 140
agency, 20, 133
aging, 110–11
Alexander, F. M., 12; technique, 12–13
Allegories of the Wilderness (Jackson), 28
analogy, 9, 41, 179
Anandamayi, 38, 49, 51, 52
Anandmayee. *See* Anandamayi
Andersen, Hans Christian, 70, 71
Anderson, Patricia, 144
ANRC. *See* Australia National Research Council (ANRC)
Arendt, Hannah, 7–8, 19–20, 58, 69–70, 148
Art of the Boyds, The (Herbst), 91
association. *See* involvement
attachment, 85
Aurobindo, Sri, 38, 39, 42
Auster, Paul, 141
Austerlitz (Sebald), 180
Australia, Aboriginal, 6
Australia National Research Council (ANRC), 114
autonomy, 20, 80, 192n8
awayness. *See* detachment

Bail, Murray, 144
Baldwin, James, 76, 77–78
Balinese culture, 1–2
Banerjee, Beena, 44–45, 46, 47, 49, 51
Bateson, Gregory, 1, 2
Baudelaire, Charles, 20
Baumann, Zygmund, 23
Becker, Ernest, 20, 192n7
beef: Sierra Leone story, 181–86; use of term, 181
behavior: and experience, 2, 13; explaining, 120, 133, 169; as habitual, 11
belief: as blueprint, 160; and experience, 2–3, 123; vs. faith, 162; and truth, 123–24, 127
Beng people, 126–27
Benjamin, Walter, 20, 176
bereavement, 122–23
Berger, John, 69
Berger, Peter, 130
Bhagavad Gita, 51
Bharati, Agehananda, 40, 46, 49, 57, 161
Big Men, 153, 181–84, 186
Black Atlantic, The (Gilroy), 71
Blacking, John, 177
black writers, 76–78
Boethius, 28
Bohr, Niels, 71
Borsodi, Ralph, 50
Bourdieu, Pierre, 118
Bowles, Chester, 53
Boyd, Arthur, 90–91

Bredsdorff, Elias, 70
Bredsdorff, Kristine, 70
Bridge of San Luis Rey, The (Wilder), 131
Brown, Norman O., 144
Broyard, Anatole, 76–77
Buber, Martin, 50
Buchanan, Scott, 49, 53
Bucket List, The (film), 163
Burghers of Calais (Rodin), 22
Bynner, Witter, 48

Camus, Albert, 42, 74
Castro, Fidel, 50
Catchpool, Gwen, 43, 49
Catholic Worker, 48, 49
Cavell, Stanley, 196n1
Cendrars, Blaise, 99
change, source of, 35–36
Childe, Vere Gordon, 115
"Christer, The" (Mayer), 50
Civil Rights Act (1960), 55
Clark, Margaret, 55–56
Cloister and the Hearth, The (C. Reade),
    136
Coleman, Ornette, 76
collective unconsciousness, 3
colonialism, 80
communities: closed, 7, 9; intentional, 36, 46,
    50, 57; unintentional, 81
Congo, violence in, 5
Congress Socialist Party (India), 41, 45
Conjuring Hope (Lindquist), 117–18, 130
Connerton, Paul, 23
Connolly, James, 68
consciousness: body, 23; and creativity, 59;
    critique on, 46; egocentric vs. sociocen-
    tric, 3, 7; false, 18; and mask, 19; oscillation
    in, 8, 35, 58
Consequences of Pragmatism (Rorty), 28
control: as acceptance, 130; and experience,
    129; and magic, 117; and philosophy, 26;
    and writing, 97–98
Coser, Lewis, 49

Dancer, Cliff, 55
Day, Dorothy, 48, 51
Delphi, Greece, 102–3
Derrida, Jacques, 166, 177, 179
Descartes, René, 161
Desjarlais, Robert, 192n8
destiny, 124–25, 135, 153

detachment, 1–3; and action, 7; and
    contradiction, 58, 73; and identity,
    193n18; methods of, 6; need for, 99, 146,
    162; and philosophy, 149; and refuge,
    36; and self/other, 122; and subjectivity,
    72; and writing, 141. *See also*
    involvement
determinism, 132
Devereux, George, 133, 171, 177
Devisch, René, 131, 133
Devonshire, Deborah, Lady, 98–99
Dewey, John, 6, 11, 12–13, 28, 147, 175
Didion, Joan, 65
difference and tolerance, 6
disease and inner peace, 107–8
dissociation. *See* detachment
Distomo, Greece, massacre, 100–101
Docili, Peter, 49
Doniger, Wendy, 53
Draper, Hal, 49, 50
Dreams in a Time of War (Ngugi), 175–76
dubria, defined, 180
dubu. See ghosts
Durrell, Lawrence, 94, 106, 110

Economic and Political Manuscripts of 1844
    (Marx), 50
economic market and magic, 117
Egan, Keith, 60, 62–65, 68
Elias, Norbert, 124
Eliot, T. S., 59, 79
Ellenberger, Henry, 18
Ellison, Ralph, 77
Encyclopaedia of Religion and Ethics
    (Hastings), 38
engagement. *See* involvement
Engels, Friedrich, 5
Erechtheion (Athens, Greece), 99–100
Essence of Christianity (Feuerbach), 50
essentialism, 76
ethnographic studies: ethics in, 167;
    fieldwork, 4–5, 6, 118–19, 168–73, 174, 188;
    innovative, 1–2; and judgment, 169; roles
    in, 8; and understanding, 171; and writing,
    8, 60, 67, 167, 172, 173–75, 179, 180, 188.
    See also social anthropology
evasion. *See* detachment
Évian Conference (1938), 89
existence, paradox of, 74
existentialism, 73, 173
expatriates, 69–73, 75, 77–78, 105–6

experience: analogies for, 9; a priori, 23–24; and behavior, 2; and belief, 2–3, 123; and control, 129; and faith, 162; and hypothesis, 6; lived, 1, 17, 72, 110, 119, 124, 174–75; and memory, 144; shared, 86; and subjectivity, 160–61, 173; transitional, 4; transitive/intransitive, 166
Eyeless in Gaza (Huxley), 11–12

faeries in Ireland, 68
Fairweather, Ian, 141–45; paintings, 142–43, 145
Fairweather, Rose, 141
faith: vs. belief, 160, 161–62; philosophical, 165; vs. reason, 127
Fermor, Patrick Leigh, 98–99
Feuerbach, Ludwig, 50
fieldwork. *See* ethnographic studies; social anthropology
fire-building techniques, 169–70
"Fire of Life, The" (Rorty), 29
Firth, Raymond, 114
Fischer, Dick, 83
Fischer, Leopold. *See* Bharati, Agehananda
Fisher, Peter, 81–85
Forsyth, Thomas, 92
Fortes, Meyer, 124–25
Foucault, Michel, 15–16, 19, 147, 148, 167
"Foule, La" (song), 20
foundationalism, 23–24
freedom, 107, 111
Freeman, Derek, 14
free will, 132
Freud, Sigmund, 13–14, 79
Fromm, Erich, 94–95
Fula people, 137–38

Gandhi, Indira, 38
Gandhi, Mahatma, 22; ashram, 42; and celibacy, 39; on rural socialism, 50; on saint's life, 73–74; and yoga, 159
Gates, Henry Louis, 76
gender identity, 28–29
Ghose, Aurobindo. *See* Aurobindo, Sri
ghosts, 85–87
Gilroy, Paul, 71
Glendalough (County Wicklow, Ireland), 62, 63
Goodson, Kendra, 165–66
Gordon, Dexter, 70–71
Gottlieb, Alma, 126–27

grace, 161
Gregory, Robert, 63
Griaule, Marcel, 147
Guangdá, Méi, 91–92
Guibert, Hervé, 15
Gupta, Brijen K., 33; background, 36–56; on God and Christ, 51; humanism of, 58; influence of, 33–34; influences on, 37–42, 48–51, 53–54; marriage and children, 53; move to New Zealand, 54–56; Pendle Hill community, 49–50; Quakerism of, 42–43, 50, 55; on retreat/engagement, 36; on social justice, 50; voyage to London, 43–44; on women, 42, 51–52

Hadden, Maude, 47, 48
Hallen, Barry, 147
Harrington, Michael, 48, 49, 50
Harris, Frank, 40
Hastings, James, 38
Heaney, Seamus, 63–64
Heidegger, Martin, 20, 29, 45, 123, 148, 171, 174
Herbst, Peter, 89–92
Herbst, Valerie, 91
Herrick, Paul, 163–65
Herzfeld, Michael, 69
Hesse, Hermann, 156, 158
Hirsch, Don, 23, 27
Hitler, Adolf, 50, 89
Ho Chi Minh, 45, 50
Hofmannsthal, Hugo Von, 59
Homage to Catalonia (Orwell), 17
hope, 28, 117–18, 120, 135
Hoselitz, Bert, 53–54, 55
Howe, Irving, 49, 50
How Musical Is Man? (Blacking), 177
human condition: ambiguity of, 133; magicality of, 30; and myth, 125–26; as paradox, 19, 69–70, 74
Human Condition, The (Arendt), 70
Humanities Research Centre (Australian National University), 23
human rights, 50
Hurston, Zora Neale, 77
Husserl, Edmund, 123, 174
Hustvedt, Siri, 141
Huxley, Aldous, 11–12

ideas and action, 12–13
identity: and balance, 167; and bonding, 141–42; and collectivity, 19; common, 129;

identity (*continued*)
    and detachment/involvement, 193n18;
    eclipsed, 91, 97; gender, 28–29; loss of, 167;
    and place of birth, 124; politics, 77–78,
    130; racial, 75–76; and relationality, 171;
    transcending, 74; as varying, 110; writer's, 17
Illich, Ivan, 175
imperturbability, 162–63
improvisation, 158
individuality, 20, 30, 74, 175, 192n8
individuation, 162
infants: and dissociation, 2, 11; and potential
    space, 122
initiation rites, 28–29
"In Search of Zora Neale Hurston" (Walker),
    77
intersubjectivity, 2–3, 118, 122, 148, 171–72, 174,
    191–92n5
Introduction to Social Anthropology, An
    (Piddington), 111
involvement, 1–3; and action, 7; and
    aloneness, 94; and contradiction, 58, 73;
    and identity, 193n18; methods of, 6; and
    philosophical thinking, 147–48, 149; as
    refuge, 36; and self/other, 122. *See also*
    detachment
Iyengar, B. K. S., 158–60

Jackson, Freya, 95–96, 100–101, 103–109,
    156–157
Jackson, Heidi, 67, 95, 103, 203n7
Jackson, Michael (pop star), 108
Jackson, Pauline, 28, 70, 103, 107
Jacob's Room (Woolf), 100
James, Henry, 4, 28
James, William, 166
Jaspers, Karl, 162, 165, 166
Journey with the Genius (Bynner), 48

Kalabari Ijo people, 125
Kamara, Alhaji Magba, 151
Kama Sutra, 40
Kant, Immanuel, 160–61
Kapferer, Bruce, 30
karma, 42, 124
Keat, Russell, 23
Kennedy, John F., 39
Kevin, Saint, 63
Keyserling, Herman, 15
Kierkegaard, Søren, 71, 74
King, Martin Luther, Jr., 34, 35

Koestler, Arthur, 35–36, 49
Koroma clan, 139, 151
Koroma, Keti Ferenke, 150–154, 186
Koroma, Samaran Bala, 151
Koroma, Sewa Magba, 148, 151, 184, 186
Koroma, Sheku Magba, 151
Koroma, Sumban Kona, 152
Krishnaprem, Sri, 42, 46, 51
Kuku Yalanji people, 81, 86
Kuranko people, 5–6, 22–23, 134–35, 139; Big
    Men, 153, 181–84, 186; and fieldwork, 67,
    168–71; fire-building techniques, 169–70;
    hierarchy among, 186; and hospitality, 168;
    initiation rites, 28; and moral person-
    hood, 148; neighborliness of, 170–71; on
    open vs. covert, 18; on others' experience,
    149; on social intelligence, 153–54;
    storytelling, 148–55
Kurtz, Glenn, 61–62

La Barre, Weston, 168–69
Laing, Alexander, 137–38, 139
Laing, R. D., 3
Lalitha Sahsarnamah, 52–53
Larsen, Nella, 75–76, 77
Lasch, Christopher, 50
lawa, defined, 93
Lawa lawa people, 87–88
Lawrence, D. H., 12, 51
Leopold II, King of Belgium, 5
Letter of Lord Chandos (Hofmannsthal), 59
Levi, Primo, 86
Lévi-Strauss, Claude, 10, 128, 148
Levy, Benny, 110
Lévy-Bruhl, Lucien, 146
liberation movements (1954–55), 50
Lindquist, Galina, 116–21, 130; illness and
    death, 118–21, 123
literacy. *See* writing
Lohia, Ram Manohar, 41, 43, 45–46, 47, 51
Lokeshwaranand, Swami, 39
Lorimer, Francine, 81–91
loss: and bereavement, 122–23; and
    intersubjectivity, 122; of personal identity,
    167; recovery from, 28, 63, 108
Love's Work (Rose), 129
Lowry, Malcolm, 70
Luxemburg, Rosa, 39

Maori, 111, 205n5
madness, 30, 67, 70, 107, 144–45

magic and control, 117
Malinowski, Bronislaw, 8, 111, 114, 146
Mamet, David, 59
Man, Das (Heidegger), 20
Man Who Died, The (Lawrence), 12, 51
Mao Zedong, 45, 50
Marah, Fasili, 135
Marah, S. B., 134–36, 180–87
Marcel, Gabriel, 172
marginalization, 90, 151
Marriage at Cana (Fairweather), 142
Marriott, McKim, 55
Martin, Virginia, 53
Martyrdom of Man, The (W. Reade), 140
Marx, Karl, 5, 39, 50
Maxwell, Val, 55
May, Hawtrey, 4
Mayer, Milton, 50–51
McCarthy era, 53
McCarthy, Patrick, 23
McGinn, Bernard, 49, 56
Mead, Margaret, 1, 2
Mehinaku people, 18
Melville, Herman, 2, 6
memory, 36, 144
Merleau-Ponty, Maurice, 23, 110, 119, 122, 123
Merton, Thomas, 34–35, 46, 48, 49, 51, 53
metaphor, 9, 10–11, 124
Midnight's Children (Rushdie), 41
Miller, Henry, 15, 107
Miller, James, 15–16
mind-body separation, 161
misfortune, explanation for, 131–32
Mitford, Deborah. *See* Devonshire, Deborah, Lady
Moby Dick (Melville), 2, 6
modernism, 94, 129
Monastery (Fairweather), 142
Montaigne, Michel de, 167–68
Moore, G. E., 40
Morgenthau, Hans, 53
Mulvaney, D. J., 114
Munz, Peter, 55
Murphy, Fiona, 60, 65, 68
Murti, T. R. V., 44
Mussolini, Benito, 50
Muste, Abraham Johannes, 47, 48, 49, 50–51
mystical experience, 161–62
myth: classical, 102; and human condition, 125–26; and superiority, 58, 125. *See also* specific myths

Narang, Rita, 46
Nehru, Jawaharlal, 38, 45
Neville, A. O., 205n15
New Age cosmology, 117
Newton, Isaac, 10
Ngugi Wa Thiong'o, 175–76
Nietzsche, Friedrich, 23, 147, 166
Nigam, R. L., 38, 41, 43, 44, 46
Nixon, Ronald. *See* Krishnaprem, Sri

observation: participant-, 7–9, 112, 118; scientific, 112, 170–71, 179
Oedipus complex, 13, 14, 125
Ogotemmêli, 147
oneness, 157, 161
Ong, Walter, 177
orality. *See* speech
Orwell, George, 17, 73–74, 107
Otherness, 8–9, 19, 76, 131, 158

pacifism, 42–43, 49–50
palka, defined, 93
Palmier, Leslie, 54, 55, 56
Panourgiá, Neni, 101–2
Paris Manuscripts (Marx). *See Economic and Political Manuscripts of 1844* (Marx)
Parlan, Horace, 71
participant-observation, 7–9, 112, 118
Parvati (goddess), 52–53
Passion of Michel Foucault, The (Miller), 15–16
Patañjali, 156, 159–60
Peirce, Charles S., 117
personhood, 148
phenomenology, 3, 19, 117–18, 173, 174
Phenomenology of Perception (Merleau-Ponty), 23
philosophy: and being-in-the-world, 147–48, 149; and control, 26; and estrangement, 149; evasive, 16; hypothesis/experience in, 6; metaphysical bias in, 146; nonempirical, 9; philosophizing, defined, 15; pragmatic value of, 6, 12, 22, 24; and self/world, 7, 23; and suspicion, 18; Western vs. non-Western, 146–47. *See also* thought; specific disciplines
Piaf, Edith, 20
Piddington, Ralph O'Reilly, 111–15
pilgrimages, 62–63, 65
Plato, 19, 24
porcupine parable, 79–80, 81
potential space, 85

Pound, Ezra, 145
Practicing (Kurtz), 61
pragmatism, 6, 12, 22, 24, 28, 126
presence. *See* involvement
public sphere vs. private sphere, 72
purges, 101–2

Quakerism, 42–43, 50, 55
Quicksand (Larsen), 75–76
Quit India movement, 37
Quong Tart. *See* Guangdá, Méi

Raboteau, Albert, 34, 35
racism in Denmark, 71
Radhakrishnan, Sarvepalli, 41, 47, 49
Radin, Paul, 146
Ramakrishna Vivekananda Mission, 39
Randall, Narena Oliver, 56
Rank, Otto, 20, 192n7
Reade, Charles, 136
Reade, Winwood, 136–40
readiness-to-hand, 171–72
reality: and appearance, 19; conditions of,
    110; hunger, 174; and thought, 10
reason, pure, 161
redemption, 63–64
Redfield, Robert, 55
reification, 17
Reiner, Rob, 163
relatedness. *See* involvement
religion, unrevealed, 129
retreat. *See* detachment
Richard, Mira Paul, 39
Ricoeur, Paul, 8, 18, 125–26, 149, 169
Rimbaud, Arthur, 140
ritual, 68
Rodin, Auguste, 22
Roosevelt, Franklin D., 89
Rorty, Mary, 27
Rorty, Richard, 22; background, 24–25,
    27; on death, 29; described, 23;
    friendship with, 27–28; influence of,
    28; interview with, 24–27; on life
    meaning, 29, 124; on philosophy,
    23–24; on poetry, 29–30; on
    poor, 32
Rose, Gillian, 121, 129
Roy, M. N., 40
Rushdie, Salman, 41
Russell, Bertrand, 40
Rustin, Bayard, 48, 49, 53

Sacks, Oliver, 177
Sahsarnamahs, 52–53
samadhi, 160, 161
Santiago de Compostela (Galicia, Spain), 62–63
Saramba myth, 187
Sartre, Jean-Paul, 1, 45, 110–11, 117, 128, 132–33
Schachtman, Max, 48, 50, 51
Scheper-Hughes, Nancy, 65–66
schizophrenia, 9
Schlatter, Colette, 47–48
Schopenhauer, Arthur, 79–80
scientific observation, 112, 170–71, 179
scientific thought, 10
Sebald, W. G., 180
Segovia, Andrés, 61
self-fulfillment, 94
self-knowledge, 102
self-sacrifice, 94
semiology, 117
separateness. *See* detachment
Seven Storey Mountain, The (Merton), 34–35
Sextus Empiricus, 166
sexuality: and jazz, 76; and spirituality, 40
shared experience, 86
Shields, David, 174
Siddhartha (Hesse), 156–57
Sierra Leone, 5–6, 67, 70, 181–87. *See also*
    Kuranko people
Sign of Jonas, The (Merton), 49
Sinhalese sorcery, 30–32
Sisyphus myth, 102, 105, 144
Siva (god), 52, 211n12
skepticism, 166
social action, 27, 34, 42, 132
social anthropology: culture shock in, 168;
    defined, 8; dilemma in, 69; engagement in,
    112–14; existential-phenomenological, 173;
    fieldwork, 4–5, 65–67, 112–13, 118–19,
    168–73, 174, 188; and judgment, 169; roles
    in, 8; on structure and agency, 133; and
    transnationalism, 72–73; and writing, 8,
    60, 67, 167, 172, 173–75, 179, 180, 188.
    See also ethnographic studies
social intelligence, 153–54
social justice, 50, 181
social science, limits of, 17
Socrates, 176
Sofka. *See* Zinovieff, Sofka
Song of Myself (Whitman), 58
Soseki, Natsume, 20
sound and writing, 175–80

Soyinka, Wole, 162
speech vs. writing, 175–80
Spinoza, Baruch, 188
spirituality and sexuality, 40
Stiegler, Bernard, 172
storytelling, 70, 148–55
subjectivity: objectivity and, 171; and relationality, 72; scientists on, 16–17; and thinking, 14
Sunyavad (doctrine of voidness), 41–42
Survey of Anglo Indian Fiction, A (Singh), 38
symbolic capital, 118

Tallensi people, 124–25
Tantric tradition, 40, 52
Terence, 128
thought: as coping strategy, 14–15; as instinctive, 148; and reality, 10; reflective, 149; scientific/nonscientific, 10; and subjectivity, 14; tradition of, 147; and world representation, 9–10, 14. See also philosophy
Tito, Josip Broz, 45, 49
tolerance and difference, 6
Totem and Taboo (Freud), 13–14
Toynbee, Arnold, 48–49
transitional phenomena, 85
Tractatus Logico-Philosophicus (Wittgenstein), 172, 173–74
Travels in the Timanee, Kooranko and Soolima Countries (Laing), 137
Trilling, Lionel, 17
Tronick, Ed, 11
Trotsky, Leon, 24, 45
trust, problem of, 70
truth: and belief, 123–24, 127; and mystical experience, 161
Turtle and Temple Gong (Fairweather), 142

unconsciousness, 18–19. See also collective unconsciousness
Urantia Book, The, 163–65

Vigh, Henrik, 180
vita activa, 7–8, 148. See also involvement

vita contemplativa, 7–8. See also detachment
Vivekananda, Swami, 38, 39
Vivisector, The (White), 144
voidness doctrine. See Sunyavad (doctrine of voidness)

waiting. See willing and waiting
Walker, Alice, 77
Warlpiri people, 92–93
Waterfield, William, 95
Webster, Ben, 71
"Weeping Willow Blues" (song), 62
Weil, Simone, 49
White, Patrick, 144
Whitman, Walt, 58
Whose Is This Song? (documentary), 129
Wilder, Thornton, 131
willing and waiting, 133–36
Winnicott, D. W., 85, 122, 123
Wiredu, Kwasi, 147
Wittgenstein, Ludwig, 40, 172, 173–74
Wofford, Clare, 45
Wofford, Harris, 45, 53
women: as anodyne, 42, 51; Vedic literature on, 51–52
Woolf, Virginia, 100
writing: anthropological/ethnographic, 8, 60, 67, 167, 172, 173–75, 179, 180; and control, 97–98; and detachment, 141; and past, 93; and personal identity, 17; and speech, 175–80; writer's block, 59–60, 64, 67
wrugbe, 126–27

Yalunka people, 137–39
yoga practice: and body consciousness, 23; branches of, 159, 160; and distancing/integration, 158–59; and faith, 161–62; integral, 39; universality of, 159–60
Yoga Sūtra (Patañjali), 159
"Yogi and the Commissar, The" (Koestler), 35
"Yonder" (Hustvedt), 141

Zinovieff, Sofka, 95–106, 204n13
zoning in. See involvement
zoning out. See detachment

TEXT
10.5/14 Jenson

DISPLAY
Jenson Pro (Open Type)

COMPOSITOR
Westchester Book Group

INDEXER
Eileen Quam

PRINTER AND BINDER
IBT Global